'The authors have an extraordinary ability to communicate complex ideas with clarity and simplicity. It is an absorbing "must read" for all those who aspire to deeper comprehension of evolving ethical challenges.'
Catherine Syms, Director of Philosophy, Religion and Ethics, Diocesan School for Girls, Auckland, New Zealand

'We all think we know what is meant by right and wrong until pressed to give a plausible account of what we mean by these terms. This is where this book begins and eventually concludes. In between it offers an admirably clear account of the key strands in ethics from the classic thinkers, via the medieval theologians to the post-Enlightenment philosophers. Whether one is an A Level student wanting a more sophisticated discussion of the ethical landscape or an undergraduate needing a very clear outline of the issues, this book has the great virtue of providing just enough to understand the scholarly debates but not so much to overwhelm.'
Michael Wilcockson, A Level Chief Examiner, Head of Philosophy, Eton College, Berkshire

'The Vardys quote John Locke: the philosopher "clears away the undergrowth so that we can see the challenges more clearly". This is precisely what this book does supremely well: bridging the gulf between philosophy and practicality in a media culture where spin and half-truth often dominate. The "supreme vice", said Oscar Wilde, was "superficiality" – here, the book is anything but – he is immensely readable and lucid especially for those not usually at home in moral philosophy; it "clears away the undergrowth" and brings clarity, simplicity and depth to puzzles and muddles that cry out for rational resolutions. In a word, this is an enlightening guide to those moral questions that don't go away. It should go to every politician, civil servant, teacher and bishop; not to mention the rest of thoughtful humanity!'
Dr Kenneth Wolfe, Emeritus Head of Philosophy and Religion, Godolphin & Latymer School, London, and Director, London Society for the Study of Religion

'For anyone wishing to wrestle with the key ethical issues of the 21st century, *Ethics Matters* is required reading. Ideal for the specialist and newcomer alike as a stimulating, accessible guide, it raises vital questions about the quality of future debate. In a world where relativism often goes untested, this book clarifies the alternatives. Our students find their own voice in this intriguing, indispensible work – highly recommended.'
Esmond Lee, Head of Religious Studies, Trinity School, Croydon

'This book will almost certainly be an important text for use by schools and universities – but is far more than a textbook. Its clear unabashed clarity of explanation will make the exciting and vital enterprise of moral philosophy accessible to a wide audience. Its use of film, poetry and prose to help unpack complex and demanding concepts make it an essential read for any serious student or layman alike. With almost evangelical commitment to their subject the authors set out to engage the reader, taking him/her on a journey through the exciting field of ethics. They draw upon wide-ranging, up-to-date and excellent scholarship to achieve a lucid and eloquent exposition of the subject. The book gives the reader the confidence to understand the issues and participate meaningfully in ethical dialogue.'
Revd Andrew Stead, Chaplain, Aldenham School, Hertfordshire

'A most welcome book and a "must" for every committed teacher and departmental library. I wish I had read it before now. Not only does it clarify theories, giving additional information, but it offers valuable insights into how some ethical theories have greater similarities than we have sometimes been given to understand and teach. Bright students will find this book accessible and helpful in raising grades.'
Judy Grill, Head of Philosophy and Religion, Churchers College, Hampshire

Ethics Matters

Peter and Charlotte Vardy

scm press

© Peter and Charlotte Vardy 2012

Published in 2012 by SCM Press
Editorial office
3rd Floor, Invicta House
108–114 Golden Lane,
London EC1Y OTG

SCM Press is an imprint of Hymns Ancient & Modern Ltd
(a registered charity)
13A Hellesdon Park Road
Norwich NR6 5DR, UK

www.scmpress.co.uk

British Library Cataloguing in Publication data
A catalogue record for this book is available
from the British Library

978-0-334-04391-1
Kindle edition 978-0-334-04450-5

Typeset by Regent Typesetting
Printed and bound by
CPI Group (UK) Ltd, Croydon, Surrey

Contents

To Petra

'only that day dawns to which we are awake:
the sun is but a morning star …'

Preface

What is the purpose of human life? Today many people aim for riches, possessions, beauty and status yet all of these pass away and fail to satisfy. The wisdom of generations, of diverse cultures, suggests that the only worthwhile aim is to live well, growing in understanding and savouring the experience of being alive. Philosophy at its best is the process of loving wisdom, the essence of life. Moral philosophy offers practical guidance to support that process. Philosophy is hard. No one pretends that it is easy. However, it is immensely rewarding. It yields something worth more than rubies: truth which offers us a form of liberation from the confines of our own perspective and our own interests and a glimpse of immortality.

Truth is awe-inspiring. It resists expression, explanation and simplification and is usually distorted by attempts to communicate it. It exists not in plain black and white but in subtle shades of grey and is hinted at in works of art, literature, even films, as well as in the lives of great men and women and their writings. In many ways truth is a puzzle, yet this should not be understood in the sense of being a mere curiosity or pastime.

This book aims to introduce students and general readers to the fascination of central ideas of enduring relevance, to give direction and inspiration to find out more and to pass on our excitement. Obviously no book, let alone one of this length and scope, can possibly cover everything and we have been selective, focusing on the western tradition in ethics and moral philosophy and trying to communicate ideas in a clear and hopefully not misleading way.

Peter and Charlotte Vardy
Adelaide, South Australia
May 2012

Introduction

There are several ways of approaching moral philosophy, all of which contribute to the discussion over how human lives should be lived.

Meta-ethics addresses the assumptions, principles and concepts on which ethical discussions rely. It seeks to understand what words such as good, bad, right and wrong really mean, to establish the origins of moral ideas and the nature of moral philosophy as a discipline. It asks whether human beings are free to make moral decisions and to be responsible for their consequences.

Normative ethics focuses on moral laws which govern actions, developing systems for deciding what to do in practical situations.

Applied ethics considers particular issues and dilemmas and analyses them, offering answers to the fundamental philosophical questions they raise.

Although philosophers today tend to focus on one of these approaches, they are not independent but rely on each other. In the past, many moral philosophers were systematic in addressing all three aspects of decision-making, but the increasing technicality and complexity of each has made this relatively rare today, with philosophers tending to rely on colleagues to fill in the gaps around their own contribution.

Since normative and applied ethics were undermined by the rise of relativism some moral philosophers have engaged in **descriptive ethics,** describing how a particular people behaves, which actions and character traits are admired, and perhaps why. This enterprise is related to biology, psychology, sociology and anthropology and is sometimes carried out within these departments in universities, rather than within the philosophy department.

The three parts of this book will focus on meta-ethics, major systems of normative ethics and selected issues in applied ethics, before considering the fundamental question of freedom and outlining a possible way forward in the two concluding chapters.

A website has been established – www.what-matters.org – for readers of this book which will include updates, suggested activities and other relevant information which readers may find interesting.

PART ONE

Meta-ethics

Truth in Ethics

Turning and turning in the widening gyre
The falcon cannot hear the falconer;
Things fall apart; the centre cannot hold;
Mere anarchy is loosed upon the world,
The blood-dimmed tide is loosed, and everywhere
The ceremony of innocence is drowned;
The best lack all conviction, while the worst
Are full of passionate intensity.
(W. B. Yates, 'The Second Coming', 1920)

Meta-ethics takes a 'bird's-eye view' of ethics. It challenges individuals to think about the assumptions, rules and concepts that are relied on in discussions about what is right and wrong and then to subject them to serious analysis. It is concerned with the origin of moral standards, whether they are real or absolute and in what sense. It is also concerned with how language is used in discussions about right and wrong and what terms such as 'right' and 'wrong' actually mean. John Locke described the work of the philosopher as clearing away the undergrowth so that we can better see the challenges ahead; in this case meta-ethics should be the first concern of every moral philosopher.

The View from the Cave

Plato (*c.* 427–347) sowed the seeds for modern meta-ethics. *The Republic* takes the form of a dialogue between various characters, each of whom represents a different way of thinking about an essential principle of moral discussions, justice.

- **Polemarchus** argues that being a just person enhances the life of the individual.
- **Thrasymachus** says that justice is whatever is in the best interests of the strong and the powerful. Morality is the creation of those in power, a system which is designed to keep them in power!
- **Glaucon** agrees that morality is a human construct, but argues that it is pragmatic, designed in order that people can live together in society.

None of these three sees justice as an absolute or 'real'; **Socrates** rejects their positions and maintains that justice is absolute and relates to 'the good' which exists independently of human perception. The dialogue shows Socrates' position to be the strongest.[1]

For Plato justice, good and truth exist, they are real in an ultimate sense. The '**Form of the Good**' exists eternally, beyond the limitations of time and space, metaphysically. Dim reflections of these absolute qualities are seen in objects and actions in the physical world and encourage individuals to contemplate the

---

1 The character of Socrates in Plato's dialogues usually seems to represent Plato's own view, and we are not sure which of the views he attributes to Socrates actually stemmed from Socrates. Socrates was Plato's teacher and inspiration and it is sad that we do not have Socrates' own account of his thinking, given the extent of his influence in western philosophy. Socrates was no academic author; his approach to philosophy was intensely practical, not to say annoying! He spent his days in the forum asking awkward questions and challenging every assumption, every unfounded belief.

It was because Socrates challenged the basis of Athenian religion and morality, because he threatened to destabilize the state by 'corrupting the young' into thinking for themselves (essentially because he engaged in meta-ethics), that he was put on trial and given the choice between death and exile. He chose to drink hemlock: being forced to deny the truth would be worse than death. Socrates became a martyr for reason; he triumphed over pragmatic politicians with truth his standard and became a hero for all philosophers. See Plato's *Apology*.

essence of goodness, which is the origin of beauty, justice and even mathematics.

In Book Seven of *The Republic* Plato used the **analogy of the cave** to explain his understanding of reality. A group of prisoners are confined underground in a cave, in almost total darkness. They are chained, facing a rock wall. The captors have a fire lit behind the prisoners and sometimes move around the cave, casting shadows of their activities against the wall. The prisoners' total reality is the shadows on the wall. They cannot conceive of the world outside. Even if one of the prisoners escaped and came back to tell them about the sun and the trees and the flowers they would simply have to kill him. It would be too unsettling to have their understanding of reality challenged, let alone to accept that they are in prison.

The film *The Matrix*[2] explores a similar idea. Neo discovers that his world is artificial, a computer-generated reality, and is given the choice over whether he stays in the Matrix or tries to leave. *The Truman Show*[3] tells the story of a man who was born and has always lived in a reality TV show. His whole world is the creation of the TV company; but one day he discovers the edge of the set and escapes.

For Plato, the task of the philosopher is to escape from the world of illusion, the shadow world perpetuated by ignorant society, to try to see things as they really are.

For Plato there is little point in discussing God in relation to moral standards. Different societies worship different gods and claim divine authority for behaving in shockingly irrational and contradictory ways. However, he argues for moral standards that are independent, universal, real, and that may be known through reason.

---

2 1999, written and directed by Larry and Andy Wachowski.

3 1998, directed by Peter Weir.

The Fog Descends

Sadly, during the twentieth century meta-ethics became obsessed with semantics, linguistic analysis, and came to undermine both normative and applied ethics. Law and moral norms were seen to be pragmatic at best and cultural constructions at worst. What can a moral philosopher do if the business of recommending how we should respond to practical dilemmas has been discredited? The alternatives seem to be to either retreat into technical and obscure meta-ethics or become a sociologist.

In northern England, people tend never to say that it rains; there may be gloam, drizzle or mizzle, it may be dank or dreary and it frequently pours down, but it rarely just 'rains'. Language is often colourful and can be used to mark territory, to divide 'insiders' from 'outsiders' and highlight newcomers. Philosophers need language to be precise, but sometimes the desire for clarity results in a proliferation of technical and obscure words which make it difficult for 'outsiders' to take part in or evaluate discussions.

Sadly, in a world where academic careers are measured by number of publications and citations some philosophers appear to have exploited this, coining yet more terms as an easy way of gaining status. Ironically, professional philosophy has actually 'planted undergrowth', obscuring the 'big questions' rather than exposing them.

What Is Truth?

There are two basic theories of truth.

- **Realists** maintain that a statement is true or false in relation to how it **corresponds** to an independent state of affairs. So: (a) 'The cat sat on the mat' is true, if – and only if – there is a cat sitting on the mat; or (b) 'Petra is beautiful' is true, if Petra conforms to some absolute standard of beauty; or (c) 'Rape is wrong' is true, if rape is wrong according to some ultimate set of values.

- **Anti-realists** maintain that a statement is true or false because it **coheres** with other statements and beliefs within a particular community or 'form of life'.[4] So 'It is wrong to tackle a person who is running' is true within a game of cricket and false within a game of rugby. 'A man may have only one wife' is true within Christian cultures and false within Islamic cultures; and the truth of statements such as 'It is good to help widows and orphans' may depend on the situation or on cultural values.

Realism and anti-realism underpin discussions in ethics as much as other philosophical discussions.

Traditionally people have accepted that claims about good, bad, right and wrong relate to real and absolute values, that the claims should correspond to truth, to the way things are objectively. During the nineteenth century, however, people began to question the existence of real values; experience of different cultures and different types of people, combined with the loosening grip of religion, suggested that values are at least culturally relative and are not absolute. What may be 'right' in one culture may be 'wrong' in another. It is not just a matter of some cultures being right and others wrong, but rather that truth actually depends on the culture we are in. What is right for one person in one set of circumstances might be wrong for another person in different circumstances. For **relativists** moral statements are true or false only to the extent that they cohere with what people accept: they are subjectively true.

---

4 The term used by Wittgenstein to indicate the community or culture within which language is understood, develops and operates.

2

Moral Realism

One can be a moral realist in several different ways. Moral statements are *either* true *or* they are false depending on whether or not they correspond – but what might they correspond to?

There are four basic alternatives:

1 **Ethical Monotheism**: Moral standards depend on the will of God, which is either directly revealed through divine commands or indirectly revealed through human nature and experience. This may be revealed in scriptures (such as the Bible, Torah or Qur'an), through the teaching of a religious institution or through conscience.
2 **Ethical Naturalism**: Moral standards depend on the common nature that all human beings share – this may or may not have been created by God.
3 **Ethical Non-Naturalism**: Moral standards exist but cannot be described or known except as a rational intuition.
4 **Synthetic Moral Realism**: We cannot prove what the foundations for moral discussion are, but it does not make sense to doubt that they are real.

Ethical Monotheism

Ethical Monotheism holds that morality depends directly on the sovereign will of God. God is supreme, created everything and has the absolute right to command what God wills. God dictates what is right or wrong. God can do as God pleases; it remains only for human beings to obey. There is no moral basis for judging God. God can even command what seems to contradict God's commands. Human beings cannot know or understand the mind of God; it is not for God to be judged by human intellect.

The Franciscan Christian tradition, mainstream Islam and some Jews hold this position; God's will is the final arbiter of morality and there can be no appeal beyond this.

The problem for human beings is how to know what it is that God commands. There are various sources for the revelation of the divine will (text(s), tradition, religious experience and reason) but there are considerable differences within religious groups as to how these should be interpreted or used. An example is biblical teaching about homosexuality. Within the Anglican (Episcopalian) Church there is little agreement over how biblical teachings should be interpreted.

- Liberals (including the previous Archbishop of Canterbury, Rowan Williams) argue that isolated references in the Bible cannot be taken literally; Christians do not kill people for wearing garments of mixed fabrics, or for being disobedient to parents. The Bible needs to be seen in the context and culture in which it was written. It contains great wisdom but specific passages should not override its general spirit.
- Conservatives and evangelicals (such as the Archbishop of York, John Sentamu, and Nicky Gumbel) criticize liberals for being pragmatic, rejecting the timeless truth of God's revelation to make Christianity acceptable to modern culture.

The **Divine Command Theory** suffers as a philosophical approach because of the difficulty of determining what God commands and how this should be applied.

Plato records how Socrates criticized the Divine Command approach to meta-ethics in his book *Euthyphro*. This is in the form of a dialogue which tells the story of Socrates' encounter with a young man (Euthyphro) to illustrate a problem with a traditional religious interpretation of 'the good'. Socrates asks whether what is good is good because the gods command it, or whether the gods only command what is good according to an independent standard. Euthyphro faces a dilemma; both alternatives are unsatisfactory:

- If goodness depends on the commands of the gods or God's command then it is arbitrary and God can be portrayed as a tyrant and therefore not worthy of worship, as whatever God commands is good just because God commands it.
- If goodness depends on an independent standard then there is a standard higher than God and God is no longer supreme.

In basic terms, most people see God (the gods) as embodying the qualities of perfection, being omnipotent (all-powerful) and omnibenevolent (all-good). But, as Socrates shows, God cannot be both. An arbitrary tyrant is not good and a god subservient to independent moral standards is not all-powerful. God, therefore, seems to be limited, either not worthy of worship or (as Bertrand Russell later argued) non-existent.

Russell formalized the argument:

1 If there is a moral law then it *either* stems from God *or* it does not.
2 If the moral law comes from God then it is arbitrary.
3 If it does not come from God then God is subject to it.
4 *Either* God is not essentially good because he is arbitrary *or* God is not ultimate because he is subject to an independent moral standard.
5 *Neither* an arbitrary God *nor* a less than ultimate God is worthy of worship.
6 Therefore there is no God.

Russell assumes that, for all believers:

1 Morality depends on God's command.
2 Limitation on God necessitates his non-existence.

His first assumption at least was misplaced; many believers are not ethical monotheists but rather adopt Ethical Naturalism.

Ethical Naturalism

Ethical Naturalism holds that human beings share a common human nature from which real and universal moral standards can be deduced. Ways of behaving which fulfil human nature are good and those that lead human beings away from fulfilment are evil.

God may be held to have given human beings their common nature, and thus morality could depend on God, but an atheist or an agnostic could also be an ethical naturalist. Aristotle held this view and did not relate human nature to God at all. What is right in naturalist ethics therefore corresponds to what leads to the fulfilment of the shared human nature, whether or not this comes from God.

For religious naturalists it is for human reason to establish how people should behave with reference to what it means to live a fulfilled human life. God may command or prohibit through prophets or teachers or through the Church – but such commands must be in accordance with reason. The mainstream Roman Catholic tradition holds this view, based on Thomas Aquinas' approach to Natural Law. The Natural Law tradition of ethics will be examined in more detail later.

Mainstream Christianity does not accept that God is a moral agent, that 'goodness' can mean the same thing in relation to God as it does in relation to human beings. For most religious people language cannot be applied **univocally** to God; at best language is **analogical**. Terms such as 'good' are true when applied to God, but because God is wholly simple (beyond the time and space which frame earthly concepts) their content is limited. Saying 'God is good' cannot imply choice or moral action; being outside time and space, God cannot change or act in the human sense. Saying that 'God is good' can only suggest that God fulfils whatever God's nature is, really that 'God is God' or, as God said to Moses from the burning bush, 'I am that I am'.[1] The Euthyphro Dilemma is misleading and irrelevant. God is not a moral agent, only fully actual. God may create human beings with a common human nature but, ethical naturalists maintain, it is this nature that grounds moral claims and not the arbitrary commands of God.

Ethical naturalists maintain that goodness can be defined in non-moral terms and that statements about 'good and bad', 'right and wrong' are true because they can be shown to be true 'scientifically', through observation and analysis of what it means to be human. What ought to be is grounded in what is. Natural Law, some forms of Utilitarianism and arguably Kantian Ethics are all naturalist approaches to moral philosophy.

Ethical Non-Naturalism

Ethical non-naturalists reject the central claim of naturalists, that goodness can be defined and understood through experience and observation. They are still realists and uphold a correspondence theory of truth, but argue that goodness may only be known through rational intuition, not on the basis of ordinary experience.

Metaethics is often traced to **G. E. Moore**'s 1903 classic *Principia Ethica*.[2] In this work Moore (1873–1958) exposed the foundations of moral philosophy in a clear and rigorous way. Understanding the writings of W. D. Ross, R. M. Hare or John Finnis depends to a large extent on understanding Moore.

Moore was a realist; he held that moral judgements are either true or false and must correspond with the actual relationship between an action or person and a standard of goodness which

---

1 For Ibn Rushd, for Maimonides and for Aquinas to be 'good' is to be fully actual, to be all that one can be and to have fulfilled all potential.

2 Terry Horgan and Mark Timmons, *Metaethics after Moore*, Oxford: Clarendon Press, 2006, p. 20.

exists independently of culture. Moore understood goodness as an absolute metaphysical reality, apprehended by reason but not dependent on experience or analysable. He did not accept that we can define or understand moral truths simply through experience and observation; the way things are is not necessarily a guide to how they should be.

For Moore 'goodness' cannot be analysed to mean just pleasure-producing. He points out that if saying 'X is good' is the same as saying 'X is pleasure' then really this is saying that 'Pleasure is good' is the same as saying 'Pleasure is pleasure'. Moore concludes that this is inadequate, arguing that it is still possible to ask, 'Is pleasure good?', which would not make sense if goodness really could be defined in terms of pleasure.

Moore compared goodness with yellowness. We would struggle to define the colour yellow without giving examples of yellow things (try it!). Yellowness cannot be defined in non-yellow terms and goodness cannot be defined in terms of pleasure or any other quality, yet we recognize yellowness and goodness. Ethics is autonomous and it is not possible to explain what is right and wrong in other terms; goodness is a **rational intuition**; not a 'hunch' but known through reason without reference to experience.

The Naturalistic Fallacy

Moore argued that philosophers such as Aquinas and Bentham depended on what he termed the 'Naturalistic Fallacy'; they observed what *is* and then moved to saying that the same *ought* to be. Writing in the lead-up to World War One Moore agreed with David Hume's conclusion[3] that the move from what is the case to what ought to be is a logical leap that does not withstand analysis. It is common for men to desire sexual pleasure, but it does not follow that this is what men should seek. The common occurrence of things does not make them right.

---

3 David Hume, *A Treatise on Human Nature*, III, 1, i.

Moore believed that this argument undermined the whole of traditional normative ethics. Natural Law, Virtue Ethics, most forms of Utilitarianism and arguably Kantian Ethics all depend on observation of human nature as the foundation for prescriptions of what human beings should be and do. Moore rejected them.[4]

Any appeal to an absolute standard that cannot be verified by observation will always be subject to criticism. It may be argued that there are fewer grounds for believing in metaphysical ideals than for believing in God and it is difficult to expect philosophers to forego grounding moral norms in experience. Also, non-naturalists rarely agree on their rational intuitions. Nevertheless ethical non-naturalism is growing in support today. Shafer-Landau argues that just as disagreement about issues in philosophy does not undermine the idea of an absolute truth, so the same applies in ethics.[5]

Synthetic Moral Realism

The synthetic moral realist argues that it is not possible to prove what the foundations for moral judgements are, but it does not make sense to doubt that they are real and that they exist independent of human culture.

The following example is given by Andrew Fisher.[6] Imagine locking up 50 different scientists from different cultures around the world in 50 different laboratories and giving them a recently fired gun. They would probably all come up with very similar

---

4 Moore may have misinterpreted Aristotle and Aquinas though. They did not move simply from what people do to what they should do. Instead they said one should observe human beings at their best and it is these examples that give us an indication of what human nature should be. Someone who beats his wife is not an example of human nature at its best.

5 Russ Shafer-Landau, *Oxford Studies in Metaethics*, Vol. 2, Oxford: Oxford University Press, 2006.

6 Andrew Fisher, *MetaEthics: An Introduction*, Durham: Acumen, 2011.

conclusions about when the gun was fired, the presence of DNA on the trigger and the type of blood on the barrel. This is because their investigations converge on the truth. Now imagine locking up 50 people around the world and asking them to come up with the ten most important moral rules – it is probable they would come up with a very similar list (do not murder, do not steal, etc.). This is because their deliberations converge on the truth.

Truth seems to be bound up with what is real – and this implies moral realism. This is also implied by progress in ethics and morality over the centuries. Many moral philosophers now accept Moore's position. Maybe Moore was right and there is no way of defining goodness. Nevertheless, in order to get around the difficulty with non-naturalism some philosophers have proposed taking some commonly accepted and useful ideas about goodness as postulates and basing morality on them. They do not suggest that these ideas are social constructs or not real, just that their reality cannot be adequately proven or expressed at present. This is Synthetic Moral Realism.

If we postulate the existence of black holes or anti-matter then we can explain things that we could not explain otherwise and scientists accept them unless or until evidence is found to the contrary. Human behaviour is best explained by the reality of moral rules, so it may be reasonable to accept that they are real unless or until evidence is presented to the contrary.

Conclusion

Moral Realism therefore, provides four alternatives. Truth claims in ethics – in other words what is right or wrong, good or bad – depend on whether a given action corresponds or not to

- God's absolute will
- human nature which may or may not be created by God
- real moral standards, known through rational intuition but which exist independently of God

- real moral standards which must exist, though we cannot describe or prove them absolutely.

Uncertainty

It is important to recognize that one can be a realist about ethics without claiming to know which ethical claims are true or false. One might say, 'Commercial surrogacy is either right or wrong, but I do not know which.' Right and wrong may correspond to a real standard (whatever that may be) but that does not mean that human beings know what right and wrong are. Some realists are also profoundly sceptical about our ability to *know* what is right. Wittgenstein was just such a sceptical moral realist.[7]

Many people today reject all the above positions. It is popular to argue that what is right or wrong is relative to culture, even to suggest that it is imperialistic to claim that polygamy, misogyny or even female circumcision is absolutely wrong. This relativistic position is tested, however, when it comes to crimes which affect people across cultural boundaries or which are so horrific that they seem contrary to humanity. Whether it is the Holocaust, genocide in Rwanda, the extermination of the disabled or the abuse of one attractive child; these cases tend to make people less accepting of cultural relativism.

The second part of this book will examine three different approaches which argue for moral realism and, therefore, absolute moral standards. Although no one normative system is without problems, as the next chapter shows, the consequences of relativism raise the stakes.

---

7 Panayot Butchvarov argues this in 'Ethics Dehumanized', in Horgan and Timmons, *Metaethics after Moore*, pp. 367–90.

3

Relativism

Moore and Wittgenstein Hit Bedrock …

As a child **Ludwig Wittgenstein** (1889–1951) was largely silent.
His wealthy family thought him slow in comparison with his
brilliant brother Paul and his accomplished sisters, and sent him
to a technical school in Vienna in the hopes that he could train
to be an engineer. Apparently Adolf Hitler attended the same
school at the same time, and was also thought to be slow. As a
young man Wittgenstein went to study aeronautical engineering
at Manchester, but one summer made his way to Cambridge. He
found out where G. E. Moore worked and arrived unannounced
at his rooms. He started to talk – indeed he talked himself into a
job (though he did not even have a degree at the time) and went
on to teach philosophy at Cambridge for the rest of his life. Wittgenstein became one of the most influential philosophers of the
twentieth century.[1]

In 1925, Moore wrote an important paper called 'In Defence
of Common Sense', in which he argued that knowledge makes
contact with the world through banal statements that it does not
make sense to doubt. For example, it does not make sense to
doubt that 'This is a hand' or 'This is a chair'. These statements
simply cannot be doubted – they are the point where questioning
comes to an end. Moore's argument leaves completely undecided
the question as to how these banal statements are to be analysed;
he is willing to accept any account which does not deny things

---

1 See Ray Monk, *Ludwig Wittgenstein: The Duty of Genius*, London:
Vintage, new edn 1991.

which I know for certain and which other people likewise know for certain. He implies that the attempt to analyse banal statements will achieve nothing.[2]

Towards the end of his career, Wittgenstein returned to the nature of these banal statements and the foundations of knowledge in *On Certainty*[3] (which was compiled from lecture notes after his death). Wittgenstein argued that we are educated into the use of language at our parents' knees; we pick up groundrules which shape our conception of reality. People do not tend to doubt these rules and cannot really comprehend, let alone communicate, a truth beyond the rules, outside the 'language-game' or 'form of life'.

Wittgenstein agreed with Moore that there is a point where it no longer makes sense to ask questions. Rather like a child who continually asks 'Why?' there comes a point when Mummy just says 'Because that is how it is – be quiet!' Wittgenstein wrote: 'when I have reached bedrock my spade is turned – then I can simply say "this is what we do".'[4] Yet Wittgenstein parted company with Moore on one issue. Moore thought that the truisms he listed are a basis for certain and universal knowledge and could be held to be true in an absolute sense, while Wittgenstein disagreed. For Wittgenstein, although truisms cannot reasonably be questioned, this does not make them absolutely true or into foundations for universal knowledge.

Wittgenstein's Language-Game

For Wittgenstein 'hand' is just a label people in one form of life assign to things that cohere with their concept and experience of hands; the word, the concept and particular experience rely on

---

2 'On Certainty', reprinted in *G. E. Moore, Selected Writings*, ed. T. Baldwin, London: Routledge, 1993, pp. 171–96.

3 Ludwig Wittgenstein, *On Certainty*, Oxford: Oxford University Press, 1969.

4 Ludwig Wittgenstein, *Philosophical Investigations*, Hoboken, NJ: Wiley-Blackwell, 2009, Section 217.

each other. **To some extent language shapes our experience of the world as well as describing it.**

Further, even within one language or culture there may be differences in how language is understood. The meaning of phrases like 'I am taking my bat home' depends on who is speaking and who is listening. In northern England the statement means 'I am fed up', but in Australia it might just mean that you are transporting a cricket bat.

Some followers of Wittgenstein argue that it follows that the same could be true of morality. It might not make sense to question statements such as 'Murder is wrong' within a culture, but that does not make them absolutely or universally true. Moral truth may depend on language, culture and other factors; judgements cannot be really or absolutely true and objective truth is effectively non-existent. For antirealists, realism is mistaken. Truth does *not* rest on correspondence and all the meta-ethical positions set out in the last chapter are to be rejected. For antirealists, moral truth relies instead on coherence, on what is accepted as true within the community. So:

- In Islam a man is allowed four wives but in Christianity only one; so it would be true to say 'Bigamy is wrong' in Scotland but not in Saudi Arabia.
- In Judaism one may not eat pork, but in Christianity this is not a problem; so it would be true to say that it is wrong to eat bacon in an Orthodox community outside Tel Aviv, but not in an Eastern Orthodox Christian community in Toronto.
- Many in the secular West consider sex before marriage to be normal, while in other traditional societies it is forbidden and may result in death. It would be true to say that a woman who was not a virgin on her wedding night had sinned in Pakistan, but not in New Zealand.
- In the Netherlands, abortion is widely accepted, while in other countries it is illegal. It would be true to say that abortion is wrong in a conservative Catholic country in South America, but false in Rotterdam.

Within Islam certain moral statements are true, within Hinduism certain statements are true and within Greece or Burma certain statements are true, but there are no absolute truths. This leads to cultural relativism. For relativists moral truth depends on what is agreed within different societies.

Truth and the Limits of Philosophy

It is worth noting, however, that, like Moore, Wittgenstein had a highly developed sense of personal morality. Yes, he doubted whether concepts of goodness and evil could be reduced, analysed and explained by philosophy but it did not stop him from being scrupulously honest. He was known to write to people he might inadvertently have misled about trivial matters to put them straight weeks after the event.[5] This was not just a habit, done to 'fit in' or to be pragmatic. Wittgenstein signed up as a private in the Austro-Hungarian army during World War One and refused to seek any 'special treatment' on the grounds of his wealth or ability to claim residence in England;[6] he left Cambridge and sought menial war-work during World War Two as well.[7] Wittgenstein was a man of exceptional integrity. When he wrote that 'Whereof one cannot speak, thereof one must be silent'[8] he did not necessarily mean that truth does not exist, just that it is beyond the limits of philosophy.

There is a real sense of modesty about Wittgenstein's claims; he wished to come to a perspicuous understanding of the world and to stop philosophers asking futile questions. He considered the attempt to describe, analyse and prove absolute foundations for knowledge futile, whether or not those foundations are real.

5 Monk, *Wittgenstein*, p. 30.

6 Monk, *Wittgenstein*, p. 30.

7 Monk, *Wittgenstein*, p. 30.

8 See Ludwig Wittgenstein, *Tractatus Logico-Philosophicus*, London: Routledge, 2001, Section 7. Quoted and discussed in Roger M. White, *Wittgenstein's 'Tractatus Logico-Philosophicus': A Reader's Guide*, London: Continuum, 2006, p. 118.

Antirealism and Postmodernism

Antirealism and postmodernism are related but are not the same. Antirealists hold on to language about truth, seeing it as grounded in culture, relative but contextually meaningful. Post-modernists go a step further and claim that meaning depends on the individual; the author of a poem may mean one thing and a reader may understand it differently. Both are valid. Nobody has a monopoly on the truth and claiming certainty is absurd. Postmodernism has been defined as an 'incredulity towards meta-narratives',[9] and its defining characteristic is scepticism towards any institution or system which claims to 'explain the human experience' or to 'possess truth' – even antirealism! Postmodern-ists are interested in the effects of perspective on perception and interpretation; they often study things in relation to gender, sexu-ality or culture. Postmodernists try to do justice to the reality of being human, which is complicated, difficult to express or under-stand, and resistant to being pinned down in simple systematic terms.

Yet, despite insisting on the limits of philosophy, denying the existence of truth is not necessarily a feature of postmodern thinking. Since 1990 'Postmodern Ethics' has developed, which tries to help people to engage with the reality of goodness and evil without prescribing or proscribing particular actions. Post-modern Ethics uses discussion, current examples and literature as ways of exploring the reality and importance of making moral decisions even if there is no absolute basis for them. Postmodern Ethics begins by encouraging people to share an ethical experi-ence rather than a set of ideas and is, therefore, individualized and highly contextual.

It is possible to see a line of inheritance from Kant to Wittgen-stein to postmodernism. Kant argued that human knowledge is coloured by perspective and that we cannot know the *Ding an*

---

9 See J. F. Lyotard, *The Postmodern Condition: A Report on Knowledge*, Minneapolis: University of Minnesota Press, 1984, p. xxiv.

sich (see page 134). Wittgenstein argued that language is a more effective barrier to knowledge than Kant admitted and postmodernism has taken this to its logical conclusion.

Hooray for Ayer?

In *Language, Truth and Logic* (1936), A. J. Ayer (1910–89) argued that the meaningfulness of statements depends on whether they can be verified through sense-experience. 'This ball is red' can be verified, and is either true or false depending on whether there is a ball and it is indeed red. However, many apparently factual statements such as 'Columbus discovered America in 1492' are difficult to verify, let alone statements about things which cannot be sensed, such as beauty, goodness or God.

The verificationists rejected as technically meaningless any talk of good, bad, right or wrong; for Ayer all ethical statements do is to express an emotional attitude – this is emotivism. It is sometimes called the 'Boo/Hurrah' theory of ethics. If someone says 'Abortion is wrong,' all they are really indicating is that they have a negative emotional attitude to abortion; if someone says 'Compassion is good,' all they are really saying is that they have a positive emotional attitude to compassion. In different societies there may, of course, be different attitudes to different moral situations and these simply reflect different emotional attitudes. The influence of verificationism is strong. Some people feel the need to put inverted commas around terms such as right or wrong for fear of appearing judgemental or ignorant.

Ayer seems to have prefigured the modern tendency to reduce complex conversations, attitudes and feelings to a combination of single words and emoticons. For example, 'I am thinking of having an abortion, but am worried that it may be wrong' becomes 'abortion ☹?', and 'I am in hospital, and one of the nurses was really kind to me' becomes 'in hospital – nurse ☺!' Verificationists might approve of social networks encouraging people to indicate their mood, likes and dislikes with simple symbols;

reducing our personalities in this way makes it much easier to 'understand' us – and classify us for marketing purposes.

It can be questioned whether reducing the scope of what can be known or meaningfully talked about to what can be empirically tested really does justice to human experience. If nothing was said about morality, if all thoughts about God were rejected and any value-judgement was laughed at then it could be argued that this would be an impoverishment of human experience. There is a danger in philosophic positions that are reductionist: the attempt to reduce complex and important ideas that may be difficult to prove to ideas that are simple and verified does violence to the depth and profundity of the ideas.

The television news might cover stories of raids on refugee camps where young girls have been captured and sold into prostitution, of a Greek shipping company which broke all the rules and caused several ecological disasters, of an African dictator who stole $4 billion in international aid money and of a Chinese factory which made its products more attractive by adding melamine powder to them, particularly to baby-milk powder – and all that we could say is 'I disapprove of those things – but I am sure that the Janjaweed, the shipping company directors, the dictator and the baby-milk manufacturers would approve and their opinion is worth as much as mine. Perhaps those things are acceptable in their culture ...'

Someone might visit an unfamiliar church and find the preacher saying how God told him in a dream that some of the children of the congregation are possessed by demons and must be exorcized by being kept in the cellar and forced to eat strange roots, at a cost of £2,000. One might hear reports of an imam telling worshippers in Gaza that it is their Islamic duty to go out and capture Israeli soldiers and give them 'a fate worse than death', because it says so in the Qur'an. In a primary school, one might be invited to attend sports day in which there are no races but just games, for which all the children get prizes for taking part. The teacher says, 'Who says we should reward only the fastest, the fittest and the strongest? In our school, we believe that it is taking part that counts.' If truth claims in ethics are rejected, then all that could be said would be, 'Well, that is an opinion. In my opinion those things are bad – but in their culture they may be perfectly acceptable. Acting to stop these things could be a form of colonialism.'

These scenarios may seem far-fetched but we can also recognize this type of thinking from general experience. Relativism and indeed the more extreme emotivism have been influential and have even come to dominate some aspects of modern life. This is despite the fact that it is impossible to verify the claims made by verificationists. There is no way to check Ayer's claim that moral judgements are equivalent to saying boo or hooray against sense-data, and therefore it could be as meaningless as those moral judgements are claimed to be.

Faith and Reason

In 1998, Pope John Paul II wrote an encyclical entitled *Fides et Ratio* (Faith and Reason),[10] in which he said that the greatest danger facing the world was not environmental catastrophe, economic cataclysm or war – but the rise of relativism and postmodernism. He wrote:

> One of the most significant aspects of our current situation, it should be noted, is the 'crisis of meaning'. Perspectives on life and the world, often of a scientific temper, have so proliferated that we face an increasing fragmentation of knowledge. This makes the search for meaning difficult and often fruitless. Indeed, still more dramatically, in this maelstrom of data and facts in which we live and which seem to comprise the very fabric of life, many people wonder whether it still makes sense to ask about meaning. The array of theories which vie to give an answer, and the different ways of viewing and of interpreting the world and human life, serve only to aggravate this radi-

---

10 Available online at http://www.vatican.va/edocs/ENG0216/_INDEX. HTM.

cal doubt, which can easily lead to scepticism, indifference or to various forms of nihilism. (Ch. 7)

He went on:

A legitimate plurality of positions has yielded to an undifferentiated pluralism, based upon the assumption that all positions are equally valid, which is one of today's most widespread symptoms of the lack of confidence in truth ... Everything is reduced to opinion ... as a philosophy of nothingness, (Nihilism) has a certain attraction for people of our time ... In the nihilist interpretation, life is no more than an occasion for sensations and experiences in which the ephemeral has pride of place. Nihilism is at the root of the widespread mentality which claims that a definitive commitment should no longer be made, because everything is fleeting and provisional.

Of course, the Pope may be wrong. Perhaps there is no meaning, perhaps life is simply a cosmic accident and the idea of moraity is no more than a set of adaptive behaviours which have evolved through natural selection to enable human genes to be perpetuated. This is the position taken by celebrity atheists and their admirers.

The consequences of such a view need to be analysed. It has come to dominate philosophy, undermine religion, and deter efforts to make the world more tolerant and principled. It is not necessarily correct.

Perhaps, as the Pope suggests, relativism leads to nihilism, to giving up on ethical issues, and may be based on flawed arguments anyway. Perhaps, however, there may be another way forward.

PART TWO

Normative Ethics

4

Normative Ethics

Meta-ethics seeks to answer higher-order questions in moral philosophy such as what words like good and bad, right and wrong may mean. By contrast, normative ethics tries to establish what is right and what is wrong by proposing systems for working out how human beings should behave and why. Normative ethics is, therefore, the basis for approaching practical issues (in applied ethics) such as abortion, stem-cell research, environmental decisions and warfare.

Some moral philosophers have focused on the rightness or wrongness of actions, arguing that certain forms of behaviour are always right or always wrong. For example, the deliberate and unlawful killing of another human person might always be wrong regardless of who carries out the action, with what intention or with what consequences. The end can never justify the means. Some people refer to such approaches as 'action-centred'; otherwise they are called absolutist or deontological, referring to the definite labelling of actions as right or wrong and to clear and universal moral duties (*deontos*, Greek for 'duty' or more literally 'function of being') which arise from this labelling. The Roman Catholic Church supports this approach, regarding certain actions as 'intrinsically evil' – that is, they are wrong in themselves. Most religions propose action-centred moral philosophies, not least because they support the administration and enforcement of law and because they provide an important role for scholars or religious authorities in determining the status of actions.

Other moral philosophers have focused on the consequences of actions, arguing that the ends may justify the means and that much depends on the particular situation. For example, perhaps even murder might be justified in extreme cases, where the outcome is somehow better than the alternative. Consequentialist (or teleological) systems see actions as right or wrong in a *relative* sense, depending on whether the results (given the particular situation) are closer to or further from some ultimate end (*telos*) which is desirable in itself for all people, such as happiness. Consequentialist systems support individuals in taking moral responsibility for their own actions, but given the difficulties in predicting outcomes and in assessing intentions it is difficult to use them as a basis for civil or religious law.

The contrast between action-centred and consequentialist ethics is well illustrated by Holman Hunt's painting of Claudio and Isabella.[1] The painting is based on a scene from Shakespeare's *Measure for Measure*. Claudio and Isabella are brother and sister. Claudio is due to hang the next day unless Isabella loses her virginity to the absent Duke's deputy, Angelo. The problem is summed up by these lines from the play which Hunt had written on the frame:

Claudio: 'Death is a fearful thing.'
Isabella: 'And shamed life is hateful.'

Claudio takes a consequentialist view of ethics, holding that the dishonour resulting from his sister losing her virginity is off-set by his continuing life, but Isabella sees such an action as inherently wrong, not justified by any consequences. Hunt was a Christian painter and the painting makes clear his position – Isabella is bathed in sunlight linking her to the outdoor scene, with its apple blossom in full bloom and a distant view of a church, a reminder of duty and Christian ethics. Claudio's contorted pose,

---

[1] The painting can be viewed online at http://www.tate.org.uk/art/slideshow?wi=1&wp=1&st=6766, accessed 25 April 2012.

as he stands manacled to the wall, indicates his troubled mind and his dishevelled dress indicates he is a passionate individual whose passions rule over his reason.

Many modern ethical disagreements originate in the difference between an action-centred and a consequentialist approach to decision-making.

Throughout history there has been a 'third way' in normative ethics, which resists calls to provide clear guidance on individual forms of behaviour and has chosen instead to consider the bigger picture, the sort of character that every moral agent should try to develop through a lifetime of decision-making. Virtue ethicists may not agree on the particular character-strengths that human beings should promote and may not provide the most practical guidance when it comes to extreme dilemmas of the type discussed in most ethics textbooks; however, they make the sensible point that dilemmas are very rare and most people deal in much lower-stake decisions on a day-to-day basis, decisions which may seem trivial but which have a cumulative effect on human personality. Most virtue ethicists agree that there is a real and universal standard for human flourishing, though they accept that some virtues may change in relation to cultural and social pressures, and they tend to be moral realists. One can describe Virtue Ethics as an 'agent-centred approach' to moral philosophy and it has had a resurgence of popularity in recent decades. Virtue Ethics is of limited use when it comes to informing the process of civil or religious law-making; however, it combines the strengths of action-centred and consequentialist systems. It allows individuals to benefit from others' wisdom about the likely effects of forms of behaviour while encouraging them to reflect and take on responsibility for their own choices.

It can be tempting to survey various approaches to normative ethics, focusing on the contrasts between them and the problems which they inevitably encounter, perhaps concluding that the whole business of discussing right and wrong is bankrupt. Of course no normative system has provided conclusive answers to questions in moral philosophy (if it had then there would be very little discussion of moral issues and the world would be a very different place). However, one of the themes of this book will be to argue that there is an underlying unity beneath different approaches. The great moral philosophers share the belief that being good consists in fulfilling our common human potential and flourishing. As the leading Catholic moral philosopher Gerard Hughes remarked, 'in a broad sense it would be fair to say that all the classical western Philosophers, from Aristotle to Bentham, tried in some way to show that morality had its basis in human nature'.[2] Clearly there are disagreements over the details of what human nature is and how we flourish, but that is not to say that there is not a common wisdom which points human beings towards a good life. This point will be explored in the coming chapters.

---

2 Gerard W. Hughes, 'Natural Law', in Bernard Hoose (ed.), *Christian Ethics: An Introduction*, London: Cassell, 1998, p. 47.

5

Natural Law

Natural Law has the longest tradition of any approach to moral philosophy. In the western tradition it has its roots in Greek and Roman philosophy and is traditionally associated with the work of Aristotle.

Aristotle

Aristotle was born in 384 BC in Macedonia, the son of a court doctor. He entered Plato's Academy at the age of 18 and was soon an intellectual rising star in Athens. Nevertheless, Plato did not make Aristotle his heir as leader of the Academy, whether because of his very different approach to philosophy or because of his connections in Macedonia (which was then the bitter enemy of Athens), and Aristotle left Athens around the time of Plato's death in 347 BC to travel and study in Asia.

In 343 BC, Aristotle became the tutor to Alexander, son of King Philip of Macedonia. He ran what was effectively an elite boarding school at Meiza for three years, teaching Alexander (as well as the future kings Ptolemy and Cassander) all subjects, from the literature of Homer to the basics of medicine and art. Alexander succeeded his father in 336 BC and quickly earned his reputation as 'the Great', going on to conquer a vast empire which stretched from Greece across Asia to the borders of India and down around the eastern Mediterranean into Egypt. He was influenced by Aristotle, who had taught him 'to be a leader to the Greeks and a despot to the Barbarians'[1] arguing that Greek civilization was better than that of Persia or other kingdoms and that the virtues of his kingship would justify his rule.

Aristotle founded his own school, the Lyceum, in Athens in 335 BC and taught there until 323 BC, when another wave of anti-Macedonian feeling led to his exile.[2] Aristotle is supposed to have said, 'I will not allow the Athenians to sin twice against philosophy,' suggesting that he would have met Socrates' fate if he had stayed. Also, Aristotle had clashed with Alexander (not being able to stomach his claim to divinity) and was suspected of involvement in Alexander's mysterious death (although there is no evidence that he was).

Most of Aristotle's writings were designed to be guides for his students and were not polished for wider publication. This may explain the marked difference in style between his writings and those of Plato. Aristotle died of natural causes in 322 BC.

Aristotle and Natural Law

Socrates, Plato and Aristotle all posited the existence of natural rights and natural justice which transcend local civil law and derive from a universal human nature. Aristotle is usually seen as the father of the Natural Law tradition,[3] because he established

---

1 Peter Green, *Alexander of Macedon*, Oxford: University of California Press, 1991, p. 58.

2 W. T. Jones, *A History of Western Philosophy*: Vol. 1, *The Classical Mind*, Independence, KY: Wadsworth Publishing, 1969, p. 216.

3 Seeing Aristotle as the father of Natural Law really started with Thomas Aquinas, who translated Aristotle and used quotations throughout his work to demonstrate its classical authority. In recent years, some scholars have disputed Aquinas' claim that Aristotle believed that there is a Natural Law deriving from a universal human nature, which largely depends on a passage in *Rhetoric* (1373b2–8). It could be that in this passage Aristotle is just arguing that there would be a rhetorical advantage in appealing to Natural Law, whether or not it actually exists, rather than claiming the existence of Natural Law. See, for example R. Corbett, 'The Question of Natural Law in Aristotle', *History of Political Thought* 30:2 (Summer 2009), pp. 229–50.

the 'scientific' inductive approach which has come to character-
ize this approach to ethics. He argued that we can discover how
people should behave by studying how people do behave; observation and rational analysis of human nature is the surest foundation for judgements about it.

The Nicomachean Ethics

In the *Nicomachean Ethics*, which contains Aristotle's fullest treatment of moral philosophy, Aristotle sees **goodness in something
fulfilling its nature**. A good oak tree is fully what it is to be an
oak tree, it is large and strong and grows and produces acorns;
similarly a good person fulfils the common human nature that all
human beings share.[4] Goodness lies in being fulfilled, flourishing,
and moral wrongdoing lies in falling short, failing to fulfil human
potential.

In Book 1, Chapter 7, Aristotle develops what is sometimes
known as his 'Function Argument'. He suggests that all beings
have a variety of **functions** (Greek *ergon*) and human beings have
a greater variety of functions than animals or plants. In order to
understand whether a being is fulfilling its potential, its nature,
it is important to understand all the functions that make up that
nature. It is only when a being is functioning well in all respects
that it can be said to be flourishing.

Hughes explains:

Aristotle held that human beings have a variety of activities
which by nature they are capable of performing: growing, re-
producing, sensing, feeling emotions, thinking and choosing.
Each of these can be performed well or badly, and each one
in the list depends upon the preceding ones in the sense that
for the 'higher' activities the required bodily infrastructures

---

4 Aristotle prefigured modern scientific method in basing knowledge on
inductive reasoning, in observing things before drawing conclusions about
them.

have to be in place and properly functioning. Some of these are activities which we share with other animals, others are characteristically human. He believes that for a human being to live a fulfilled life, all these activities must be functioning well. Though a fulfilled life will, of course, involve keeping healthy and sleeping and digesting and so on, what makes it fulfilling is not these background activities but the activities of intellectual understanding and contributing to society. Human beings are thinking social beings.[5]

It is clear that for Aristotle a fulfilled, flourishing, *good* human being is one who lives healthily (obviously) in order to contribute peacefully, work, prosper, philosophize, have children and pass on wisdom. These could be seen as the **basic human goods** of Aristotle's Natural Law. A good life, for Aristotle, is one which has these characteristics. The human being is functioning well, fulfilled and therefore, he argues, happy.

Aristotle argued that all human beings have **natural rights**,[6] such as the right to self-preservation, simply by virtue of being human. These cannot be alienated or taken away by a particular community. It is this idea of rights that underlies the United States Declaration of Independence. When asked once what was the philosophy underlying the Declaration of Independence, Thomas Jefferson replied: 'All its authority rests ... on the harmonizing sentiments of the day, whether expressed in conversation, in letters, printed essays, or in the elementary books of public right, as Aristotle, Cicero, Locke, Sidney, &c.'[7] This stands in contrast to those who hold that human rights are conferred by society or depend on a social contract.

---

5 Gerard W. Hughes, 'Natural Law', in Bernard Hoose (ed.), *Christian Ethics: An Introduction*, London: Cassell, 1998, p. 52.

6 See Fred D. Miller Jr, 'Aristotle and the Origins of Natural Rights', *The Review of Metaphysics* 49:4 (1996), pp. 873–907.

7 Thomas Jefferson, Letter to Henry Lee, 8 May 1825.

Goodness and Fulfilment

For Aristotle, pleasure arises from 'unimpeded activity',[8] from the fulfilment of a function. Sleeping, eating and having sex are all human functions and pleasure can be attained by fulfilling them, but focusing entirely on bodily functions would lead human beings to neglect higher human potentialities and leave a significant part of human nature unfulfilled. The implication is that higher pleasures are derived from fulfilling higher functions and so for an individual to seek to fulfil their entire human nature will over-ride any short-term sacrifices they have to make in order to pursue their higher potentialities.

Aristotle argues that human beings always act to pursue what they see at the time as being good, but sometimes this is an **apparent good** rather than a **real good**. Rationally human beings can appreciate the need to consider broader fulfilment but sometimes they can be caught up in the moment and neglect the longer-term implications of focusing on the fulfilment of a specific short-term need.

The final good for man, according to Aristotle, is *eudaimonia*. This is a difficult term to translate (and scholars still debate what it means precisely); however, it seems that it lies in a complete and fulfilled life, a life characterized by rational actions, both practical and theoretical.[9] Since all human beings share a common human nature, it will be possible to work out which actions contribute to human fulfilment and which do not.

Aristotle and Virtue

For Aristotle, virtuous behaviour treads a middle line between extremes. For example, courage is a virtue and lies between rash-

---

8 Aristotle, *Nicomachean Ethics*, trans. W. D. Ross, Oxford World Classics, Oxford: Oxford University Press, rev. edn 2009, 1153b7–12.

9 J. L. Ackrill, 'Aristotle on Eudaimonia', in A. Rorty (ed.), *Essays on Aristotle's Ethics*, London: University of California Press, 1980, pp. 26–7 is a useful defence of this point.

ness and cowardice. A good life is one which seeks out the golden 'mean' of behaviour.

Aristotle saw Natural Law and Virtue Ethics as two sides of the same coin, not as separate approaches to ethics. It was not until much later that moral philosophers in this tradition chose to focus on the status of actions rather than on the status of agents. Other moral philosophers using Natural Law, including Thomas Aquinas, have seen the importance of considering the bigger picture, the total character of a moral agent rather than just their actions, when reflecting on human goodness.

Both Aristotle and Aquinas understood that character and actions cannot be separated when discussing moral philosophy, that actions make up character and it is impossible to be a good person and do bad things – though bad people do apparently good things every day. They both appreciated that behaving like a good person, cultivating the virtues as habits, makes individuals more inclined to do good things.

The Development of Natural Law

From the early third century BC the **Stoics** developed and transformed Natural Law. Stoic philosophy was based on the existence of a universal human nature and a definite order to the universe. Stoics moved from this basis to the existence of a virtuous way of living in accordance with nature, which appealed to rational people independently of local laws and cultures.

The Stoics taught that it was good to be directed by reason and resist having judgement clouded by the passions. A good life began with the cultivation of reason, contemplation of the nature of things and a decision to act well. Maintaining a focus on the ultimate end of life and the pleasure which this brings enables the Stoic to accept the temporary suffering that living a good life inevitably involves. In this respect, Stoic philosophy has parallels in Buddhist philosophy, in teaching that seeing the truth and deciding to live well enables people to accept suffering and, through peace of mind, achieve ultimate happiness.[10]

Like Plato and Aristotle (and Buddhist thinkers), Stoic philosophers taught that cultivating virtuous habits is an important part of a good life. For the Stoics the virtues were wisdom, courage, justice and temperance. Unlike other proponents of Natural Law, the Stoics argued that suicide was right in extreme circumstances when it would be impossible to go on living a virtuous life (for example in cases of terminal illness or when forced to live under tyranny), though in other circumstances it would be wrong as it would impede any progress towards fulfilment and goodness.

Influenced by Stoicism, the great Roman orator **Cicero** (106–43 BC) wrote:

True law is right reason in agreement with nature; it summons to duty by its commands, and averts from wrongdoing by its prohibitions. And it does not lay its commands or prohibitions upon good men in vain, though neither have any effect on the wicked. It is a sin to try to alter this law, nor is it allowable to attempt to repeal any part of it, and it is impossible to abolish it entirely. We cannot be freed from its obligations by senate or people, and we need not look outside ourselves for an expounder or interpreter of it. And there will not be different laws at Rome and at Athens, or different laws now and in the future, but one eternal and unchangeable law will be valid for all nations and all times, and there will one master and ruler, that is, God, over us all, for he is the author of this law, its promulgator, and its enforcing judge. Whoever is disobedient is fleeing from himself and denying his human nature, and by reason of this very fact he will suffer the worst penalties, even if he escapes what is commonly called punishment.[11]

---

10 To find out more, listen to http://www.bbc.co.uk/programmes/p003k9fs (accessed 25 April 2012), or explore modern Stoicism by searching for Jules Evans' numerous blogs, articles etc.

11 Cicero, *De Re Publica, De Legibus*, trans. Clinton W. Keyes, London: Heinemann, 1970, *De Re Publica* Book 3, paragraph 22, p. 211.

Cicero is sure that there is a single Natural Law for all people, that this law places demands on rulers and that it has its origin in our common human reason and ultimately God.[12]

Christianity and Natural Law

It is clear that Christians had been influenced by Natural Law for centuries before Thomas Aquinas used it as the basis for a new systematic Christian moral philosophy, which was accepted as a definitive exposition of Catholic doctrine in 1879 by Pope Leo XIII (although in practice it had been accepted long before that). The Apostle Paul seems to reflect Cicero's thinking in his Epistle to the Romans[13] and Augustine of Hippo wrote: 'Natural Law is the light of understanding placed in us by God through which we know what we must do and what we must avoid,' and 'These rules are written in the book of that light which we call truth and are imprinted on the heart of man as a seal upon wax.'[14] He famously remarked that '*lex iniusta non est lex*' (an unjust law is not really a law).[15]

---

12 It is easy to see why early Christians, frequently persecuted at the whim of local rulers, seized on Cicero's work and used it as a foundation of Christian moral philosophy. It enabled them to move from saying that laws which discriminated against them disagreed with Christ's teaching to saying that these laws disagreed with universal Natural Law, that enforcing them was sinful and would earn punishment in the next life even if not in this.

13 Romans 2.14. A. J. Carlyle, *A History of Medieval Political Theory in the West*, Vol. 1, London: Blackwood, 1903, p. 83.

14 Quoted in the Catechism, http://www.catholicity.com/catechism/the_moral_law.html, accessed 14 February 2012.

15 Quoted by Andrei Marmor in 'The Nature of Law', *The Stanford Encyclopaedia of Philosophy* (Winter 2011 edition), ed. Edward N. Zalta, http://plato.stanford.edu/archives/win2011/entries/lawphil-nature/, checked 14 February 2012.

Thomas Aquinas

Thomas Aquinas was born in 1225 in Roccasecca, Italy and studied to enter the Church at the University of Naples, where he was introduced to the works of Aristotle, the Muslim philosopher Averroes (Ibn Rushd) and the Jewish philosopher Maimonides.

At the age of 19, Aquinas rebelled against his family, who wanted him to become a Benedictine and progress to become an abbot like his brother. He tried to join the Dominicans in Rome. Aquinas' family captured him en route and had him imprisoned for two years, but this did not diminish his enthusiasm to become a Dominican – which he eventually managed to do in 1244 by escaping from his window by night!

In 1245, Aquinas travelled to Paris to study under Albert the Great, the great Dominican scientist who applied Aristotle's method to study the natural world. Aquinas was older than many of his fellow students, rather plump and quiet, but his teacher recognized his brilliance, saying 'We call him the dumb ox, but in his teaching he will one day produce such a bellowing that it will be heard throughout the world.'[16] Aquinas became regent master of theology at the University of Paris between 1256 and 1259 and returned to Paris from 1269 and 1272 to deal with the rise of 'radical Aristotelianism' at the university.

Aquinas died in 1274, three months after having a powerful religious experience which led him to see his work as having limited value, saying '*mihi videtur ut palea*'[17] – it all seems like straw to me.

Aquinas was responsible for a great body of work, much of which served to provide strong philosophical foundations for Christian doctrine. Other church leaders saw the re-emergence of Aristotle, and the Islamic philosophy of Averroes which developed Aristotelian ideas, as a threat. Aquinas on the other hand saw that it could be used to systematize Christian belief, ensuring

---

16 Eleonore Stump, *Aquinas*, London: Routledge, 2003, p. 3.

17 Brian Davies, *The Thought of Thomas Aquinas*, Oxford: Oxford University Press, 1993, p. 9.

that it appealed to reason and would have wide-ranging and last-ing appeal while society progressed and as Islam (which had no problem with using philosophy to explore and defend faith at this time) continued to push at Europe's borders.

Although Aquinas' work was eventually accepted,[18] his writings were condemned by the Bishop of Paris in 1270 and again in 1277 for promoting Aristotelian ideas, and he remained a controversial figure for decades after his death while the dispute between the supporters of Aristotelian philosophy and those who saw it as a threat to Christian faith rumbled on. Nevertheless, Aquinas was canonized in 1323 and was used to defend Catholic doctrine against Protestant 'heresies' at the Council of Trent (1545–63), the *Summa Theologica* being placed on the altar next to the Bible. The Church eventually realized the importance of using reason to explore and defend faith (as *Fides et Ratio* makes clear).

Aquinas and Natural Law

Aquinas adopted Aristotle's ethics with relatively few modifications. Nevertheless, Aquinas was a Christian and this meant that he had to place Aristotle's view of the world within the context of a single divine creator. It also required him to import the principle that the universe had a beginning and will have an end (neither of which Aristotle accepted), and that the characteristics of order and purpose that are apparent in all things are the result of a divine will.[19] Aquinas relied on revelation as authority for these beliefs.

If the universe was created by God and everything in it has a clear order and purpose, it is simple to argue that things behave in an orderly way and fulfil their purpose because of God's will. Aquinas argues that evil has no positive existence but results

18 Aquinas became one of the 'doctors of the Church' in 1567.

19 To be clear, Aristotle was not a theist and held to a very limited view of God as the unmoved mover which explained motion.

from a lack of something good and that 'it belongs to a prudent governor' to create ugly foundations that a great building may stand strong, or to place silent pauses in a chant that the music may sound sweeter.

Non-human beings have no choice about how they act: as Hughes puts it, 'the non-human parts of creation reflect the eternal law in a deterministic way: they inevitably behave according to the natures they have'.[20] On the other hand, human beings have been created with free-will and have both choice and moral responsibility. 'Unlike rocks or trees human beings can come to understand the kinds of beings they are, and are free to live in a way which corresponds to that understanding, or to refuse to do so.'[21]

Part of human freedom is the ability to understand Natural Law through reason; if humans did not understand how they should behave they could not be held morally responsible for making wrong choices. Every human being can use reason to work out what is morally right and is, therefore, morally accountable.

Aquinas accepted Aristotle's view that human nature includes animal functions (living, growing, eating, sleeping, sex), higher animal functions (such as working and contributing to society) as well as distinctively human functions (reasoning, free action). He accepted Aristotle's argument that we experience pleasure as a result of fulfilling each of these functions and that we experience more pleasure, true happiness, from fulfilling our entire nature than from fulfilling any single function within it.

For both Aristotle and Aquinas fulfilling our higher human functions will involve making choices and sacrificing immediate short-term pleasures for wider fulfilment. Human beings should not aim for base pleasure, but should aim for total fulfilment and true happiness: as Aquinas wrote, 'nor can pleasure itself be the ultimate end, but it is a concomitant of it'.[22] Where Aquinas

---

20 Hughes, 'Natural Law', p. 48.

21 Hughes, 'Natural Law', p. 48.

22 Thomas Aquinas, *Selected Writings*, ed. and trans. Ralph McInerny, London: Penguin, 1998, p. 270.

differs from Aristotle is in his belief that 'God is the ultimate end of the intellectual substance'.[23] He argues that 'since happiness is the proper end of the intellectual nature, it must come to an intellectual nature according to what is peculiar to it',[24] and that 'the ultimate felicity of man lies substantially in knowing God with his intellect'.[25]

For Aquinas 'knowing God' is the most distinctive human function and key to human fulfilment. It is clear, however, that 'knowing God' is related to the free exercise of rationality and it may not be that different from Aristotle's concept of wisdom and the contemplation of truth that he identifies with *eudaimonia* in Book 10 of the *Nicomachean Ethics*.[26]

Although in the *Summa Contra Gentiles* Aquinas is at pains to detail how human happiness does not lie in pleasure, honours, glory, riches, worldly power, possessions, the senses, artistic activity or even in the exercise of the virtues,[27] it is clear that each of these things has the potential to give us some pleasure and contribute in part to the fulfilment of human nature.[28] In *Summa Theologica* II, i question 4 article 5 Aquinas argues that 'there are two kinds of happiness, one imperfect which is had in this life, and the other perfect, which consists in the vision of God. But it is manifest that the body is required for happiness in this life ...'[29]

Aquinas does not disagree with Aristotle's definition of a good life. He just believes that it cannot be complete unless the highest

23 Aquinas, *Selected Writings*, p. 270.

24 Aquinas, *Selected Writings*, p. 268.

25 Aquinas, *Selected Writings*, p. 270.

26 Thomas Nagel, 'Aristotle on Eudaimonia' and Ackrill, 'Aristotle on Eudaimonia', in A. Rorty (ed.), *Essays on Aristotle's Ethics*, London: University of California Press, 1980 are useful in explaining what Aristotle meant by this term.

27 Aquinas, *Selected Writings*, pp. 272–9 (from *Summa Contra Gentiles*, Book 3).

28 In the *Summa Theologica* II, i, question 2 Aquinas explains how we derive happiness from each of these things, but 'the ultimate end of anything lies in its perfected state, hence the part is for the sake of the whole as for its end'.

29 Aquinas, *Selected Writings*, p. 530.

human capability is fulfilled through the rational contemplation of the truth, God. He wrote:

> If man's ultimate happiness does not lie in those external things which are called the goods of fortune, nor in goods of the body, nor in the goods of the soul whether of the sensitive part or in the intellectual part, in the acts of moral virtue, nor in any intellectual activities pertaining to action, namely art and prudence, it remains that man's ultimate happiness lies in the contemplation of the truth. This is the only activity of man that is peculiar to him and is in no way shared by the other animals.[30]

The Precepts of Aquinas' Natural Law

Aquinas goes on to explore which principles of action or 'precepts' follow from Natural Law.

The most universal precept, **the primary precept of practical reason**, is '*bonum est faciendum et prosequendum et malum vitandum*' or 'good is to be done and pursued and evil avoided' (though on its own this is not particularly practical in forming moral decisions!). As Murphy explains:

> No one can in acting simply pursue good – one has to pursue some particular good. And Aquinas holds that we know immediately, by inclination, that there are a variety of things that count as good and thus to be pursued – life, procreation, knowledge, society, and reasonable conduct (ST IaIIae 94, 2; 94, 3) are all mentioned by Aquinas (though it is not clear whether the mentioned items are supposed to constitute an exhaustive list).[31]

---

30 Aquinas, *Selected Writings*, p. 280.

31 Mark Murphy, 'The Natural Law Tradition in Ethics', *The Stanford Encyclopedia of Philosophy* (Winter 2011 edition), ed. Edward N. Zalta, http://plato.stanford.edu/archives/win2011/entries/natural-law-ethics/.

Aquinas argues that on the most basic level human beings function as animals. Like animals it is natural for human beings to live, grow, eat, sleep and reproduce, ensuring survival. On a higher level, human beings have the potential to function socially, offering friendship and love, and growing in knowledge and wisdom. On the highest level, human beings function religiously and have the potential to know God and contemplate the truth. All of these functions are good and contribute towards the greater good of human fulfilment; it follows that acting to support any of these goods would be a **primary precept of Natural Law**.

It follows from the primary precepts of Natural Law and how all human beings function that they should uphold certain absolute principles, for example 'thou shalt not kill' and 'thou shalt not steal' (Exod. 20). These become **secondary precepts** of Natural Law which rationality suggests must be applied **consistently**, that is, not in some circumstances only but universally with no exceptions. This gives rise to the Catholic teaching that certain actions are 'intrinsically evil' – wrong in themselves.

Good and Bad Actions

Aquinas believed that human beings always pursue what they think to be good, but this may be an **apparent good** rather than a **real good**.[32] Aquinas wrote that 'evil acts in virtue of a defective good', we think we are pursuing the good but may be mistaken either because the action is poorly motivated ('to give alms for the sake of vainglory is bad'[33]) or because it prioritizes a lesser good such as personal happiness outside the context of the greater good of human fulfilment. Nevertheless, Copleston wrote:

> As Augustine says, there are some things which cannot be justified by any alleged good intention ... if I steal money from

---

32 Aquinas, *Selected Writings*, p. 566 (*Summa Theologica* II, i, question 18 article 1).

33 Aquinas, *Summa Theologica* I, ii, question 20, article 1.

a man in order to give it to someone else, my action is not justified by my good intention ... it is not possible to father on Aquinas the view that the end justifies the means.[34]

Human beings are rational and acting for an apparent good is not a justification for doing something that is obviously wrong.

Aquinas also makes a distinction between **interior acts** and **exterior acts** in human behaviour. Exterior acts are those observable by another, while interior acts, such as intention and knowledge, are not directly observable, although they are more significant in God's judgement of us. Aquinas' thinking about what makes an action good or bad is sophisticated and subtle, which contrasts with how it is sometimes presented.

As Longford wrote:

[T]he secondary precepts all have to be interpreted in the context of the situation, and it is here that the flexibility of Natural Law arises. At one point [Aquinas] argues as follows 'The first principles are altogether unalterable, but its secondary precepts ... although they are unalterable in the majority of cases ... can nevertheless be changed on some particular and rare occasions ...' Aquinas argues 'the more you descend into the details the more it appears how the general rule admits of exceptions, so you have to hedge it about with cautions and qualifications'.[35]

This flexibility of the Natural Law approach is often not recognized by some who appeal to it as a basis for morality today.

Aquinas and Virtue

Like Aristotle, Aquinas saw that cultivating positive habits of mind and will is the first step in living a good life. Aquinas

---

34 Frederick Copleston, *Thomas Aquinas*, Harmondsworth: Penguin, 1955, p. 207.

35 M. J. Longford, *The Good and the True: An Introduction to Christian Ethics*, London: SCM Press, 1985, p. 204.

believed that one needs one's reason to be perfected by the virtues in order to understand how the primary precepts of Natural Law apply in practice.[36]

Aquinas divided four **cardinal virtues** (prudence, temperance, justice and fortitude) from three **'theological virtues'** (faith, hope and charity). The cardinal virtues are natural and appeal to our reason as a result of our experience of nature. They are binding on everyone. The theological virtues are revealed by God and are required for us to achieve total human fulfilment in knowing God; humans may not appreciate these virtues without grace.

Law and Morality

Civil law can only be concerned with external actions. It is not able to forbid all wrong deeds, let alone punish them. There are some areas of human affairs that human law cannot control and it should not pretend otherwise. For example, no society has prevented the practice of prostitution and (despite our reasonable disapproval of it) Aquinas suggested that it should be tolerated.[37] He wrote:

> [A]ccordingly in human government also those who are in authority rightly tolerate certain evils, lest certain goods be lost, or certain evils be incurred: thus Augustine says [*De Ordine* 2.4] 'If you do away with harlots, the world will be convulsed with lust'.[38]

Aquinas was not troubled by the limitations of civil law because he maintained that God's eternal law can direct what

---

36 http://www.aquinasonline.com/Topics/natlaw.html, accessed 15 February 2012.

37 See Vincent M. Dever, *Aquinas on the Practice of Prostitution*, Essays in Medieval Studies 13. Available online at http://www.illinoismedieval.org/ems/VOL13/13ch4.html.

38 Aquinas, *Summa Theologica* II, ii, question 10 article 11, quoted by Dever, *Aquinas*.

human law cannot. God will judge us on how close each of us has come to total fulfilment. Although it is clear that a good person would not do bad things, it is perfectly possible for a good person to do good things with bad consequences or for a bad person to do good things for bad reasons.

Influences on Aquinas, and the Influence of Aquinas

Aquinas' thinking has given rise to some controversial Catholic teachings, particularly in sexual ethics. Aquinas actually suggests that each part of the human body is determined to be used for a particular end and that choosing to use it differently is unnatural and sinful. For example, the genitals are determined to be used for reproduction so using them purely for pleasure where there is no possibility of reproduction would be wrong. He details in *Summa Contra Gentiles* 3:122 how depositing semen anywhere but in a vagina is sinful, so anal or oral sex, sex with an animal, masturbation and contraception would all be wrong. When discussing masturbation and sodomy he wrote:

[W]herever there occurs a special kind of deformity whereby the sexual act is rendered unbecoming, there is a determinate species of lust. This may occur in two ways: First, through being contrary to right reason, and this is common to all lustful vices; secondly, because, in addition, it is contrary to the natural order of the venereal act as becoming to the human race: and this is called 'the unnatural vice.'[39]

Given that Aquinas' thinking on sexual ethics has been enormously influential, affecting the lives of literally billions of people, it is important to consider the extent to which it is a necessary part of his broader moral philosophy rather than the product of medieval attitudes and influences. Some scholars have suggested

---

39 Aquinas, *Summa Theologica* II, ii, question 154 article 11, quoted by Dever, *Aquinas*.

that Aquinas may have sought to justify attitudes which would not necessarily follow from his general philosophy because it was prudent to do so.

Gareth Moore OP (1948–2002) noted that

> there are two basic elements which converge in the Stoic attitude to sex. First, for many Hellenistic thinkers the world was a purposeful place ... Proper human action was action which respected and was in harmony with the purposes found in nature; it also respected the natural purposes of human organs [which] ... was clearly reproduction ... Second, if somebody did not engage in sexual activity in order to have children, the alternative was that they were doing it for pleasure. There was a suspicion of pleasure in the Hellenistic world ... To do anything for the sake of pleasure was, in much Greek thought, unworthy and dangerous and it also subverted the natural order of things.[40]

Moore implies that it could be that Aquinas adopted the general negativity towards sex (at least for any purpose other than propagating the species) that was common in the world of Classical philosophy as well as in Scripture without really re-examining and evaluating it. This could have been in order to accommodate doctrine and enjoy a peaceful life!

Richard Gula argues that Aquinas' argument in relation to sex seems to rely on a different interpretation of Natural Law from that which he uses elsewhere – which is suspicious. As background it is important to understand that by the second century AD Roman jurists interpreted 'Natural Law' in two distinct ways.

- **Ulpian** (AD 170–228) argued that Natural Law is 'the generic rule of action common to humans and to animals'; good humans should behave in the way that most humans do be-

---

have.[41] Hoose refers to Ulpian's approach as the '**order of nature**' approach to Natural Law.[42]

- **Gaius** (AD 130–80) argued that Natural Law has its origins in reason and is based on how people *should* act, not just on how people *do* act. Gaius pointed to Aristotle's analysis of human functions, saying that if it is a human function to be rational then behaving rationally is natural to human beings. Hoose refers to Gaius' approach as the '**order of reason**' approach to Natural Law.

Gula argues that although Aquinas generally follows Gaius' 'order of reason' interpretation of Natural Law, in relation to his teaching on sex 'the influence of Ulpian is quite evident'.[43] He argues that Aquinas' 'vacillation between the "order of nature" and the "order of reason" as the basis of moral teaching ... has caused great confusion in Catholic moral thought'.

However, Paterson concludes that

[t]he same kind of functionalist [order of nature] argument (albeit occurring in less sensational contexts) is used time and again elsewhere in ST (for example, a human being has two eyes; a human being normally has two eyes; two eyes promote better sight than one eye; ergo it is good for a human being to have two eyes). If voluntary actions involving the genitals accord with natural teleology they are judged fitting and virtuous, if not, they are judged unfitting and vicious.[44]

This might suggest that the influence of Ulpian coloured Aquinas' thought more generally than Gula supposes and that his teaching on sex sits comfortably within his general approach.

41 Richard Gula, *Reason Informed by Faith: Foundations of Catholic Morality*, New York: Paulist Press, 1989, pp. 222–3.

42 Lecture notes provided by Bernard Hoose for Candle Conferences Ltd. 'Living the Good Life' conferences, Autumn 2011.

43 Gula, *Reason Informed by Faith*, p. 225.

44 See Craig Paterson and Matthew S. Pugh, *Analytical Thomism: Traditions in Dialogue*, Aldershot: Ashgate, 2006, p. 181.

Nevertheless, Aquinas was certainly capable of making his reasoning accommodate pillars of doctrine. He argued that celibacy was justified in the pursuit of the greater good of knowing God, writing that 'the precept about generation applies to the whole community, which not only must be multiplied corporeally but also make spiritual progress. And so sufficient progress is made if some only attend to generation, while others give themselves to the contemplation of divine things ...'[45] The Apostle Paul had advocated celibacy in his Epistle to the Romans, Jesus was apparently celibate, and the Church had definitively demanded that all priests be celibate (and avoid close contact with women who were not related to them) since the twelfth-century Lateran Councils. There is, therefore, evidence that Aquinas did import attitudes which a Natural Law approach on its own would not necessarily justify.

Perhaps because Aquinas' work has been imbued with such authority by the Church, it has become difficult to question it. Some scholars claim that Catholic Natural Law is not really based on reason, and because discussion is discouraged there is no legitimate forum for Catholics to explore whether this point is valid. Suppressing discussion seems to highlight the willingness of the Church to promote unity over truth and to prize tradition over what might better serve God, humanity and reason. Exerting authority may have had the effect of weakening Catholic moral philosophy rather than strengthening it. For example, in practice it is clear that many Catholics disobey church teaching on a daily basis, particularly in the developed world. In 2011, the Guttmacher Institute reported that 98 per cent of American Catholic women of reproductive age had used artificial birth-control.[46] Nevertheless, church teaching continues to have a significant effect on rates of HIV infection in Africa and South America. This

45 Aquinas, *Summa Theologica* I, ii, question 152 article 2 ad.1, quoted in Dever, *Aquinas*.

46 http://www.guttmacher.org/media/inthenews/2012/02/15/index.html, accessed 14 March 2012.

gives the impression that Catholic orthodoxy relies on ignorance of its philosophic foundations and promotes injustice and, while this impression may be wrong, there seems little way of Catholics challenging current moral thinking without being denounced by the institution they seek to defend.

Natural Law in Other Ancient Traditions

Natural Law is not an exclusively western approach to moral philosophy and, although the western tradition is the focus of this book, it is right to acknowledge where similar moral reasoning has influenced other cultures.

Confucius (551–479 BC)

'Confucius' was the name applied to the Chinese philosopher 孔子 by the Jesuit Matteo Ricci, one of the founders of the mission to China in the sixteenth and seventeenth centuries. Confucius was born in Qufu, now in the Shangdong province of China, in 551 BC. He was not a systematic philosopher, but became a 'sage' or wise man whose life and thought has had a profound influence on Chinese society ever since. He had a long and varied life, working as everything from a cowherd to justice minister in Lu, and died in 479 BC. Confucius was the father of a rich tradition of scholarship in China which is known in the West as 'Confucianism'.

Confucian Ethics: Another Variety of Natural Law?

Confucian ideas have clear parallels in the western tradition. Like Plato, Confucius suggested that good and just government depends upon the moral and cultural qualities of the ruler and his officials. Like Aristotle, Confucius suggested that personal morality derives from a noble, humane, cultured, trustworthy and just character.[47] Confucian ethics are based on the 'golden rule', often identified with Christianity but present within all major world faiths:

子貢問曰：“有一言而可以終身行之者乎”？子曰：“其恕乎！己所不欲、勿施於人。

Zi gong (a disciple of Confucius) asked: 'Is there any one word that could guide a person throughout life?' The Master replied: "How about "shu" [reciprocity]: never impose on others what you would not choose for yourself?'[48]

Many scholars have suggested that Confucianism is a variety of Natural Law ethics, which derives moral norms from a definition of what it is to live well. For example, Joseph Needham wrote: 'The Confucians adhered to the body of ancient customs, usage, and ceremonial, which ... unnumbered generations of Chinese people had instinctively felt to be right – this was the li and we may equate it with Natural Law.' The emphasis on living virtuously certainly seems to fit in with Aristotelian and Thomist thinking and appeals to modern virtue ethicists, who point to Confucianism in support of their argument that although virtues and moral norms may be defined differently in different cultures there is a core of human wisdom concerning how to live well.

There is, of course, a key difference between Confucianism and most western systems of Natural Law.[49] Confucianism is not strictly grounded in any 'scientific' account of what it is to be

---

47 Steven Greer and Tiong Piow Lim, 'Confucianism: Natural Law Chinese Style?', *Ratio Juris* 11:1 (1998), pp. 80–9.

48 Confucius, *The Analects*, trans. David Hinton, Berkeley, CA: Counterpoint Press, 1999, XV, 24. Many Confucian ideas have parallels in Christian moral philosophy; indeed this, coupled with the lack of a personal God, meant that Jesuit missionaries felt that it would be possible for Chinese people to be Confucian and Christian simultaneously – until Pope Benedict XIV banned Chinese Catholics from practising traditional Chinese rituals in the mid eighteenth century.

49 Joseph Needham, quoted by R. P. Peerenboom in *Philosophy East and West* 40:3 (1990), p. 309.

human, but rather relies on 'the aesthetic judgement of exemplary persons (**jun zi**)'[50] to define its 'primary precepts'. This makes Confucianism rather more akin to a non-naturalist Natural Law system (such as that of Finnis – see page 65) than to the functionalist systems of Natural Law derived from, say, Ulpian. Nevertheless, Confucianism holds that human beings come to know how to be good from reflecting on nature, knowing the natural way of things, and from rational contemplation, as well as from being immersed in culture and tradition and so learning from the wisdom of others,[51] so it is fair to make the comparison.

Confucian moral philosophy begins with the concept of virtue or *de*. In Chinese thought virtue is not a static personal quality; it is the power that somebody has to bring others towards moral behaviour. Virtue is not just important for the individual; the existence of virtuous people, leaders, is important for the whole of society. Virtue is something which needs constant work. Nobody wants to follow somebody who is complacent; we are attracted to people who are constantly refining themselves and cultivating their strengths.

The basic characteristics of Confucian virtue are

- Ren (仁, Humaneness)
- Yi (義, Righteousness or Justice)
- Li (禮, Propriety or Etiquette)
- Zhi (智, Knowledge)
- Xin (信, Integrity).[52]

These are supplemented by the additional virtues of

- Zhong (忠, Loyalty)
- Xiao (孝, Filial piety) and
- Jie (節, Continency).

---

50 Peerenboom, *Philosophy*, p. 309.

51 Xinzhong Yao, *An Introduction to Confucianism*, Cambridge: Cambridge University Press, 2000, p. 158.

52 Dagobert D. Runes, *Dictionary of Philosophy*, New York: Philosophical Library, 1983, p. 338.

Human beings have a duty to cultivate these characteristics and become virtuous for their own benefit and, more importantly, for the benefit of society.

The aim of Confucian moral philosophy is not to achieve salvation from this life, but rather to be fulfilled in this life and contribute to making society better – in this respect Confucius is very similar to Aristotle who had no idea of life after death (except in one disputed text). The Confucian concept of immortality (*buxiu*) suggests the lasting effects of virtue, words and works in this world rather than any supernatural eternal life.

Confucianism has attracted criticism for stressing the importance of etiquette, loyalty and duty to parents on the same level as becoming fully human or acquiring knowledge. Some argue that the presence of these virtues has contributed to an extreme conservatism in Chinese society which leads to people being unwilling to think for themselves and challenge authority, even when this has perpetuated ignorance, injustice and oppression. It would be wrong for somebody to prioritize etiquette when this would impede the fulfilment of one or more of the other virtues – say justice and humaneness – but this has happened and does happen. Confucian values were and still are imparted through a rigorous system of education in China, which may have stifled the process of free and balanced thinking in the cause of ensuring that this thinking was properly informed.

Despite claims to the contrary, Confucianism is not a purely secular tradition; it has a profound sense of religiosity and spirituality,[53] despite having no sense of a personal God. It is founded on the belief that reality is generated from an uncaused cause that is heaven, which gives rise to all things which exist in a dynamic state of change. As such it influenced Deism in Enlightenment Europe, particularly through the work of Leibniz.

53 Xinzhong Yao, *Introduction to Confucianism*, p. 155.

Natural Law and Islam

In the tenth century, the great Afghan Islamic legal philosopher **Al Maturidi** stated that human beings can know of the existence of God and the basic difference between right and wrong (such as that killing, stealing, excessive drinking and fornication are wrong) without revelation, through reason and experience. 'Averroes' is the western name for the twelfth-century Moorish scholar Ibn Rushd.[54] In his commentary on Plato's *Republic*, he wrote that human beings can know that killing and stealing are wrong (and can therefore grasp the basic principles of Islamic sharia law – to protect religion, life, property, offspring and reason)[55] through reason and without direct revelation. Both Al Maturidi and Averroes anticipated Aquinas' later position.

In the eleventh century, the Persian philosopher **Al Ghazali** suggested instead that actions are good when they relate to one or more of five *'basic goods'* (religion, life, reason, lineage and property); however, he did not see these deriving from 'scientific' observations of human nature or directly from reason but rather from the revealed truth of the Qur'an and the Sunnah. Al Ghazali anticipated the difficulties in moving *from an is to an ought*, from partial observations of human nature or rational ideas shaped by personal experience to universal moral claims. He got around this basic difficulty with Natural Law by appealing to revelation. Today, Al Ghazali's teaching on Natural Law is the basis for the controversial concept of *Istislah* (literally 'the public interest' – what will result in one or more of the basic goods) in Islamic law, which Muslim jurists may appeal to when there is no clear textual authority relating to a particular situation.

Istislah was the basis for a relatively liberal school of thought within Islamic jurisprudence in the twentieth century, particu-

---

54 Averroes was a master of Aristotelian philosophy, and it was through his work in translating and developing Aristotelian thought that Aquinas and his European contemporaries began to engage with it and consider its place within the Christian tradition.

55 Henry Corbin, *History of Islamic Philosophy*, trans. Liadain Sherrard and Philip Sherrard, London: Kegan Paul International, 1993, p. 39.

larly associated with **Rashid Rida** (1865–1935). Rida argued that Islam was being strangled by its reliance on tradition and authority and its suppression of innovation or practical rational thought. He wrote: 'What a heinous crime is being committed, then, by these ignorant persons who call themselves the Ulema of Islam?'[56] Rida suggested that text- or tradition-based rulings should always be set against the most basic principles derived from the Qur'an and Hadith, such as 'no harm, no retribution' – where the specific ruling would go against the basic principle it should be dropped. For example, if a ruling had the effect of treating women unequally it should be set against the basic Qur'anic principle of the equality of the sexes and the ruling should be set aside. In practice, this means that Islam could be compatible with liberal human rights and support progressive laws which would otherwise seem 'unislamic'; indeed before the recent revolution the Egyptian Supreme Court had accepted this approach.[57]

Criticisms of Natural Law

Natural Law has, of course, attracted criticisms.

Is and Ought

Versions of Natural Law rely on what Moore called the '*Naturalistic Fallacy*', moving from an analysis of how things *are* to claims about how they *should be*. To put it simply, the way things are is not necessarily a good guide to the way they should be – how

---

56 *Tafsir al-Manar*, Vol. IV, Cairo, 1375 (1956), p. 240, quoted as part of a useful article at http://www.mideastweb.org/Middle-East-Encyclopedia/muhammad_rashid_rida.htm, accessed 17 December 2011.

57 Rida was no conventional liberal and has been seen by some as the father of modern Islamism – he issued a fatwa against those who translated the Qur'an and campaigned for a new Caliphate, a union of independent Islamic states across the Middle East under a supreme spiritual and political ruler.

students behave at lunchtime is not necessarily representative of how they should be behaving according to the school rules! As Moore pointed out, goodness in actions is recognized in cases which are rare and often defy logic – in self-sacrifice, in unrecognized and thankless kindness and service. It is not clear that 'goodness' really is rooted in experience of how human beings generally operate, in a rational analysis of efficient human functioning. No definitive explanation has been provided to support what seems to be a leap in logic in the foundations of Natural Law – and this could undermine its credibility, as well as that of other naturalist normative systems.

Human Nature

Versions of Natural Law may also be criticized because they fail to provide a consistent account of human nature or one which resists cultural influence, despite relying on the claim that there is a common human nature and that we can describe and analyse it. If variations between the accounts of human nature offered by, say, Aristotle and Aquinas are taken to suggest that how human nature is understood depends on culture, then the basic principle that absolute and universal moral laws may be grounded in a scientific and rational observation of a common human nature is undermined. Nevertheless, one could argue that the accounts of human nature put forward by Aristotle and Aquinas share much more than they do not despite coming from very different contexts, and this could actually support the idea that there is a single human nature.

Legalism v. Personalism

The lists of secondary precepts that most versions of Natural Law provide are rigid and seem to put principle ahead of people. Both situationists and proportionalists agree that there is a tension between the Christian law of love and the legalism which characterizes some versions of Natural Law. There are cases in which people seem to be sacrificed unjustly – such as in denying effective pain-relief to terminally ill patients or in forcing women with ectopic pregnancies to have their fallopian tubes removed rather than having laser treatment.[58] On the other hand, having a strong code of ethics is useful: it provides clear guidance and prevents people who are often ill-equipped to make decisions (let alone in the stress of the moment) from doing wrong for lack of support.

Freedom and Responsibility

Kantians point to the erosion of individual freedom and rationality which results from following rules unquestioningly and from acting out of habit – and both these can be fostered by obedience to Natural Law ethics. However, Kant fails to offer a convincing alternative to moral education involving rules and cultivating virtues (see Chapter 10).

Injustice

Utilitarians point to the many cases in which upholding a rule causes more pain than pleasure, suggesting that this makes Natural Law supportive of injustice. This does, of course, depend on how justice is defined. They might also hold that Natural Law takes no accounts of the situation or consequences and this is a possible weakness.

---

58 'The good effect must not be obtained by means of the evil effect; the evil must be only an incidental by-product and not an actual factor in the accomplishment of the good': although the 'Principle of Double Effect' may justify doing something when a possible secondary side-effect is negative, it cannot make it acceptable to do something in the clear knowledge that the effects will be negative. Pain medication must be limited to that which will not directly shorten life and treatment chosen that is not directly designed to terminate pregnancy. See http://www.catholicreference.net/index.cfm?id=33215.

Baptized Reason

Catholic Natural Law has been criticized for accommodating pillars of doctrine such as priestly celibacy, which otherwise seem inconsistent with the principles of Natural Law – this has led to its being referred to as *'baptized reason'*. Although most Catholics seem satisfied that theological insights can helpfully amplify philosophic reasoning, it must be accepted that importing theological assumptions will be controversial.

Conclusion

The basic principles of Natural Law are simple: all human beings share a common human nature; some forms of behaviour are morally wrong because they lead people away from fulfilling their real potential and other types of behaviour help people to move closer to human fulfilment. The problems arise in defining human nature and human fulfilment.

The basic idea that some moral choices diminish us and take us away from fulfilment underpins many works of literature and films. In *The Lord of the Rings*, Smeagol makes choices that turn him into a pathetic creature dominated by his wish for 'the precious', and in *Harry Potter*, Lord Voldemort makes choices that end with his becoming a pathetic example of what it is to be human. Many people find Natural Law appealing but struggle to accept the harsh and inflexible rules which have been derived from it. In the twentieth century, a number of philosophers attempted to develop the basic principles in different ways, and it is to these developments that we now turn.

6

Natural Law and Virtue Ethics Today

Two of the most important modern proponents of 'New Natural Law' or 'neonaturalism' are the American Catholic **Germain Grisez** (b. 1929) and the Australian **John Finnis** (b. 1940).

Germain Grisez

Grisez is a practising Catholic who became fascinated with Aquinas' philosophy while at a Jesuit university. He became one of the foremost thinkers in the field of Catholic moral theology, refining and developing Aquinas' thought within the bounds of Catholic doctrine and providing guidance on how Catholics should respond to modern moral dilemmas, from contraception to nuclear proliferation.

Grisez said of Aquinas:

> He wasn't primarily interested in philosophy; he was interested in doing theology, and you didn't have to have a tight ethical theory and tight moral arguments in his day because in general the big arguments weren't going on in the area of ethics. So the theory in Aquinas is no more refined and perfected than it needed to be, and it didn't have to be very refined and perfected for his purposes. It is sound as far as it goes and very suggestive, but it's not honed and not worked out carefully. He is a gold mine of a starting-place, he's got a lot of good ideas, but he doesn't have any coherent overall theory of ethics, and

he doesn't equip you to argue the issues and solve the problems as they've been posed in modern times.[1]

Grisez made his name defending church teaching on contraception. In *Contraception and the Natural Law* (1965) he developed a meticulous argument that 'the choice to contracept is a choice against the human good of procreation and as such can never be justified, since it is never morally right to turn one's will against a good of the person, not even for the sake of some other good'.[2] He was not afraid to criticize other Natural Law arguments which he considered defective. As a result of this work, Grisez played an important role in the controversy surrounding the publication of the papal encyclical *Humanae Vitae* in 1968[3] and was the chief theological advisor to the US Church in 'selling' the Church's teaching to enraged American Catholics.

Grisez went on to develop Catholic responses to abortion, euthanasia and the nuclear deterrence (with John Finnis) as well as producing a number of guides to Catholic moral philosophy and the philosophy of religion.

The hinge of Grisez's restatement of Natural Law is that human beings have real freedom and real moral responsibility; the stakes are so high that we must confront the difficult decisions that reason and faith call us to make, realizing that short-term happiness is nothing in relation to the long-term and big-picture consequences of falling short of our natural God-given potential.

---

1 Quoted in Russell Shaw, 'The Making of a Moral Theologian', reprinted in *Ethics, Metaphysics, and Politics: Essays on Grisez*, ed. Robert George, Washington, DC: Georgetown University Press, 1996, and in the March 1996 issue of *The Catholic World Report*. The text is available online at http://www.ewtn.com/library/HOMELIBR/GRISEZ.TXT, checked 15 February 2012.

2 Quoted in Shaw, 'Moral Theologian'.

3 This restated the Church's teaching on contraception and made it clear that the use of *all* forms of artificial birth control, including the pill, were sinful. The encyclical caused a near-schism in the Church, with many priests and scholars, as well as countless ordinary Catholics, dissenting and ignoring the teaching.

In the three-volume *The Way of the Lord Jesus: Moral Theology* (Franciscan Herald Press, 1983) Grisez set out the 'basic human goods' or primary precepts of his Natural Law. In summary, for Grisez, a good human life involves:

- self-integration
- practical reasonableness
- authenticity
- justice
- friendship
- religion
- life and health
- knowledge of truth
- appreciation of beauty
- playful activities.

As with Aquinas, for Grisez all human actions are good in that they relate to at least one of these human goods (real or just apparent) but they may well be misplaced, serving a short-term single good rather than long-term total human fulfilment. One of Grisez's more controversial points is that a person should never choose to act directly against a basic good; to do so would be 'to make a choice to destroy, damage or impede that good in one or more instances'.[4] This rules out the possibility of intentionally sacrificing one good for the sake of another,[5] or for the sake of overall human fulfilment. So, for instance, as 'life' is included in the list of basic goods, abortion or euthanasia will be absolutely

---

4 G. Grisez and R. Shaw, *Beyond the New Morality: The Responsibilities of Freedom*, South Bend, IN: University of Notre Dame Press, 3rd edn 1988, pp. 135–6.

5 This would rule out many cases of so-called 'double effect': for example, using a condom to prevent the transmission of HIV (that is, to promote the good of health) would also knowingly stand in the way of using sex as permitted by the Church and would thus go against the goods of religion, truth, justice, etc. Similarly, using large doses of morphine to ease suffering in a terminally ill patient in the knowledge that it will shorten life by days or weeks may be questionable because it would intentionally go against life and health.

ruled out. The basic goods are therefore given equal and infinite weight; no other factors can outweigh them.

Grisez's work has been criticized, by Catholics and non-Catholics alike, for its extreme conservatism and for the assumptions it seems to import into the framework of Natural Law. Like Aquinas, Grisez puts his naturalistic moral reasoning in the context of Scripture and Christian doctrine, and his interpretations are not universally accepted. Tom Deidun wrote:

> Germain Grisez has written that according to Veritatis Splendor 'passages such as 1 Corinthians 6:9–10 mean exactly what they say: those who do certain kinds of acts, such as adultery and sexual perversion, will not inherit the Kingdom ...' Whether or not such passages mean exactly what they say (or what Grisez says they say) one must first establish what they do say. A sure way of aborting this task is to ignore the Greek text and to neglect to ask what the terms used would have meant to Paul and his hearers.[6]

The problem is that, instead of basing his approach to Natural Law on observation of what a fulfilled human life should be like (as Aristotle sought to do), Grizez imports theological assumptions which non-Catholics as well as many Catholics would not accept in order to arrive at conclusions that are acceptable to his Church. This can be argued not to be good philosophy.

John Finnis

Finnis was educated at St Peter's College, Adelaide and the University of Adelaide, where he won a Rhodes scholarship to University College, Oxford, in 1962. At Oxford, Finnis became a specialist in the philosophy of law (jurisprudence). He

---

6 Tom Deidun, 'The Bible and Christian Ethics', in Bernard Hoose (ed.), *Christian Ethics: An Introduction*, London: Cassell, 1998, p. 16; he is referring to an article in *The Tablet* by Grisez (16 October 1993) and it is a point that has also been made by Nicholas Lash.

is currently Professor of Law at University College, Oxford and at the University of Notre Dame, teaching jurisprudence, political theory and constitutional law.

Finnis studied Aquinas because he provided an alternative theory of the nature and origins of the law to the relativist approach which was dominant in the 1960s and which suggested that 'law is a social construction'.[7] For Finnis, as for Aquinas, law and morality are closely related; Aquinas believed that what is morally and what is legally right ought to be the same thing. Finnis was seeking a universal basis for law which could be the foundations of international law and a basis for judging certain laws or whole legal systems in some countries to be flawed, even if they have the support of government and/or people. For example, if the law in Afghanistan makes teenage girls who have been gang-raped guilty of adultery and forces them to face either marriage to an attacker or prison then what grounds do people in Australia have for criticizing this position?[8] If law is socially constructed then there is no basis for judging it from outside that society.

In *Natural Law and Natural Rights* (Oxford University Press, 1980), Finnis developed a new version of Aquinas' Natural Law which, he argued, could be the basis both for moral philosophy and for law. He tried to get around standard criticisms of Natural Law, such as those listed at the end of the previous chapter.

Controversially, Finnis starts with the argument that Aquinas, properly interpreted, was an ethical non-naturalist. He argues that the 'basic goods' of Natural Law appeal directly to reason without any need to make particular observations of nature. Jean Porter criticized Finnis for this, arguing that he speaks of basic human goods as if they were Platonic forms enjoying an independent existence of their own and is mysterious, not being clear

---

7 Finnis makes this point in 'The Priority of Persons', available online at http://fds.oup.com/www.oup.co.uk/pdf/0-19-826858-0.pdf, accessed 16 February 2012.

8 http://articles.cnn.com/2011-12-17/asia/world_asia_afghanistan-rape-interview_1_attacker-afghan-president-hamid-karzai-afghan-law?_s=PM: ASIA, accessed 25 April 2012.

about their logical or ontological status.[9] Craig Paterson also rejects Finnis' argument, concluding that,

> spurred on, no doubt, by laudable motives of 'intellectual rescue'... [Finnis] distorts the historical Aquinas by interpreting Aquinas as if he were wearing an analytical pair of spectacles, enabling himself, so equipped, to 'reconstruct' Aquinas as a post-Enlightenment compatible thinker.[10]

Robert George has attempted to defend Finnis, saying that the basic human goods are irreducible, self-evident truths, but this does not convince many meta-ethicists.[11]

Finnis argues that unless law is grounded in what it is to be human and relates to a moral code, then human beings will not see that following the law is morally right and will obey it only out of habit or fear while the tools of civic education and enforcement endure. They will not feel that the law has the moral authority to coerce people, to use prison and even death as a punishment. Finnis claims that a law can be legally valid, even if unjust, but that there can be no moral justification for enforcing an unjust law.

Take for example, the novel and film *The Reader*.[12] Hana Schmidt, an illiterate factory worker at Siemens, was assigned by her employer to become an SS guard in charge of a work-

---

9 Jean Porter, 'Basic Goods and the Human Good', *The Thomist* 47 (1993), pp. 27–49.

10 Craig Paterson, 'Aquinas, Finnis and Non-Naturalism', in Craig Paterson and Matthew S. Pugh, *Analytical Thomism: Traditions in Dialogue*, Aldershot: Ashgate, 2006, p. 177.

11 See Gerard Bradley and Robert George, 'The New Natural Law Theory: A Reply to Jean Porter', *American Journal of Jurisprudence* 39 (1994), pp. 303–15. Ethical non-naturalism is deeply unfashionable today, largely because of J. L. Mackie's criticism of it: what is to stop anybody from developing a list of non-natural moral ideas on the basis of what appeals to them? What makes Finnis' list of basic human goods more or less authoritative than that of Grisez, or Aquinas, or Aristotle? Finnis' approach does not even have the strength of appealing to a 'scientific' analysis of human nature.

12 By Bernhard Schlink, directed by David Hare, 2008.

party from a concentration camp. She was contractually obliged and arguably coerced to follow orders, choosing set numbers of women to send back to the camp gas-chambers to make way for new, stronger, prisoners. At her trial, the prosecutor says that she should have refused, knowing that choosing one woman rather than another would make her complicit in an appalling crime against humanity; she replies, 'What would you have done?' Finnis would support the prosecutor's line of argument, saying that just because what Hana did was legal at the time in Germany does not make it morally right or acceptable in relation to the universal human laws which underpin rights. If more people had made a stand and refused to co-operate, then the Holocaust could not have happened; as Edmund Burke famously remarked, 'All that is necessary for evil to triumph is that good men do nothing.'

Finnis' version of Natural Law has had a wide influence on the world of politics and law. In *Natural Law and Natural Rights*, he set out the 'basic human goods' of his system as:

- life
- knowledge
- aesthetic appreciation
- play
- friendship
- practical reasonableness
- religion ('all those beliefs that can be called matters of ultimate concern; questions about the point of human existence')
- 'the marital good' (added in the 1996 edition).

Finnis' approach to normative ethics offers an interesting alternative to the more obviously faith-based approach of, say, Grisez.[13] However, it would be a mistake to see it as secular. In Peter Singer's *A Companion to Ethics*, Stephen Buckle argues that Finnis' list of proposed basic goods seems plausible until it becomes clear that in their application Finnis intends to support

---

13 Paterson, 'Aquinas', p. 172.

the moral viewpoint of the Catholic Church on a range of controversial issues, including contraception and masturbation.[14]

Grisez and Finnis are not alone in proposing new versions of Natural Law, suitable for the modern world and seemingly (although this is debatable) taking account of post-Enlightenment insights into human nature. In recent decades, a number of Catholic scholars have proposed a more radical reworking of natural law known as 'Proportionalism', a move which has caused a great deal of controversy and which provides the major dividing line in Catholic ethics today. Proportionalism has been firmly rejected by the Church despite appealing to many moral philosophers and ordinary Catholics.

Proportionalism

Scholars such as Bernard Hoose and Louis Janssens take issue with Grisez and Finnis, seeing them to be too inflexible and legalistic to be serious about their claim to put people at the centre of moral philosophy. Hoose, Janssens and other proportionalists claim that their approach has support in early texts, even in the spirit of Aquinas' Natural Law, which acknowledges the complexity of real situations and the need to qualify every attempt at a moral law in the light of the diverse and demanding circumstances we operate in.

There will always be the need for right reason and judgement in the application of Natural Law. While the Church has tried to reduce this by providing exhaustive guidance and support, proportionalists would argue that the only way to teach people to be good is to let them make real decisions. For example, imagine that your mother is teaching you to drive.

• Should she eliminate all risk and insist that you spend several years studying the Highway Code, watching driving videos,

---

14 Stephen Buckle, 'Natural Law', in Peter Singer (ed.), *A Companion to Ethics*, Oxford: Blackwell Publishers, 1997, Chapter 13, p. 171.

using simulators and watching her – before she eventually allows you to drive a dual-controlled car around a track on Sundays.

• Or should she sit next to you and let you practise on her car (after some grounding in theory and practice in the car-park) before taking your test and setting out solo?

The traditional approach of the Catholic Church has been to eliminate risk, teaching that followers (if they are to remain followers) should be guided by detailed teaching and by trained priests in all matters, never 'going solo'. The reasonable justification for this is that the stakes are incredibly high and that the Church has a responsibility, both to members and society at large, to ensure that God's teaching is acted upon. There is a sense in which (through baptism) individual Catholics confirm their trust in the Church, agree to let it make decisions for them, and therefore earn salvation.

Proportionalists would argue that this approach is unrealistic and possibly counter-productive. People need to learn to be good people, not just obedient Catholics. These are not necessarily the same thing. It is perfectly possible, as Aquinas himself noted, for a bad person to do good things for the wrong reasons. Many obedient Christians do what they do out of fear, lack of imagination, habit, or to 'fit in', gain prestige or other advantage. Are these really good people?

Many people are never really tested in this life; despite the impression given in ethics textbooks it is relatively rare to have to make big decisions about abortion, euthanasia, war, capital punishment or the environment. Although it is a much-vaunted statistic that a third of western women have an abortion, this means that two-thirds do not – and many who do abort do so when they are very young and unaware of the reality of the choice. Most people are not in a position to influence the law and simply go along with what others have decided. They may enjoy offering their opinion in class-discussions, over a drink with friends or in a radio phone-in, but this is usually just an articulation of what they have been taught to believe and not a reasoned response to a full survey of the evidence.

Perhaps this is why the issue of contraception has had such an impact. It was the cause of Catholics encountering a moral dilemma in real life and unusually having to make a decision for themselves – and in practice this has meant that the large majority of Catholics use contraception even though it is forbidden by their Church. Church teaching forces 'obedient Christians' to consider whether to accept the paternalistic authority of the Church or to exercise freedom. It is sad that exercising freedom has so often been identified with rebelling against the Church. Proportionalists argue that it would be better if the Church could embrace free and responsible adults, rather than seeing them as a threat. This is the motivation of scholars such as Hoose, who rejects Grisez's absolutist approach, seeing it as opposed to Grisez's supposed focus on freedom and moral responsibility.

Taking Grisez's example about lying (or using violence) to protect an innocent from a murderer, Hoose wrote:

In spite of what Grisez says, resorting to violence when trying to protect an innocent person from a would-be murderer could well be described as an act of desperation (although one would certainly be hoping, in such a situation, that it would work, as would be the case if one lied instead). Moreover, resorting to violence might also be described as something that divides the inner and outer aspects of the self, especially if one is at heart a peace-lover (and, indeed, a peace-maker). As for attacking and impeding community, is anything better designed for that than violence? Grisez, of course, refers to real community, but real community is already under attack from the would-be murderer. If there are cases in which the existence of such attacks renders a proportionate use of violence justifiable, surely something similar can be said for lying. If it is helpful to call it the lesser evil, then let us do so.[15]

---

15 Bernard Hoose, 'Towards the Truth about Hiding the Truth', *Louvain Studies* 26 (2001), pp. 74–5.

Proportionalists, like all other proponents of Natural Law, begin by reflecting on what it is to live a good life. The list of 'basic human goods' proposed by most proportionalists is compatible with those proposed by Aquinas, or Grisez, or Finnis – the difference comes in how these goods are applied. As Hoose wrote:

> [P]roponents of this way of thinking hold that, when trying to judge whether a proposed action is right or wrong, we need to take into account all the goods and evils that are involved in that particular case. This includes taking into account unintended but foreseeable side effects of our action.[16]

Proportionalists argue that people should take a complete and long view of each action and its particular context. They stress that no two situations are identical and it is important to consider all the effects an action will have, positive and negative. It is clear that no action has entirely positive, or entirely negative, effects and it is for the individual to judge what is appropriate to do in the situation.

To take an example used by Bernard Hoose, what is good for Margaret (an adult) is not necessarily good for Mary (a child) – we may tell the unvarnished truth about the violent death of a friend to Margaret, while shielding Mary for her own benefit. Would not telling Mary the details of a car-crash be morally wrong? Is the only moral alternative to this to say nothing? Would it not be better from every human point of view to break the news gently and suggest that the death was peaceful – at least until time elapses and the child develops sufficiently to cope? Hoose concludes that 'in short, then, a proportionalist takes the norm into account, but also considers other factors'.[17]

Hoose qualifies this by saying that:

---

16 Lecture notes provided by Bernard Hoose for Candle Conferences Ltd. 'Living the Good Life' conferences, Autumn 2011.

17 Hoose, lecture notes.

it is sometimes mistakenly reported that proportionalism is about finding a proportionate reason for doing what one knows to be morally wrong. This is simply not the case. It is in fact about trying to discover what is the morally right thing to do in any particular set of circumstances. We should always do only what, in conscience, we judge to be morally right, and we should never do what we judge in conscience to be morally wrong.[18]

As W. D. Ross pointed out, justice does not refer to the production of the greatest sum of good; it refers rather to the right distribution of good.[19]

Modern Virtue Ethics

Virtue Ethics and Natural Law are, as set out in the previous chapter, two sides of the same coin – they both relate directly to human fulfilment. Today, to get around the problems inherent in using Natural Law to guide specific actions, some scholars have adopted an agent-centred 'virtue' approach, arguing that we should focus less on specific actions and precepts and more on the character traits which will help us to achieve our ultimate fulfilment, individually and as a people. Obviously this is not new, taking its cue from Aristotle and Aquinas, but modern Natural Law virtue ethicists suggest that agents should be the focus of moral philosophy, not the search for an action-centred system.

Examples of contemporary virtue ethicists who build on the Aristotelian idea of human flourishing, identifying character traits or moral habits which serve this end and recommending that these be cultivated as habits, are Elizabeth Anscombe, Alistair MacIntyre, Philippa Foot, Rosalind Hursthouse and Michael Slote.

18 Hoose, lecture notes.

19 W. D. Ross, *The Right and the Good* (1930), Part II, available online at http://www.ditext.com/ross/right2.html.

Although the approach proposed by each virtue ethicist is distinctive, almost all modern Virtue Ethics show their dependence on Aristotelian philosophy, from which three key concepts are regularly imported. These concepts are *arête* (excellence or virtue, that is, character traits that should be cultivated in order to flourish), *phronesis* (practical or moral wisdom, that is, discussions about the nature of the virtues or human flourishing which should begin with experience), and *eudaimonia* (usually translated as happiness or flourishing, that is, what virtue ethics aims to achieve – see page 76).

A New Approach to Ethics

Modern Virtue Ethics can be traced back to a 1958 article by **Elizabeth Anscombe** (1919–2001) called 'Modern Moral Philosophy' in which she criticized the traditional normative approaches of Natural Law, Kant and Mill, which focus on actions, and argued that (like Aristotle) moral philosophers should consider what it really means to be human and live a good life.[20] In 1985 **Bernard Williams** (1929–2003) developed this idea, arguing that morality has become too concerned with abstractions, considering actions outside of their contexts, ignoring the different situations people find themselves in which affect their freedom and thus their responsibility.[21] People are different and people develop; situations are different and they develop as well. Williams argues that traditional moral philosophy has reached its limit and there is a need for a new approach to ethics, an approach which looks at the bigger picture and engages with the real world, which does not dwell on blame but guides people towards a better life.

---

20 G. E. M. Anscombe, 'Modern Moral Philosophy', *Philosophy* 33: 124 (January 1958). Available online at http://www.philosophy.uncc.edu/mleldrid/cmt/mmp.html.

21 Bernard Williams, *Ethics and the Limits of Philosophy*, Cambridge, MA: Harvard University Press, 1985.

Both Anscombe and Williams took inspiration from the practical approach to philosophy found in the work of Plato and Aristotle. Philosophy was not, for the Greeks, an abstract and technical discipline confined to academic papers which few people read – it was an attitude and a way of living, the practice of loving wisdom and applying it to life's challenges.

Alistair MacIntyre (b. 1929) and *After Virtue*

In 1985, MacIntyre's *After Virtue* set out progress towards a new Virtue Ethic and outlined some of the challenges to be addressed. Importantly, MacIntyre noted the existence of different virtue-theories within different cultures; for example, the virtues in Ancient Greece differ from those suggested by Aquinas in medieval Christian Europe and again from those proposed by feminist writers in the present-day USA. He argued that although this might suggest that goodness is relative, in fact different theories of what is virtuous are underpinned by the principle that goodness depends on moral integrity. Cultures and philosophers may differ in how they describe a good life and positive character traits, but there is a unifying idea of what it means to be fully human.

Since the late 1980s, Virtue Ethics has become a complex and often confusing area. Very broadly speaking, 'whereas deontology and consequentialism are based on rules that try to give us the right action, virtue ethics makes central use of the concept of character. The answer to "How should one live?" is that one should live virtuously, that is, have a virtuous character,'[22] and Virtue Ethics offers a 'third way' in ethics, which rejects looking at actions or consequences in isolation, but looks at character as a whole. Attempts to describe how a fully functioning human being operates, to isolate and describe the virtues, to deal with the challenges presented by a realistic account of being human,

22 Nafsika Athanassoulis, http://www.iep.utm.edu/virtue/, accessed 1 April 2012.

and to apply Virtue Ethics to practical issues have been many and diverse, with some different accounts using the same terminology in different ways and others using different terminology to refer to the same things.

Modern Virtue Ethics has been concerned to build on a range of insights from philosophy, sociology and psychology, compiling a full account of how virtuous (that is, good) people behave which could then be used to instruct others. It is no coincidence that there has been new interest in the fields of 'Positive Psychology' and 'Values Education' in the last quarter century. It is important to recognize, therefore, that while Catholic Natural Law remains locked into the categories put forward by Thomas Aquinas, modern virtue ethicists seek to use a broader understanding of what it means to live a fulfilled human life based on modern science.

Virtue Ethics soon developed two principal branches: eudaimonism and agent-based ethics.

Eudaimonism

Eudaimonism looks back to Aristotle's Function Argument (see above, page 35) and asks how a fully functioning human being would behave; the idea being that when a person functions well, virtuously, they will be both good and live a fulfilled life. One important function of being human is to be rational; it follows that rational, consistent action is a necessary part of being fulfilled and good. In this way Virtue Ethics shows its debt to Kantian thinking (page 51) as well as Aristotelian philosophy. Good examples of virtue ethicists who advocate eudaimonism are Rosalind Hursthouse and Philippa Foot.

Agent-based Ethics

This approach to Virtue Ethics is an attempt to get around the problem that Virtue Ethics depends on the 'naturalistic fallacy' and moves from an observation of how human beings do behave to claims about how they should behave. Michael Slote once argued that we recognize the virtues intuitively, rather than as a result of experience.[23] Virtues are the characteristics of admirable people, who are not necessarily just fully functioning or successful people, but distinctive individuals with strength of character. Instead of moving from saying that fulfilled people generally share such a characteristic, therefore they should cultivate it, particular traits, rather, may be admired and chosen just because they are admirable.

Criticisms

Virtue Ethics has been criticized for being impractical and offering little guidance on responding to modern dilemmas. Advocates point out that most people rarely encounter the sort of dilemmas that textbooks dwell on and that it is actually more practical for normative ethics to focus on the sort of moral decisions that everybody must face every day, how to live a life of integrity and move towards fulfilment. It follows that people who develop positive habits such as honesty and fidelity will be better equipped to make sensible big decisions and that it respects each person's freedom and rationality not to be heavy-handed in prescribing laws.

Virtue Ethics may encourage people to focus in on their own character development, rather than looking outwards to the effects of each action on others. This criticism, most associated with Scanlon,[24] could be held to apply to all major normative systems and to leave acting according to the apparently unnatural impulse to sacrifice one's own interests for others as the only option. It would be possible to argue that virtuous behaviour does

23 M. Slote, *From Morality to Virtue*, New York: Oxford University Press, 1992.

24 T. M. Scanlon, *What We Owe Each Other*, Cambridge, MA: Harvard University Press, 1998.

not just benefit an individual but would benefit humanity if every individual cultivated it: therefore the imperative to cultivate a virtue is a rational imperative or duty rather than a selfish urge.

Finally, Virtue Ethics has been criticized because, although it claims to embrace the differences between people and situations and the developmental character of both, it fails to respond to the problem of moral luck. Some people just have better opportunities or capabilities to cultivate the virtues than others and there seems little way to avoid the conclusion that circumstance or luck plays a part in determining moral status. This in turn suggests that people are not entirely free and may not be entirely morally responsible, two conclusions which virtue ethicists, along with most other moral philosophers, would be reluctant to accept.

Conclusion

The Natural Law tradition remains enormously influential not least in the international legal scene with the International Criminal Court prosecuting leaders for 'crimes against humanity' on the basis that certain actions go against the common human nature that all human beings share. To reject this assumption would lead to the demise of the International Criminal Court and the whole idea of there being absolute standards against which crimes such as genocide can be judged. The problem remains of defining human nature as well as what it means to live a fulfilled life – and this continues to be greatest challenge for modern versions of Natural Law and Virtue Ethics. There is, perhaps, a real need to bring together different disciplines including philosophy, psychiatry, psychology, anthropology and even theology to address the question, 'What does a fulfilled human life look like?' Sadly, such an inter-disciplinary approach is a rarity in modern universities, yet if the Natural Law tradition is to flourish it needs to be well grounded and to draw on the latest research.

7

Classical Utilitarianism

In some ways, Utilitarianism is the polar opposite of Natural Law. As a consequentialist system, Utilitarianism encourages people to consider the outcomes of their actions and assess whether their choices have produced the largest amount of happiness possible. Clearly, Natural Law would not usually allow individuals such a level of freedom in making or justifying their own choices. Utilitarianism suggests that, given the right situation, any action might be a good one – even murder or theft. Natural Law would dispute this, arguing that some actions are always and absolutely wrong, regardless of the situation.

Nevertheless, there is a greater degree of similarity between Natural Law and Utilitarianism than is often considered.

- The reasoning process each system employs is similar. Both Natural Law and Utilitarianism start with an analysis of human nature, of what makes human beings flourish. Although the definition of human nature provided by Aristotle, Aquinas or Grisez is more prescriptive than the simple definition of human beings as rational pleasure-seekers offered by Bentham, the systems go on to suggest that actions which serve the fulfilment of human nature are good and actions which inhibit it are bad.
- Both systems are teleological; actions are justified in relation to the ends they produce. Most forms of Natural Law take a very long view of the effects of our actions, whereas most versions of Utilitarianism take a shorter view; however, there are

versions of Natural Law which encourage people to consider more immediate effects and versions of 'Rule Utilitarianism' which insists on the importance of maintaining some general principles because of the bigger-picture benefits that doing so brings.

- Natural Law and Utilitarianism are both concerned with human flourishing and achieving a reduction in human suffering. 'Happiness' is notoriously difficult to define and it is hard to reach agreement over which actions generally contribute to it, yet both systems attempt to deal in it in their own ways.

Theological Utilitarianism

Given this level of similarity it is, perhaps, not surprising that the first 'utilitarians' (recognizing that this term is used anachronistically) were also Christians, steeped in the naturalistic moral philosophy of the Church. **Thomas More** (1478–1535), **Erasmus** (1466–1536) and **Bishop George Berkeley** (1685–1753) all put forward arguments for ethical hedonism within a Christian framework. Of course, these theologians did not have the same conception of what pursuing pleasure might involve as later moral philosophers.

For Thomas More, our desire for happiness will motivate us to act as God wishes in every respect – because we have certain knowledge that there will be reward in heaven and eternal punishment in hell. Pascal's famous wager[1] makes a similar assumption.

Bishop Berkeley wrote what can only be understood as an argument for strong Rule Utilitarianism.

In framing the general laws of nature, it is granted we must be entirely guided by the public good of mankind, but not in the ordinary moral actions of our lives. Such a rule, if universally observed hath, from the nature of things, a necessary fitness

---

1 Blaise Pascal, *Pensées* 233.

to promote the general well-being of mankind: therefore it is a law of nature. This is good reasoning. But if we should say, such an action doth in this instance produce much good and no harm to mankind; therefore it is lawful: this [would be] wrong. The rule is framed with respect to the good of mankind, but our practice must be always shaped immediately by the rule.[2]

Hutcheson and Moral Sense

Francis Hutcheson (1694–1746) is probably the best-known early utilitarian, and was acknowledged as an inspirational teacher by later utilitarian philosophers. Originally Irish, he studied and later taught at the University of Glasgow, where the economist Adam Smith was one of his students. Smith went on to develop a system of moral philosophy which owed much to Hutcheson.

A Presbyterian minister, Hutcheson argued that people can understand good and evil without knowledge of and revelation from God through a 'moral sense',[3] which we all possess and which, if we follow it, allows us all to be good and to stand worthy of any metaphysical reward. Building on Berkeley's work, Hutcheson suggested that human beings naturally approve of things that bring pleasure and naturally disapprove of things that cause pain. He argued that people prefer a happy and contented society to turmoil and wrote that 'the highest moral approbation is the calm, stable, universal goodwill to all' or 'the greatest good of the greatest number'.[4] In this way Hutcheson argued that people naturally choose what will bring about the greatest good.

---

2 *The Works of George Berkeley Part Two*, trans. G. N. Wright, Whitefish, MT: Kessinger Publishing, 2004, Vol. 2, p. 17.

3 Moral sense theory is also known as 'sentimentalism' by meta-ethicists. Hutcheson, Adam Smith and David Hume were all sentimentalists, believing that morals have their roots in the emotions, not the reason. Modern sentimentalists include Slote and Blackburn.

4 Francis Hutcheson, *An Essay on the Nature and Conduct of the Passions and Affections, with Illustrations on the Moral Sense* (1742).

These views brought Hutcheson into conflict with the Presbyterian authorities from 1738. His argument could mean that non-Presbyterians (and even non-Christians) could be in as good a position to achieve salvation as those who filled the pews every Sunday.

Paley and Beneficent Design

William Paley (1743–1805) wrote *Natural Theology*, the standard text at Cambridge for those studying the natural sciences in the nineteenth century, and which is best known today for its famous 'watchmaker' argument for the existence of God. He is often presented as a bumbling clergyman from the sticks (he was Archdeacon of Carlisle). Nevertheless, Paley was actually a major moral philosopher, a radical utilitarian, who advocated re-examining all our accepted beliefs and argued in favour of women's rights, against slavery, for the Americans in the War of Independence – even against private property.

Paley went further than Hutcheson by arguing that because God is perfectly good he must will us to be happy, further that God's will is the same as a command and following a commandment is a duty, so trying to be happy is a moral and religious duty. Both Hutcheson and Paley engaged with the work of David Hume (see below), accepting his scepticism about traditional religious moral philosophy while retaining a belief in God and the existence of real moral values.

Paley's moral philosophy dominated the curricula in American colleges in the late eighteenth and early nineteenth centuries and may explain why Utilitarianism has not been seen as being in opposition to religion in the USA. The fact that Utilitarianism became associated with secular humanism in the UK owes much to Jeremy Bentham, a contemporary of Paley's.

Jeremy Bentham (1748–1832)

Bentham began his career as a lawyer and made his name by criticizing William Blackstone (1723–80), a Judge and Tory politician whose work was of immense importance in establishing the constitution and law in England (and later in the USA). In 1776, Bentham published *A Fragment on Government* criticizing as 'a fiction' a passage in Blackstone's *Commentaries on the Laws of England* (1766) which suggested that the English legal system approximated to Natural Law more closely than any other. Bentham was appalled by the state of English law, seeing it as a mess of custom, taboo and attempts at tyranny.

He argued that religion was an unsuitable basis for law, because it was inherently mysterious and because it sometimes seemed to call on people to suppress their nature, to choose to suffer, on the strength of threats from religious authorities who could not verify their positions through logic or evidence. Bentham wrote:

> [T]he principle of asceticism never was, nor ever can be, consistently pursued by any living creature. Let but one tenth part of the inhabitants of the earth pursue it consistently, and in a day's time they will have turned it into a Hell.[5]

It is worth saying that both Hutcheson and Paley would probably have agreed with Bentham's analysis.

Bentham advocated subjecting English law to a rational analysis and sweeping away any laws which are not socially useful, which do not contribute to the greatest happiness for the greatest number. People should be equal before the law; the law should be rationally intuitive so far as it is possible. It simply wasn't fair to judge and punish people according to laws they have no hope of understanding without the benefit of a substantial and appro-

---

5 Jeremy Bentham, *An Introduction to the Principles of Morals and Legislation* (1823), Vol. 1, p. 21. Available as a free e-book at https://play. google.com/store/books/details?id=oogJAAAAQAAJ&rdid=book-oogJAA AAQAAJ&rdot=1.

priate education. Any reasonable person should be able to work out how to behave and so may be judged as fully responsible. For Bentham, the function of law is to award punishment and rewards and to maintain a just balance between them, so helping society to grow ever happier.

Bentham wrote, 'The age we live in is a busy age; in which knowledge is rapidly advancing towards perfection';[6] he was playing his part by pushing to reform the law, making it serve and progress change. His ambitions were to reform British politics and through them British society, to create a 'pannomion', a complete utilitarian code of law, accessible and rational schools and universities, and 'panopticons', prisons designed to completely remove liberty and privacy from inmates and so to deliver the severest possible humane punishment. Bentham wrote that panopticons would be 'a new mode of obtaining power of mind over mind, in a quantity hitherto without example'.[7] He believed that they would re-train criminals, giving them the sense that somebody is watching them when they act. It is fair to say that Bentham never really achieved his ambitions (he died just before the Great Reform Act was passed in 1832), but his influence lives on – and not just through his mummified corpse attending council meetings at University College London.

Although Bentham and Paley would have shared many opinions, Bentham was more directly influenced by the work of **David Hume** (1711–76).

David Hume

Hume applied for chairs of Philosophy at the Universities of both Edinburgh and Glasgow and was turned down because of his

---

6 Jeremy Bentham, *A Fragment on Government*, available online at http://www.constitution.org/jb/frag_gov.htm.

7 *The Works of Jeremy Bentham, Published under the Superintendence of His Executor, John Bowring* (1834), Boston, MA: Adamant Media Corporation, 2001, Vol. 4, p. 39.

atheism and his supposedly heretical writings. He was forced to make a living by working as a private tutor, a librarian and a secretary and by publishing works he hoped would be popular. In the eighteenth and nineteenth centuries Hume was best known as a historian; his six-volume *History of England* was published between 1754 and 1762 and was a bestseller despite being over a million words long. Hume's main ethical writings were Book 3 of his *Treatise of Human Nature* (1740), his *Enquiry Concerning the Principles of Morals* and some of his essays, such as that 'On Suicide'.

For Hume, a sceptic, nothing can be said to be known unless it can be experienced and tested through the senses. Moral laws are not empirically testable or verifiable so therefore we cannot know that murder is wrong or that helping others is good.

Hume argued that reason is the 'slave of the passions', that moral distinctions are not derived from reason, but from sentiment and attitudes fostered by the emotions. He wrote: 'Morals excite passions, and produce or prevent actions. Reason itself is utterly impotent in this particular. The rules of morality, therefore, are not conclusions of our reason …'[8] Hume was much more cynical about human nature than either Hutcheson or Smith. For Hume, the only reason for doing something moral is the pleasure that we feel that following a moral principle will give us, the sense of satisfaction in our conscience or 'impartial observer', the comfort we gain from 'fitting in' with social expectations and our upbringing, or the real approval of other people; conversely, avoiding 'immoral actions' is a matter of avoiding emotional discomfort, disapproval and of course punishment!

Hume encouraged people to cast away social conditioning and think through ethical questions from scratch. In practice, Hume's applied ethics are blunt and controversial. For example, take Hume's famous essay 'On Suicide', which he left to be pub-

---

8 David Hume, *A Treatise of Human Nature* (1740), Oxford: Oxford University Press, 1967, p. 325. A good summary of Hume's moral philosophy can be found at http://plato.stanford.edu/entries/hume-moral/.

lished posthumously in 1783.[9] In it Hume argues that suicide is no more a rebellion against God than is saving the life of someone who would otherwise die; he caricatures the 'Natural Law' approach to ethics, suggesting that it should recommend leaving everything to nature and not intervening to change the course of things in the smallest detail. If we really do discover how we ought to behave from observations of how nature is, then why do we practise medicine or use the law to protect the vulnerable? Surely nature dictates that only the fittest do and therefore should survive and breed?

Hume argued that suicide does not violate a duty to society. He compares suicide with becoming a total recluse, which is not normally considered to be immoral, although this would not justify a suicide that has significant effects on others. As for duty to self, Hume takes it to be obvious that there can be times when suicide is desirable, though he also thinks it ridiculous that anyone would consider suicide unless they first considered every other option. With reference to the emotions that are likely to be triggered by suicide, clearly they are likely to be negative. One's decision may be coloured by a sense that the conscience or impartial observer is judging the action, the worry about what others may think, worries about being denounced by the Church and denied a Christian burial – or even fear of punishment should the attempt fail. According to Hume, none of these is a rational reason; all are emotional or sentimental responses to the situation. He concluded, 'if it be no crime, both prudence and courage should engage us to rid ourselves at once of existence, when it becomes a burden' and, famously, 'the life of a man is of no greater importance to the universe than that of an oyster'.[10]

---

9 The text of this essay, which was withdrawn from publication by Hume during his lifetime because of the storm advance copies caused, is now online at http://www.anselm.edu/homepage/dbanach/suicide.htm, accessed 3 October 2011.

10 David Hume, 'On Suicide', written in 1755, published in 1777.

Bentham's Utilitarianism

John Stuart Mill coined the term 'Utilitarianism' when he edited Bentham's works. Bentham argued that both the law and our concept of what is right should be based on the understanding that humans pursue happiness and avoid pain. In Chapter 1 of *An Introduction to the Principles of Morals and Legislation* (1781), he begins with the observation that 'nature has placed mankind under the governance of two sovereign masters, pain and pleasure. It is for them alone to point out what we ought to do, as well as to determine what we shall do.'[11] For Bentham, as for Aristotle and Aquinas, the law should be based on moral philosophy, which should in turn be based on a clear and scientific account of human nature. However, for Bentham 'every law is an infringement of liberty', therefore laws should be kept to a minimum in order to preserve liberty, which he saw as the foundation of happiness.

Bentham saw human beings as **psychological egoists** and did not appeal to the existence or nature of God to underpin his theory of human nature or moral duty. Unlike Hume, Bentham did not see that the sentiments provide sufficient motivation for people to behave morally. He tried to build on ethical hedonism using the principle of rational equality, arguing that, although 'in every human breast ... self-regarding interest is predominant over social interest; each person's own individual interest over the interests of all other persons taken together',[12] we recognize that all human beings are fundamentally equal and that it serves utility to treat others as we would want to be treated. This is why Bentham's utilitarian maxim suggests that we should 'always act so as to produce the greatest happiness for the greatest number' rather than just acting hedonistically.

---

11 Jeremy Bentham, *An Introduction to the Principles of Morals and Legislation*, Chapter 1:1, available online at http://www.Utilitarianism.com/jeremy-bentham/index.html, accessed 13 April 2012.

12 Jeremy Bentham, *Book of Fallacies*, Part V, Chapter IX. Not in print but available online at http://archive.org/details/bookoffallaciesfoobent.

Bentham argued that it is irrational to expect human beings to suppress their nature and act contrary to their own interests and the pursuit of pleasure; however, reason suggests that what is good for the majority of people in society will eventually be good for most individuals; we cannot expect others to consider our interests if we fail to consider others' interests. Yet Utilitarianism is radically different from hedonism. It is obvious that decisions which maximize the number of people made happy would sometimes make the person making the decisions immediately unhappy. High standards of rationality and altruism are expected of the utilitarian.

Bentham's approach bears some similarities with that of Kant (see page 147), whose work is often presented as being diametrically opposed to it.

- They agreed about human nature, seeing human beings as rational pleasure-seekers.
- They agreed that it cannot be a moral duty to act against one's own interests and that it is irrational to expect somebody to do something that they cannot do or that is against their nature.
- They agreed that it is good to follow reason in determining what will result in the greatest good.
- Further, Bentham and Kant agreed that people should work out a course of action in each situation, because following rules and acting out of habit or fear rather than freely applying one's reason to each situation is to fail to fulfil human potential,[13] though obviously they differed in which actions they would see follow from this reasoning!

Famously, Bentham devised a 'felicific calculus' (later called a hedonic or hedonistic calculus) to ease the process of decision-making. He wrote:

---

13 Bentham went so far as to write that 'he who thinks and thinks for himself, will always have a claim to thanks; it is no matter whether it be right or wrong, so as it be explicit. If it is right, it will serve as a guide to direct; if wrong, as a beacon to warn' (*Works*, Vol. 10).

Sum up all the values of all the pleasures on the one side, and those of all the pains on the other. The balance, if it be on the side of pleasure, will give the good tendency of the act upon the whole, with respect to the interests of that individual person; if on the side of pain, the bad tendency of it upon the whole.[14]

In essence, he recommends that people assess actions according to the following formula:

$$\frac{\text{Pleasure}}{\text{Pain}} \times \text{Number Affected} = \text{'Score'}$$

Although the business of assigning values to the pleasure or pain caused by any course of action is difficult and although it is tricky to know how many people will be affected by a decision, the criteria outlined below and the calculus were aimed to provide a defensible rationale to underpin decision-making. The idea is that once various courses of action have been 'scored' it is relatively easy to make 'objective' comparisons.

Bentham immediately saw a difficulty with using the utilitarian maxim 'always act so as to produce the greatest happiness for the greatest number' as the basis for a normative approach to ethical decision-making. How could pleasure be quantified effectively, let alone ranked according to quality? The measurement of pleasure, pain, happiness and sadness is incredibly difficult and Bentham was not insensitive to this. In Chapter 4:4 of *An Introduction to the Principles of Morals and Legislation* (1781) Bentham listed seven criteria which form the 'felicific calculus'. The pleasure produced by an action will be greater or less, according to:

- its intensity
- its duration
- its certainty or uncertainty
- its propinquity or remoteness [how near or far off the pleasure is]

14 Bentham, *Introduction*, Chapter 4:5.

- its fecundity [likely to produce other pleasures]
- its purity [dependent on pain?]
- its extent; that is, the number of persons to whom it extends or (in other words) who are affected by it.

The calculus, though much derided, forms the basis of modern risk-assessments and is used to derive 'Quality Adjusted Life-Year Scores' (QALYS) on which funding is often allocated in today's public health services.

Unusually for his time, Bentham argued that pleasures from any source can be assessed side by side, that 'intellectual pleasures' for one example should not be counted as inherently superior, though they may produce more fruitful and long-lasting pleasures. This meant that Bentham's Utilitarianism was **egalitarian**; people from any social class, race, religion or gender could be counted as equals before the calculation. Contrary to popular opinion, Mill actually misquoted Bentham when he claimed that Bentham said that 'pushpin is as good as poetry'.[15] Bentham's actual argument was rather more sophisticated, though it did allow that there is nothing to stop a popular game or art form producing more pleasure than an elitist one.

Thomas Carlyle (1795–1881) attacked Bentham's Utilitarianism, calling it 'pig philosophy', and it was in response to this jibe that Bentham's godson John Stuart Mill formulated his own version of Utilitarianism.

John Stuart Mill (1806–73)

Mill was brought up by his father (the economist and historian James Mill) to be an asset to society and his education was on

---

15 J. S. Mill, 'Bentham', in John Stuart Mill, *Utilitarianism, On Liberty, and Essay on Bentham*, ed. M. Warnock, New York: New American Library, 1974, p. 123. The closest actual reference is from Bentham's *Rationale of Reward*, Book 3, Chapter 1, paragraphs 8–9: 'The utility of all these arts and sciences, – I speak both of those of amusement and curiosity, – the value which they possess, is exactly in proportion to the pleasure they yield ...'

strict Benthamite lines. Although James Mill had been ordained in the Church of Scotland, he became a disciple of Bentham and shielded his son from religious instruction[16] and its effects while coaching him in every other discipline from the age of three. As a result, Mill became a child-prodigy, reading David Hume and Edward Gibbon before he was seven. He began Greek at four and Latin at eight. At twelve, he was learning theoretical chemistry and classical economics.

By his late teens, Mill had established a reputation as a firebrand journalist; he railed against the established values of his time. One morning in 1823, on his way to work at the East India Company, Mill came across the body of a newborn infant in St James's Park. It had been strangled and abandoned. Mill's response to this was to distribute leaflets written by Richard Carlisle[17] explaining how to use the contraceptive sponge. For this, he was arrested, tried and imprisoned for a few days.[18] He was 17. Following this, Mill became ever angrier and ever more productive. Obviously a workaholic, he began the mammoth and important task of editing Bentham's work. Mill himself said that he was a 'Benthamite reasoning machine' during this period.

When this task came to an end in 1825, Mill began to struggle emotionally. Despite the fact that he had earned respect as one of the foremost intellects of his generation, he felt lost and began to question Benthamism. David Hume, who went through a similar intellectual and personal crisis a century earlier, resolved it through 'claret and riding'.[19] Mill's self-medication involved tears and the poetry of Wordsworth. He claimed that Wordsworth transformed his thinking and gave him access to a range of

16 Mill was never able to bring himself to believe in God, although later in life he advocated a 'Religion of Humanity' and was influenced by the French philosopher Auguste Comte (1798–1857), who saw the purpose of religion as being primarily practical, about the benefits of practising religion rather than objective truth. Effectively he saw sociological value in religion.

17 Richard Reeves, *John Stuart Mill: Victorian Firebrand*, London: Atlantic, 2007, p. 1.

18 Francis Mineka, *Mill Newsletter* 8:1 (1972).

19 Roy Porter, *The Enlightenment*, London: Penguin, 2000, pp. 89–90.

human emotions from which he had been barred by the narrowness of his education.

In 1828, Mill took part in a debate on human perfectibility, during which he said 'the passions are the spring, the moral principle only the regulators of human life'.[20] He condemned the followers of Bentham for their neglect both in theory and practice of the cultivation of feeling and their 'undervaluing of poetry and of Imagination generally as an element of human nature'.[21] After this, he developed a much broader understanding of Utilitarianism, grounded in our common humanity and the good of society as a whole. It is essential to understand the difference that this made to Mill's approach; to equate Bentham and Mill is to make a major error.

Mill's general approach to philosophy was more journalistic than systematic; he developed his thinking through articles, popular books and political speeches and tended to base his claims in appeals to common sense rather than in technical argument. He worked collaboratively, particularly with the early feminist Harriet Taylor (the love of his life whom he married after the death of her husband and who, he said, influenced him more than anyone else). Mill always intended his work to lead to discussion and a practical improvement in society.

Following his exposure to Wordsworth, Mill's understanding of pleasure was more sophisticated than that of Bentham, but also more elitist. Against Carlyle, Mill argued that Utilitarianism did not have to be 'pig philosophy'. He argued that 'higher pleasures' (including finding joy in truth, beauty and virtue) are intrinsically more worthwhile than 'lower pleasures' and famously declared that he would rather be 'Socrates dissatisfied than an ordinary mortal satisfied, a human being dissatisfied than a pig satisfied'.[22]

---

20 J. S. Mill, *Speech on Perfectibility*, available online at http://www.utilitarian.org/texts/perfectibility.html.

21 *Autobiography of John Stuart Mill*, Charleston, SC: Forgotten Books, 2010, p. 112.

22 J. S. Mill, *Utilitarianism*, Chicago, IL: University of Chicago Press, 1906, p. 260.

Defending his position, Mill said, 'It is quite compatible with the principle of utility to recognize the fact that some kinds of pleasure are more desirable and more valuable than others.'[23] He went on:

I never wavered in the conviction that happiness is the test of all rules of conduct, and the end of life. But I now thought that this end was only to be attained by not making it the direct end. Those only are happy ... who have their minds fixed on some object other than their own happiness ... The cultivation of the feelings becomes one of the cardinal points in my ethical and philosophical creed.[24]

It seems that Mill was suggesting something much closer to the Utilitarianism of Hutcheson and Smith than that of Bentham, not a million miles away from Virtue Ethics or even Kantian Ethics, that people should cultivate 'moral feelings' and act according to principles designed to serve the greater happiness, hoping that personal happiness may result indirectly from this.

For Mill being human involves 'the desire for perfection, the accusing or approving conscience, the sense of honour and dignity, the love of beauty, order, power as an instrument of good and the love of action'.[25] Mill had a broad view of education, grounded in freedom. He wrote that 'whatever helps to shape the human being, to make the individual what he is, or hinder him from being what he is not ... is part of his education'.[26] Mill would be critical of much modern education. He wrote:

---

23 Mill, *Utilitarianism*, Chapter 2.

24 Quoted from Mill's *Autobiography* in Alan Sell, *Mill on God: The Pervasiveness and Elusiveness of Mill's Religious Thought*, Aldershot: Ashgate, 2004.

25 J. S. Mill, 'Bentham', Section 3, available online at http://www.laits.utexas.edu/poltheory/jsmill/diss-disc/bentham/bentham.s03.html, accessed 13 April 2012.

26 J. S. Mill, inaugural address to the University of St Andrews 1867; available online at http://oll.libertyfund.org/?option=com_staticxt&static file=show.php%3Ftitle=255&chapter=21681&layout=html&Itemid=27.

It is, no doubt, a very laudable effort in modern teaching to render as much as possible of what the young are required to learn, easy and interesting to them. But when this principle is pushed to the length of not requiring them to learn anything BUT what has been made easy and interesting, one of the chief objects of education is sacrificed ... [education] is training up a race of people who will be incapable of doing anything that is disagreeable to them.[27]

For Mill, education involved developing the whole person. The stress today on results, academic tests and league tables he would have seen as 'selling out' to an impoverished view of humanity. Mill had a much more developed view of human nature than Bentham, one which valued actions which are difficult and principled, which produce little personal or immediate pleasure, one which did not differ so much from that of Aquinas or Aristotle. Many philosophers do not recognize this but Mill has a profound sense of what human fulfilment represents which could easily have derived from Aristotle – although there is no evidence that it did.

Like Kant, Mill believed that human nature necessarily involves caring for others and that human fulfilment lies in acting on principle for the good of others. He therefore developed a 'religion of humanity' whose cornerstone was altruism. Mill was an early sociologist, wanting religion to be useful to society. He was sceptical about traditional views of God but, like **Auguste Comte** (1798–1857) and, of course, Kant himself, Mill considered that a rational form of religion had an important motivating function.[28] He wrote:

[A]sk yourself whether you are happy, and you cease to be so. The only chance is to treat not happiness, but some end ex-

27 Mill, *Autobiography*; also available in the Routledge Collected Works series as *Autobiography and Literary Essays*, pp. 53, 55.

28 Arguments recently re-hashed by Alain de Botton in *Religion for Atheists: A Non-Believer's Guide to the Uses of Religion*, London: Hamish Hamilton, 2012.

ternal to it, as the purpose of life. Let your self-consciousness, your scrutiny exhaust themselves on that and, if otherwise fortunately circumstanced, you will inhale happiness with the air you breathe.[29]

In other words, happiness cannot be sought directly. Mill called people to altruism, arguing that this will lead to happiness as a by-product. It cannot be emphasized strongly enough how different this understanding of Mill's Utilitarianism is from the impression given in many introductory books: Mill's Utilitarianism is fundamentally unselfish and has a great deal in common with some forms of religious ethics.

Unlike Kant and unlike most advocates of Natural Law, Mill remained confident that humans are able to work out the likely results of their actions for themselves. He did not see **the problem of prediction** (predicting the consequences of actions) as an insurmountable obstacle to consequentialist ethics. Nevertheless, he wrote that:

a theory which considers little in an action besides that action's own consequences ... will be most apt to fail in the consideration of the greatest social questions ... for these ... must be viewed as the great instruments for forming the national character, or carrying forward the members of the community towards perfection or preserving them from degeneracy.[30]

Mill advocated a much longer view of utility. Decisions must be made by individuals now for the long-term good of society. Mill was one of the first to argue for environmental conservation and population control, suggesting that tough decisions are necessary in the short term to preserve the greater happiness in the longer term.

---

29 Mill, *Autobiography*, Routledge Collected Works, p. 147.

30 *The Collected Works of John Stuart Mill, Volume X – Essays on Ethics, Religion, and Society* (1833), available online at http://oll.libertyfund.org/simple.php?id=241.

Henry Sidgwick (1838–1900)

In the later Victorian period, Utilitarianism was developed by Henry Sidgwick at the University of Cambridge. His work was described by John Rawls as the 'first truly academic work in moral theory, modern in both method and spirit'.[31] Schultz claims that 'Utilitarians from G. E. Moore and Bertrand Russell to J. J. C. Smart and R. M. Hare down to Derek Parfit and Peter Singer have acknowledged Sidgwick's *Methods* as a vital source for their arguments.'[32]

Sidgwick's most important work was *Methods of Ethics* (1874) which was modelled on Aristotle's *Ethics* and started from first principles. He was a meta-ethicist before his student G. E. Moore made that term and that approach well known (see page 12ff.). He wrote:

> I have desired to concentrate the reader's attention, from first to last, not on the practical results to which our methods lead, but on the methods themselves. I have wished to put aside temporarily the urgent need which we all feel of finding and adopting the true method of determining what we ought to do; and to consider simply what conclusions will be rationally reached if we start with certain ethical premises, and with what degree of certainty and precision.[33]

Sidgwick's ethics were sophisticated; he acknowledged Kant as one of his masters[34] and had been convinced by Joseph But-

---

31 J. Rawls, 'Kantian Constructivism in Moral Theory', *Journal of Philosophy* 77 (1980).

32 Barton Schultz, 'Henry Sidgwick', *The Stanford Encyclopedia of Philosophy* (Spring 2011 edition), ed. Edward N. Zalta, available online at http://plato.stanford.edu/archives/spr2011/entries/sidgwick/.

33 Henry Sidgwick, *Methods of Ethics*, 1907 edn, p. viii.

34 Sidgwick agreed with Kant about the rationality of first principles, but disagreed with Kant when it came to goodness lying only in a good will and in defining a good action only as one which is made freely and consciously. Sidgwick could not see how we can establish if free-will is real or simply an illusion – so he sidestepped the issue. Sidgwick's ethics were more teleological

ler[35] to abandon Bentham's psychological egoism. He believed, with Mill, that human beings are capable of genuine altruism, of acting for others' interests without the expectation or hope of any reward.[36] He argued that the will is (at least possibly or in part) motivated by reason, not just by selfish desires for pleasure. For Sidgwick, moral principles are non-natural. He understood right to mean 'reasonable' or 'objective', an 'ultimate and unanalysable notion'. According to Schultz 'his student Moore was willing to declare the methods untainted by the "naturalistic fallacy"'.[37]

Sidgwick argued that a good action was one which produced the maximum amount of pleasure and that Utilitarianism was the best available ethical system. He saw pleasure in terms of universal flourishing; although Sidgwick maintained that no man should act so as to destroy his own happiness, he advocated making decisions with a long and rational view of what pleasure is.

Sidgwick 'seemed to recognize that the mental states we call pleasures are a mixed bag as far as their phenomenal properties are concerned'

> ... [W]hat pleasures have in common is not something internal to them – their peculiar feeling tone, or whatever – but something about us – the fact that we like them, enjoy them, value them, find them satisfying, seek them, wish to prolong them, and so on.[38]

---

than Kant's: he saw good actions in terms of the foreseeable results they produced, not in terms of the mythical *summum bonum*. See J. B. Schneewind, *Sidgwick's Ethics and Victorian Moral Philosophy*, Oxford: Clarendon Press, 1977, p. 420.

35 See the final chapter of this book.

36 See the final chapter of this book and the essay by William K. Frankena in Bart Schultz (ed.), *Essays on Henry Sidgwick*, New York: Cambridge University Press, 1992.

37 Schultz, 'Henry Sidgwick'.

38 L. W. Sumner, *Welfare, Ethics and Happiness*, Oxford: Clarendon Press, 1996, p. 86.

This would make Sidgwick the father of the Ideal Utilitarianism proposed by Moore (sometimes called 'Aesthetic Utilitarianism') and of modern Preference Utilitarianism, both of which will be explored in the next chapter.

Act and Rule Utilitarianism

The terms 'Act Utilitarianism' and 'Rule Utilitarianism' were not really used until the mid twentieth century.[39] The distinction is between forms of Utilitarianism which recommend new decisions being made in every situation and forms which base more or less absolute rules on the principle of utility. It can nevertheless be useful to consider how they might relate to the Utilitarianism of Bentham and that of Mill.

Contrary to popular opinion, Bentham did not suggest that people apply the felicific calculus to each new situation. In *An Introduction to the Principles of Morals and Legislation*, Chapter 4:6, he wrote: 'It is not to be expected that this process should be strictly pursued previously to every moral judgment, or to every legislative or judicial operation. It may, however, be always kept in view ...' In practice, he wanted to use Utilitarianism as the basis for law. It follows that he would have accepted people following rules when those rules were based on the principle of utility and when they seemed to serve justice – that is, except when the circumstances showed that the rule was inappropriate or inadequate. He does not really, therefore, fit clearly into either the 'act' or 'rule' camp.

Similarly, Mill suggested that individuals work out the consequences of each action for themselves but also that rules and moral education will be necessary in order to bring people to

---

39 They are discussed by J. J. C. Smart, 'Extreme and Restricted Utilitarianism', *Philosophical Quarterly* 6:25 (October 1956); by R. Eugene Bales in *Act Utilitarianism vs. Rule Utilitarianism*, Garden City: Doubleday, 1968; and by J. J. C. Smart and Bernard Williams in *Utilitarianism: For and Against*, Cambridge: Cambridge University Press, 1973.

the point where they are capable of rational moral decision-making.[40] Mill stressed the long-term and big-picture effects of actions, which would tend to support people acting on principles such as 'Do not lie', 'Do not steal' and 'Do not kill'. It is clear that Utilitarianism only justifies making exceptions to such principles when the immediate, near and certain effects of actions are prioritized, as Bentham seemed to advocate.

Both Bentham and Mill discussed how utilitarian principles can and should be used in practice as well as in theory; neither ignored the need to consider both what Herbert Spencer called 'Absolute Ethics' (how things should be in an ideal world where law and morality were brought together) and what he called 'Relative Ethics' (how things are in reality). Bentham and Mill seem to suggest that though we should be act utilitarians in ourselves, there will still be a need for rules or laws (based on the principle of utility) to guide people who are not willing to be or capable of being rational. Ideally act utilitarians' decisions would be the same as those made to conform to the law.[41] Bentham and Mill wanted small-government, they wanted the law to be reduced as much as possible, and in this case the probability for conflict between the individually right and the legally right thing to do would be lower than it is at present. The 'act' and 'rule' distinction may therefore be too crude to accurately reflect the position of classical utilitarians.

---

40 Whether Mill's ethics are really rule-consequentialist is controversial (J. O. Urmson, 'The Interpretation of the Moral Philosophy of J. S. Mill', *Philosophical Quarterly* 3:10 (January 1953), pp. 33–9; Roger Crisp, *Mill on Utilitarianism*, London: Routledge, 1997, pp. 102–33).

41 David Lyons argued in *Forms and Limits of Utilitarianism*, Oxford: Oxford University Press, 1965, that 'a plausible formulation of rule-Utilitarianism would make it recommend the same actions as act- Utilitarianism, so the two kinds are "extensionally equivalent" and there is no practical difference between the two'.

Criticisms of Classical Utilitarianism

What is Happiness?

It is immediately apparent that Utilitarianism, whether in the version of Hutcheson, Bentham, Mill or Sidgwick, suffers from the difficulty of defining pleasure. How can one person tell what will really make another happy – or what will really cause another to suffer? When an educated guess is wrong, a utilitarian calculation may be rendered completely incorrect.

Predicting and Measuring Pleasure

Despite Bentham's 'felicific calculus' the task of measuring the outcomes of actions is not precise or consistent. Different people will rank and compare different sensations differently – they will also include different groups of people in their calculations. The 'problem of prediction' is one which no consequentialist system of ethics has satisfactorily dealt with. To what extent can we work out what the precise effects of our actions will be before we act? If actions are only justified in relation to effects then moral luck will play a huge part in determining whether people are good or bad.

Take, for example, Nicholas Montserrat's *The Cruel Sea*.[42] Captain Hawkins authorizes depth charges being dropped on what he takes to be an enemy submarine, despite survivors of an earlier shipwreck being in the water; he does not realize that the sonar is misleading and there is, in fact, no submarine. He causes the deaths of many of his own men without intending to, by doing what he has been ordered to do. Is Hawkins an evil man? Few people would say so, though his conscience plagues him for the rest of his life. Nevertheless, utilitarians have to contend with the gap between how people predict consequences and how things actually turn out.

---

42 Charles Frend, 1953.

Subjectivity

This leads to the important criticism that Utilitarianism, despite claiming to offer a naturalistic, 'scientific' and 'objective' approach to moral philosophy, may just provide a fig-leaf for selfish behaviour. People are often able to twist utilitarian calculations to suit themselves and, even when they have the best intentions, their subjective perspective must colour their understanding of the effects of actions.

Take the popular film and musical *Dirty Dancing*.[43] The protagonist, 'Baby', lies to her father to get the money for another girl to get an abortion. She is naïve. Coming from a sheltered background, she does not realize that abortion is illegal or dangerous and that her actions might have had the effects of causing or facilitating death or serious injury. She does not think about the effects of her father finding out. According to Utilitarianism, based on what Baby knew at the time when she lied, she probably did the right thing – and yet when the decision is considered with the benefit of hindsight she was wrong.

Responsibility

If people disregard all rules, then the world becomes difficult and frightening – and the stakes are high. Perhaps not all people are capable of taking 100 per cent of the responsibility for thinking through and making moral decisions. People often have an unrealistic view of their own rational and moral capabilities, being unaware of deficiencies in their knowledge, and may consciously or subconsciously be twisting things to their own advantage anyway. Combine this with the realities of having to weigh things up using a felicific calculus in the heat of the moment and it is probable that Utilitarianism is unworkable.

---

43 Emile Ardolino, 1987.

There May Be Value in Suffering

Utilitarianism is predicated on the desirability of pleasure and the undesirability of pain and suffering. While it is obvious that pain may be useful, and feeling no pain may be actively dangerous, even suffering may have a real value. This is a point often made by Christians or other religious people, who believe that suffering may be directly linked to character development and a re-ordering of priorities away from material concerns. Even some atheists and agnostics acknowledge that a life devoid of suffering may be a shallow life that does not feature a full range of experience.

Mob-rule

Another assumption made by Utilitarianism is that the interests of 'the greatest number' must prevail. It may be that it is right, even if not popular, to stand up for the rights of individuals or minorities. What most people think they want does not necessarily serve the long-term happiness of most people.

This problem was highlighted in relation to democracy itself by the British Prime Minister Lord Salisbury at the turn of the twentieth century, who stood up for the right of the educated elite to act in the best interests of others who lack the understanding to know what is good for them. Plato made a similar point and rejected democracy as a result, as electoral decisions are then made by the mass of people many of whom are poorly educated and politicians pander to their short-term desires rather than acting in the best interests of a country on a long-term basis. The power of the media is enormous and powerful interest groups control newspapers, TV and internet media and can use these to persuade ordinary people to vote to foster the interests of those in power.

Levelling Down

If pleasures are seen to be equal and poetry is as good as push-pin, then Utilitarianism may argue to promote more accessible pleasures, perhaps removing support for 'higher art forms' which can only be enjoyed by a few. The Romans had immensely popular gladiator fights which distracted the population; in Britain cock fighting and bull baiting were popular sports; and, across the world today, sport distracts people and provides entertainment arguably preventing them from thinking more deeply about the meaning and purpose of life. Plato might well have said that sport is an effective way of keeping the majority of people in the cave of ignorance (see page 5).

Shaky Foundations

Bentham does not try to conceal his move from saying that human beings do seek pleasure to saying that when they do then they are doing as they ought. So far as he is concerned all that 'ought' can mean is that an action conforms with the principle of utility. This is the classic 'naturalistic fallacy', which would argue that it is not possible to derive what people ought to desire from what they do desire. Many men enjoy pornographic magazines and videos and derive pleasure from these – but arguably this is a lower form of pleasure which, the Natural Law tradition of ethics would say, diminishes people and leads them away from fulfilling their full potential. Mill's insistence on higher and lower pleasures recognizes this problem in a way that some other utilitarians do not.

Lack of Transparency

Imagine that the family of an elderly person with dementia decides to murder him in order to inherit; nobody is likely to find out. The utility of the murder depends on people not finding out. If three possible scenarios are compared:

1 the murder goes ahead in secrecy,
2 the murder is found out and punished or
3 the murder of elderly people becomes legal,

it may be argued that the most happiness is produced by the murder going ahead in secret. Sidgwick wrote:

> [T]hus a Utilitarian may reasonably desire, on Utilitarian principles, that some of his conclusions should be rejected by mankind generally; or even that the vulgar should keep aloof from his system as a whole, in so far as the inevitable indefiniteness and complexity of its calculations render it likely to lead to bad results in their hands.[44]

Bernard Williams criticized Sidgwick in 1985 for this, claiming that his ethics were elitist and hypocritical and referring to them as **Government House Utilitarianism**, seeking to justify decision-making based on the principle that nobody will ever know.[45]

Conclusion

The basic principle of Utilitarianism is simple; those actions which maximize pleasure are good and those which minimize pleasure or cause pain are bad. The problem comes in deciding what pleasure means, whose interests are to be taken into account and how this is to be measured; none of these problems can be definitively solved and most versions of Utilitarianism stand open to abuse. If pleasure is defined in terms of human fulfilment then Utilitarianism may have more in common with the Natural

---

44 Quoted by Julia Driver, 'The History of Utilitarianism', *Stanford Encyclopedia of Philosophy* (Summer 2009 edition), ed. Edward N. Zalta, available online at http://plato.stanford.edu/archives/sum2009/entries/Utilitarianism-history/.

45 Bernard Williams, *Ethics and the Limits of Philosophy*, Cambridge, MA: Harvard University Press, 1985.

Law tradition of ethics than is often supposed; however, the consequentialist character of Utilitarianism gives it a flexibility that the Natural Law tradition lacks.

8

Developments in Utilitarianism

R. M. Hare's Preference Utilitarianism

R. M. Hare (1919–2002) was White's Professor of Moral Philosophy at the University of Oxford from 1966 until 1983 and taught both Bernard Williams and Peter Singer during this time.

In 1981, Hare described Preference Utilitarianism,[1] a system which has become very popular in academic circles for both its flexibility and its coherent meta-ethical foundations. In basic terms, Preference Utilitarianism defines right actions as those which are *in the interests of* or fulfil the 'preferences' of the greatest number of sentient beings involved.

Preference Utilitarianism acknowledges that every person's experience of satisfaction is unique, since what is good and right depends solely on individual preference and there can be nothing that is in itself good or bad. Nevertheless, it gets round difficulties with predicting outcomes, defining and measuring pleasure and pain, as the preference utilitarian can only consider what is in the interests of those involved, taking their preferences into account when known.

Hare also developed 'Two-Level Utilitarianism', applying common sense to the discussion of whether Utilitarianism should be applied in each situation (Act) or used as the basis for moral rules (Rule). He suggested that rules make life simpler and thus serve greater happiness, but that people should not follow them when

---

1 R. M. Hare, *Moral Thinking: Its Levels, Method, and Point*, Oxford: Oxford University Press, 1981, Chapter 8.

they seem inappropriate or seem to produce more pain than pleasure. In practice, this approach seems close to that of Bentham.

Peter Singer (b. 1946)

Singer is probably the best-known preference utilitarian today. The son of Viennese Jews who escaped to Melbourne during the Second World War, Singer studied at Oxford before teaching in Melbourne and at Princeton, where he is currently Ira W. DeCamp Professor of Bioethics. Singer is known for trying to practise what he preaches, giving a proportion (20 per cent) of his salary to charity and saying publicly that, were it legal, he would have euthanatized his elderly mother, so that the money spent on maintaining her poor quality of life could have been better spent in Africa in accordance with his argument for the redistribution of wealth. In *Practical Ethics* (*1979*), he wrote that 'helping is not, as conventionally thought, a charitable act that is praiseworthy to do but not wrong to omit; it is something that everybody ought to do'.[2]

Although best known for his controversial views on animal liberation and personhood – Singer argues that some animals have a better claim to moral status than young children or the very disabled – his work actually attempts to unpack what is in people's interests, what it is that we should be seeking to maximize through utilitarian decisions. Singer argues that different people have different interests and these require different treatment.[3] Everybody has an interest in avoiding pain but other interests depend on people's capabilities and situation. Some people have a more significant interest than others in the same thing – a homeless person has more interest in a flat than somebody wanting a holiday home and a lonely person has more interest in a friendship than somebody who is surrounded by people.

---

2 Peter Singer, *Practical Ethics*, Cambridge: Cambridge University Press, 1979, p. 230.

3 Singer, *Practical Ethics*, p. 230.

Moral status depends upon capacity to experience pain or enjoy things and ultimately the desire to keep on living, and therefore status may be assigned on a 'sliding scale' with some people or beings counting for more because of their greater degree of sentience, and even with people going through stages of more or less moral worth within the same life. For example, a young child has relatively limited ability to suffer or enjoy life, but this will change with age and may diminish again towards death. A terminally ill person may have little desire to carry on living, and this would make killing them less wrong than it would be to kill a vital person as it would frustrate fewer desires and not be contrary to their interests.

It is important to note that Singer is not concerned with trivial pleasures or pains, but with deeper enjoyment or suffering. Like virtue ethicists, Singer tries to account for the developmental nature of human life and the differences between people. Nevertheless, Singer's openness to assign moral status on a sliding scale and to take into account the minute differences between situations may make his 'practical ethics' rather impractical. Who is really to judge what someone's interests are, which person's interests are more significant than others and why? Is anyone sufficiently objective to make such calculations without allowing personal prejudices to affect their judgement? Singer's ethics may well be open to abuse and leave vulnerable people open to abuse. It also, of course, rejects any absolute value for human life or any idea of 'natural rights' (rights that are universal or innate).

Singer attempts to counter this possibility by suggesting that people should rise above their personal concerns and make ethical judgements as if addressing a universal audience or acting in front of an 'impartial observer'.[4] This is significant; doing what is right is not just pragmatic and related to what people find out. We should always act in such a way that we would be happy for others to follow the precedent, as if everybody is watching. This

---

4 This is a device much discussed by other moral philosophers, from Hutcheson and Smith through to R. M. Hare.

ensures that decisions are made fairly and consistently, not self-ishly and opportunistically.

Peter Singer is concerned to 'widen our circle of ethical concern', and he holds it is 'speciest' to give moral priority to human beings simply because they are a different species from animals or even the environment without rational grounds for so doing. This leads to what some may regard as an unacceptable conclusion – for instance that the life of an adult gorilla may be worth more than an unwanted newborn human baby if the interests of both are compared and if the potential to suffer and to exercise preferences is taken into account. In addition he tackles a failure of more traditional utilitarian schemes by seeking to do two things:

1 To widen the circle of ethical concern to include all sentient beings and, in particular, those in the Third World. Too often utilitarianism is thought to promote the interests of a relatively narrow group of people without a particular society or region and Singer resists this. This will have an impact on business ethics which will be discussed later (Chapter 14).

2 To demonstrate that a failure to act is itself an ethical failure. As an example, albeit not one derived from Singer himself, to spend money on a high-end and expensive mobile phone or an expensive pair of shoes when for the same money one could buy a cheap phone or pair of shoes and feed and clothe a child in Africa for a year is morally unacceptable. When those in the rich world fail to share their wealth with those in real need or develop economic policies that favour those in the West, this represents a failure.

Singer, therefore sets out a real challenge to many traditional ethical systems – not least those that deem themselves to be 'religious' – and, while coming from a firmly atheistic viewpoint, his approach to ethics can be seen to have much in common with a religious imperative.

Like Hare, Singer sees the continuity between Kantian deontology (see page 143) and Utilitarianism: genuinely acting in the interests of humanity involves universalizing our actions and considering others as equal with ourselves. Like Mill and like Kant, Singer seeks to justify people's acting according to universal principles on the grounds that this will bring them deeper and more lasting happiness than acting pragmatically would. He points to Mill's suggestion that 'the only chance is to treat not happiness, but some end external to it, as the purpose of life. [And] ... you will inhale happiness with the air you breathe'.[5]

Act or Rule Utilitarianism?

Rule Utilitarianism has been proposed as a way of providing clear moral or legal guidelines, justified according to the principle of utility without the need for a religious paradigm or sophisticated naturalistic reasoning. It has been criticized by the Australian philosopher **J. J. C. Smart** (b. 1920)[6] who is currently emeritus professor at Monash University. A preference utilitarian, Smart rejects all forms of Rule Utilitarianism because:

1 Rule Utilitarianism collapses into Act Utilitarianism; there is nothing stopping rules from being incredibly specific and therefore the two forms are 'extensionally equivalent'.
2 If there is a limit on what can be a rule then under some circumstances the rule utilitarian would have to prefer following a rule even when it is not in the greater interest. Smart calls this 'superstitious rule worship'.

Smart is perhaps best known for his 'deluded sadist' thought experiment. He wrote:

---

5 Quoted from Mill's *Autobiography* in Alan Sell, *Mill on God: The Pervasiveness and Elusiveness of Mill's Religious Thought*, Aldershot: Ashgate, 2004.

6 J. J. C. Smart, 'An Outline of a System of Utilitarian Ethics', in J. J. C. Smart and B. Williams (eds), *Utilitarianism: For and Against*, Cambridge: Cambridge University Press, 1973, pp. 3–74.

[L]et us imagine a universe consisting of one sentient being only, who falsely believes that there are other sentient beings and that they are undergoing exquisite torment ... he takes delight in these imagined sufferings. Is this better or worse than a universe containing no sentient being at all? ... I suggest that the universe containing the deluded sadist is the preferable one.[7]

This is often used to criticize Utilitarianism, particularly Act Utilitarianism, for moral bankruptcy and making no distinction between different types of pleasure, weighing 'impure pleasures' such as that of the sadist directly against 'pure pleasures'. Remember, Bentham argued that pleasures from different sources should be counted as equal.[8]

The Repugnant Conclusion

Derek Parfit (b. 1942) has applied Utilitarianism to contemporary moral challenges such as those of global warming and climate change. He suggests that Classical Utilitarianism, along with other normative systems of ethics, was formed in small communities in relation to a less technologically advanced world and cannot cope with situations in which world-changing events are caused by millions of trivial actions.[9] For example, Mendola observes that:

common sense does not determinedly suggest that it is grossly immoral to buy an SUV for idle urban use, or even a big yellow Humvee. It is not customary to claim that an individual act can

---

7 Smart, 'Outline', p. 25.

8 James Baldwin attempted to argue against Smart by suggesting that 'whoever debases others is debasing himself', whether in thought or actual deed; and Rawls suggested that self-respect is the most significant primary good of all. Quoted in Geoffrey Scarre, *Utilitarianism*, London: Routledge, 1996, p. 158.

9 Joseph Mendola, *Goodness and Justice: A Consequentialist Moral Theory*, Cambridge: Cambridge University Press, 2006, p. 308.

be grossly wrong when its negative effects on other people are imperceptible.[10]

Bentham's felicific calculus predisposes act utilitarians to prioritize pleasures or pains that are certain and near at hand over those which are more indistinct or long term, and this may make this approach inadequate to deal with real challenges which require people to act for the longer term.

Further, if one takes a long view of the pain and pleasure caused by an action and does not consider there to be a *qualitative difference* between different forms of pleasure or pain then one might reasonably suggest that the small increase in happiness caused to, say, 50,000,000 anti-Semitic Europeans by the removal of Jewish competition in German businesses would outweigh the suffering of 6,000,000 Jews in concentration-camps. Measuring total pleasure in this way leads to what Parfit has called the 'repugnant conclusion': that is, that a world containing a large number of slightly happy people would be better than one containing a smaller number of very happy people. It might then be a moral duty to have many children, because an existing person can feel more pleasure than a non-existent one: thus, even if the individual pleasures of living in a grossly overpopulated world are small, they outweigh the larger pleasures of a smaller number of people.

Negative Utilitarianism

Seeking to maximize pleasure is not easy; it is difficult to define, measure and predict what will cause pleasure. An alternative, suggested by **Karl Popper** (1902–94), is 'Negative Utilitarianism'. Popper argued that 'it adds to clarity in the fields of ethics, if we formulate our demands negatively, i.e., if we demand the elimination of suffering rather than the promotion of happiness'.[11] It is

---

10 Mendola, *Goodness and Justice*, p. 309.

11 Karl R. Popper, *The Open Society and Its Enemies*, London: Routledge, 2nd edn (revised) 1952, Vol. 1, Chapter 9, note 2.

reasonably clear what pain and suffering are, it is easier to begin measuring them medically or psychologically and it seems easier to predict that something will cause pain and suffering than that it will cause happiness.

R. N. Smart quickly pointed out that Popper's Negative Utilitarianism would justify and even encourage us to seek the quickest and least painful method of destroying the world. This is known as **the pinprick argument**: that is, that in seeking to avoid the pain of a pinprick (let alone the birth of one more child born to be sick, age and die) then the negative utilitarian would sanction nuking the planet, always providing that Armageddon was quick.[12]

Nevertheless, Smart's criticism was not the end of Negative Utilitarianism. Although some followers are rather pessimistic about the future and may support the 'voluntary human extinction' movement,[13] Abolitionists tend to have a really optimistic view of the future and believe that technology can and should be used to eliminate the causes of human suffering, thus making the world progressively happier. Many Abolitionists are doctors, scientists and IT innovators. The James Martin Twenty-first-Century School at the University of Oxford[14] brings together leading thinkers in disciplines from psychology to politics, law to literature, genetics to game theory to advance research into how to tackle the 'big problems' currently facing humanity.

Transhumanism

Transhumanism describes a movement which argues that there is a 'Hedonistic Imperative',[15] a moral duty to use human talents to

---

12 R. N. Smart, 'Negative Utilitarianism', *Mind* 67:268 (1958), pp. 542–3, available online at http://www.utilitarianism.com/rnsmart-negutil.html.

13 See http://www.vhemt.org/.

14 http://www.oxfordmartin.ox.ac.uk/.

15 This is the title of the philosopher David Pearce's book on Abolitionism and Transhumanism, a sort of manifesto for the movement, which is available online at http://www.cosmiclol.com/david-pearce-the-hedonistic-imperative.pdf.

reduce suffering and maximize pleasure in whatever way is possible – including that of making human beings better than they
could be naturally. Humanity+[16] is an organization based in New
York which seeks to promote this agenda through cultural events
and research. Transhumanism may seem like the preserve of sci-fi
fanatics, but it is influential.

In the text of a talk given at a 2007 conference David Pearce
said:

> I predict we will abolish suffering throughout the living world.
> Our descendants will be animated by gradients of genetically
> pre-programmed well-being that are orders of magnitude richer
> than today's peak experiences.
>
> It's technically feasible to engineer the well-being of all sen-
> tience and retain most but not all of our existing preference
> architecture. The three technical options for abolishing suffer-
> ing that I've presented – wireheading [the direct stimulation
> of the pleasure centres of the brain via implanted electrodes],
> designer drugs and genetic engineering – aren't mutually ex-
> clusive.[17]

This may seem like a far-out argument; but Pearce founded the
World Transhumanist Association with his university friend Professor Nick Bostrom, who is now a leading light of the Philosophy faculty at the University of Oxford and an associate of the
James Martin School.

The basic principle behind transhumanist projects has been
called into question by several philosophers and science-fiction
writers. **Robert Nozick** (1938–2002) gave the example of an
experience machine.[18] He asks us to imagine that people on this
machine believe they are surrounded by friends, winning Olym-

16 See http://humanityplus.org/.

17 The text of the talk is available online at http://www.hedweb.com/
abolitionist-project/index.html.

18 R. Nozick, *Anarchy, State, and Utopia*, New York: Basic Books, 1974,
pp. 42–5. See also the movie *The Matrix* which brings this dilemma alive.

pic gold medals and Nobel Prizes, having sex with their lovers – doing whatever gives them the greatest balance of pleasure over pain. Although they have no real friends or lovers and actually accomplish nothing, people on the experience machine get just as much pleasure as if their beliefs were true. Moreover, they feel no (or little) pain. Nozick argued that (assuming that the machine is reliable) it would seem irrational not to hook oneself up to this machine if pleasure and pain were all that mattered, as hedonists claim. Since it does not seem irrational to refuse to hook oneself up to this machine, hedonism seems inadequate. It seems to overlook the value of real friendship, knowledge, freedom and achievements, which are lacking for the deluded people on the experience machine.

Transhumanist philosophers such as David Pearce would, of course, dispute this. It all comes down to whether enhanced human experiences are seen to be real, whether it is fair to say that somebody who is happy (or who does not suffer) because of drugs, devices or even their genetic makeup is deluded. The transhumanists take a basic view of pleasure which Aristotle, Aquinas or Mill would reject – all these philosophers would focus on a much broader vision of fostering human fulfilment which cannot be defined in mere pleasure terms.

Motive Utilitarianism

Motive Utilitarianism was first developed by **Robert Merrihew Adams** (b. 1937)[19] and has been described as a 'middle way' between Act and Rule Utilitarianism, as well as a distinct approach in its own right.

Adams tries to relate moral philosophy to how human beings actually think and behave. Drawing on psychological research, he argues that human beings are passionate and emotional and that we do much better with positive goals than with negative

---

19 Robert Merrihew Adams, 'Motive Utilitarianism', *Journal of Philosophy* 73:14 (1976), pp. 467–81.

prohibitions. He proposes that human beings should start by developing the skills, inclinations and mental focuses that are likely to be most or at least highly useful (that is, happiness-producing) in the real-world situations they are likely to face, rather than in the dramatic hypothetical situations seemingly so common in textbooks and articles on ethics. Motive Utilitarianism is, in fact, strikingly similar to the Virtue Ethic that Adams went on to describe in later works.[20]

Bernard Williams' Critique of Utilitarianism

Bernard Williams (1929–2003) was a great critic of Utilitarianism, though he remained a moral relativist. In *Morality: An Introduction to Ethics* (1972), he criticized both deontology and Utilitarianism and tried to focus ethics back on helping real people in real-life situations. He was suspicious of any systematic attempt at moral philosophy – or philosophy in general – and his main contribution was as a sceptic, in the manner of Hume. He caused people to think again at what had become accepted truths, subjecting them to rational scrutiny and discarding falsehood, however useful or comfortable it had become.

Williams often used examples to make his points.

Take Jim, a botanist doing research in a South American country led by a brutal dictator. One day he finds himself in the central square of a small town facing 20 Indians who have been randomly captured and tied up as examples of what will happen to rebels. The captain who has arrested the Indians says that if

---

20 In *How to Make Good Decisions and Be Right All the Time: Solving the Riddle of Right and Wrong*, London: Continuum, 2008, Iain King develops a quasi-utilitarian system compatible with consequence-, virtue- and act-based accounts of ethics. Look at the work of Dr Martin Seligman at Harvard, at websites such as http://www.authentichappiness.sas.upenn.edu/Default.aspx and http://www.ted.com/talks/martin_seligman_on_the_state_of_psychology.html and http://www.positivepsychology.org.uk/pp-theory/strengths/112-from-what-is-wrong-to-what-is-strong.html and http://www.viacharacter.org/www/.

Jim will kill one of them, the others will be released in honour of Jim's status as a guest, but if he does not, all the Indians will be killed.[21]

For most consequentialist theories all that matters is the outcome; an act utilitarian would tell Jim to kill one of the men. However, Williams argued that there is a crucial moral distinction between a person being killed by me, and being killed by someone else because of an act or omission of mine. The utilitarian loses that vital distinction, turning us into empty vessels by means of which consequences occur, rather than preserving our status as moral agents, as human beings. He argued that moral decisions must preserve our integrity, although many would sympathize with the idea that it may be better to sacrifice one life than to lose 20. The same type of example can be applied to the torture of possible terrorist subjects which can be justified on utilitarian grounds since it would save lives – the problem becomes where the compromises stop.

Williams went on to observe that we do not really judge actions by their consequences. For example, if only a few people were shot for speeding on motorways then speeding would soon stop. The felicific calculus could justify the shootings by the happiness that the absence of speeding and of course the absence of injuries, death, unnecessary environmental pollution and depletion of natural resources would bring. Williams argued that any moral theory which justifies shooting people for speeding is barbaric and a long way from describing how people actually do behave. We should therefore reject Act Utilitarianism.

Williams also rejected Rule Utilitarianism. He argued that implementing a rule such as 'Nobody should be subject to judicial murder' on the grounds of the increase in general happiness caused by a prohibition on capital punishment relies on our making a calculation about the status of actions such as murder that most of us know to be wrong. For Williams, we should reject any system that reduces moral decision-making to a few algorithms, because any systematization or reductionism of the decision-

---

21 See Smart and Williams, *Utilitarianism: For and Against*, pp. 98ff.

making process will inevitably distort its complexity. The process of calculating moral status also enables us to set aside our moral sense, making us more likely to accept immoral principles.

Conclusion

Modern versions of Utilitarianism have tried to account for the criticisms levelled at the classical approaches of Bentham, Mill and Sidgwick. They have examined the nature of pleasure and pain and have suggested that neither may adequately express what it is that human beings should seek or avoid. For many contemporary utilitarian philosophers, what it means to flourish is closely linked to human fulfilment, and, therefore, like Natural Law ethicists they are reflecting on what it means to live a fulfilled human life.

Those utilitarians who focus on the higher potentialities of being a human have much more in common with Natural Law ethics than those who think of pleasure or happiness purely in short-term, hedonistic terms. Even Peter Singer, at a conference in Oxford with Catholic moral philosophers in 2011,[22] found that they had much more in common than might have been expected. Of course, there are differences – Singer does not see there being any essential, ontological difference between humans and animals and life is not an absolute value for him. Nevertheless the commonalities are surprising and Singer's view of human fulfilment is sophisticated and a long way from the relatively simplistic approach of Bentham.

Modern utilitarians have explored the difficulties in predicting, measuring and comparing outcomes and the extent to which people can really be expected to weigh consequences in relation to each action. They have confronted the possible consequences of Utilitarianism, what it might be seen to justify in terms of bar-

---

22 student.thetablet.co.uk has a useful teaching resource based on a *Tablet* article about this conference in the teachers' section.

baric and inhumane behaviour. Nevertheless, Utilitarianism remains a controversial approach to decision-making and this may account for some scholars seeking to merge its best attributes with aspects of Kantian Ethics, Virtue Ethics or Christian Ethics, all of which have a better reputation for respecting the sanctity of life and upholding basic moral norms.

9

Situation Ethics

G. E. Moore (1873–1958) strongly disagreed with what he saw as the hedonistic approach of the classical utilitarians. Moore believed that the good included far more than what could be reduced to pleasure. Like Plato, Moore believed in the metaphysical existence of ideals which we know intuitively to be worthwhile, independently of experience or how they affect individuals. For Moore and his followers in the 'Bloomsbury Group', beauty was intrinsically valuable. He called on people to maximize the ideals of goodness, beauty and justice rather than simple happiness.

Moore's system, which combined flexibility and personal responsibility with the desire to promote ideals, struck a chord with many Christians in the first half of the twentieth century. For 'situation ethicists', an action may be justified if it is more **loving**. Of course, love is no easier to define than happiness or Moore's ideals. It is true that in 1 Corinthians 13.4–6 Paul wrote:

> Love is patient, love is kind. It does not envy, it does not boast, it is not proud. It is not rude, it is not self-seeking, it is not easily angered, it keeps no record of wrongs. Love does not delight in evil but rejoices with the truth. (NIV)

However, situation ethicists differ in their interpretation of Christian love (*agape*) and what it might justify in terms of action.

William Temple and Dietrich Bonhoeffer were among those who became disillusioned with the legalism of traditional Christian moral philosophy.

William Temple (1881–1944)

Temple was one of the first acknowledged 'situation ethicists'. Anglican Archbishop of York and later Archbishop of Canterbury during the Second World War, he actually visited the troops in Normandy after D-day. One biographer has told how during the Second World War Temple

> worked for famine relief in war-ravaged countries and pleaded with the British government to make the safety of European Jews a primary concern. In his writings, sermons, and broadcast addresses to the nation, he denounced Nazism as idolatry, but maintained that while the use of force to resist evil might be necessary, the English were to bear no ill will towards the Germans and resist thoughts of revenge. He advocated humane treatment for German prisoners of war. Sin, he reminded his listeners, was universal, and both sides in the war had cause for repentance. Even as German bombs were falling on English cities, Temple urged the nation to look beyond the war to a time of forgiveness and reconciliation.[1]

Temple had an influence over the British second only to that of Churchill during this period.

Temple relished the experimental nature of the moral life, seeing life as an adventure in which people must take every opportunity to glorify God by putting people ahead of power as God did by sending God's Son to become human and die for our sins. For Temple, God's only absolute law was the law of love:[2] all other laws are to be interpreted through the principle that God is love and intends only for human beings to love one another. He wrote that 'on freedom all spiritual life depends, and it is astonishing and terrifying that the church has so often failed to understand

---

1 Richard Schmidt, *Glorious Companions: Five Centuries of Anglican Spirituality*, Grand Rapids: Eerdmans, 2002, p. 256.

2 Alan Suggate, *William Temple and Christian Social Ethics Today*, Edinburgh: T & T Clark, 1987.

this';[3] he would have seen the level of moral responsibility placed on individuals by Utilitarianism as one of its strengths and as compatible with a life of faith, lived as Luther put it *coram deo* (before God).

Although Temple's ethics may not seem to have much in common with classical Utilitarianism, they are consequentialist and are concerned to act in the interests of as many people as possible. It would be a mistake to see the desired end of Temple's ethics or of any other form of Situation Ethics as happiness; however, few modern forms of Utilitarianism are satisfied to use this word either, preferring to speak of 'the good' or 'best interests' as the consequence to be desired.

Dietrich Bonhoeffer (1906–45)

Bonhoeffer was a Lutheran pastor in the run-up to the Second World War and became a leader in the Church's opposition to Nazism in Germany. In 1937 the activities of the Church were all but outlawed and Bonhoeffer's seminary was closed; he went to England but decided to return when war broke out and was recruited into the resistance in 1940. By 1943, he had completed his *Ethics* and had become a key player in a plot to assassinate Hitler, acting as courier and diplomat to the British government on behalf of the resistance, ensuring support in bringing an end to hostilities should the plot succeed. It did not and Bonhoeffer was executed, along with members of Military Intelligence, in 1945.

How did a Lutheran pastor justify plotting a political assassination? Like Temple, Bonhoeffer questioned the possibility of moral certainty[4] and saw life as an adventure in which we have to take risks, being guided by the spirit and example of Jesus, who was love incarnate. Actions cannot be justified in advance;

---

3 William Temple, *Christianity and Social Order*, London: SCM Press, 1950, p. 69.

4 Dietrich Bonhoeffer, *Ethics*, London: SCM Press, 1995, p. 231.

they can only be 'eschatologically justified' by God when individuals come to be judged. Bonhoeffer wrote that 'before God self-justification is quite simply sin'. People simply have to try to do what they think is right before God, in the knowledge that they are quite possibly wrong and that sin will be punished. Human beings are free and responsible and this calls them to action; doing nothing is to participate in evil. Assassinating Hitler may well be wrong and may well be condemned by God, but Bonhoeffer maintains that it is still better to have made a positive free choice than to have fallen short of human potential by not engaging. 'What is worse than doing evil,' Bonhoeffer notes, 'is being evil.'[5] His ethics are focused on resisting evil and on matters of life and death; they have little to say about more mundane everyday choices.

Bonhoeffer argues that when we are 'assaulted by evil ... it is not only what is said that matters, but also the man who says it'.[6] This is crucial in understanding Bonhoeffer's ethics; he had much in common with modern virtue ethicists in focusing on character and the effects that actions have on who we are as whole and rounded people. He tried to account for the unique nature of each situation and the particular factors that each individual has to deal with. Like Virtue Ethics, Bonhoeffer's ethics does not provide much clear direction on what to do or not do. In fact he calls attention to the problems inherent in seeking ethical direction or justification, suggesting that appealing to reason, or to dogma, to conscience, to private virtue or to duty may all lead people to abnegate responsibility and collaborate with evil. Nevertheless, Bonhoeffer offers a powerful alternative to legalistic Natural Law or simplistic Utilitarianism, one which puts the free and thinking individual centre stage without underestimating what is at stake in the decision-making process.

---

5 Bonhoeffer, *Ethics*, p. 67.
6 Bonhoeffer, *Ethics*, p. 267.

Joseph Fletcher (1905–91)

Fletcher is most usually associated with Situation Ethics and wrote the clearest and most controversial statement of it. He began by researching William Temple's ethics, which influenced his thinking on medical, social and business ethics. Although he was Dean of St Paul's Cathedral in Cincinnati during the Second World War and lectured at Harvard (1944–70), he was suspected of communism during the McCarthy era. He lost his faith while writing *Situation Ethics: The New Morality* between 1963 and 1966,[7] thereafter becoming a humanist and focusing on issues in medical ethics. He died in 1991.

Fletcher was very practical in his understanding of Christian Ethics and deplored both the Church's failure to engage with the major issues of our time and its tendency to discourage Christians from taking personal moral responsibility by laying down inflexible rules for them to follow.

Fletcher began by going back to Mark 12.28–31.

'Which commandment is the first of all?' Jesus answered, 'The first is, "Hear O Israel: the Lord our God, the Lord is one; you shall love the Lord your God with all your heart, and with all your soul, and with all your mind, and with all your strength." The second is this, "You shall love your neighbour as yourself." There is no other commandment greater than these.' (NRSV)

He suggested that there are three possible approaches to Christian moral philosophy.

1 **Legalistic** (includes Catholic Natural Moral Law and Protestant Biblical Literalism)
2 **Antinomian** (includes those, such as Kierkegaard or Bonhoeffer perhaps, who act on 'conscience' or 'revealed insight' without reference to laws)

---

7 Joseph Fletcher, *Situation Ethics: The New Morality*, London: SCM Press, 1966.

3 **Situational** (a middle way which applies the Christian principle of agape to each situation).

Fletcher argues that the situational approach is the only appropriate response to real ethical dilemmas. It values individual freedom, puts people first and acknowledges the genuine diversity of circumstances. It guards against acting on selfish impulse or whim, and respects the values of the community (*agape*), but is sufficiently flexible to operate in the real world.

Fletcher argues that the situationist must always uphold the law of love, which is accepted *a priori* (that is, without further justification); but the situationist must also respect the laws of his/her community, only breaking these laws if they clearly go against the law of love in the particular situation. Fletcher is assuming a Christian foundation with love as the fundamental rule in the universe – but this is an assumption and, as such, can be rejected. It is important to recognize that Fletcher is not proposing an absolute relativism. He encourages individuals to reflect on laws and gives them the option of determining their own action in specific circumstances in response to a clear absolute – the law of love.

Fletcher detailed **Four Working Principles** as the basis for his approach to Situation Ethics, namely:

1 **Pragmatism** – The course of action must be practical and work.
2 **Relativism** – All situations are always relative; situational ethicists try to avoid such words as 'never' and 'always'.
3 **Positivism** – The whole of situational ethics relies upon the fact that the person freely chooses to believe in *agape* love as described by Christianity.
4 **Personalism** – Whereas the legalist thinks people should work to laws, the situational ethicist believes that laws are for the benefit of the people.

He never really argues for these principles, but rather assumes that they will appeal to common sense. The **Six Fundamental**

Principles go a long way to explaining how Fletcher's system would work in practice:

1 'Only one thing is intrinsically good; namely love: nothing else at all.' (p. 56)
2 'The ruling norm of Christian decision is love: nothing else.' (p. 69)
3 'Love and Justice are the same, for justice is love distributed, nothing else.' (p. 87) 'Justice is Christian love using its head, calculating its duties, obligations, opportunities, resources ... Justice is love coping with situations where distribution is called for.' (p. 95)
4 'Love wills the neighbour's good, whether we like him or not.' (p. 103)
5 'Only the end justifies the means, nothing else.' (p. 120)
6 'Love's decisions are made situationally, not prescriptively.' (p. 134)

In keeping with Fletcher's practical approach to moral philosophy, he uses a series of examples to encourage reflection and to make his case for Situationism. It is worth considering or discussing some of these yourself.

A. *The Mental Hospital*

An unmarried female patient with schizophrenia is raped by another patient and becomes pregnant. State law only permits abortion on 'therapeutic grounds', that is, to avoid risk to the mother's life. Should the patient be given an abortion?[8]

B. *The Insurance Problem*

Fletcher writes:

---

8 Fletcher, *Situation Ethics*, p. 37.

I dropped in on a patient at the hospital who explained that he only had a set time to live. The doctors could give him some pills (that would cost $40 every three days) that would keep him alive for the next three years, but if he didn't take the pills, he'd be dead within six months. Now he was insured for $100,000, double indemnity and that was all the insurance he had. But if he took the pills and lived past next October, when the insurance was up for renewal, they were bound to refuse the renewal, and his insurance would be cancelled. So he told me that he was thinking that if he didn't take the pills, then his family would get left with some security, and asked my advice on the situation.[9]

C. Means to an end?

Fletcher writes:

[I]n Ukraine, Mrs. Bergmeier (a POW) learned through a sympathetic commandant that her husband and family were trying to keep together and find her. But the rules allowed them to release her to Germany only if she was pregnant, in which case she would be returned as a liability. She turned things over in her mind and finally asked a friendly Volga German camp guard to impregnate her, which he did. Her condition being medically verified, she was sent back to Berlin and to her family. They welcomed her with open arms, even when she told them how she had managed it. And when the child was born, they all loved him because of what he had done for them. After the christening, they met up with their local pastor and discussed the morality of the situation.[10]

In each case, Fletcher implies that *agape* dictates that 'sometimes you've got to put your principles to one side and do the right thing'.

---

9 Fletcher, *Situation Ethics*, p. 166.
10 Fletcher, *Situation Ethics*, p. 165.

Criticisms of Situation Ethics

Agape?

Arguably, Situation Ethics confuses the concept of agape. If love 'is not rude, it is not self-seeking, it is not easily angered, it keeps no record of wrongs. Love does not delight in evil but rejoices with the truth. It always protects, always trusts, always hopes, always perseveres' (1 Cor. 13), as the Apostle Paul wrote, then can it really justify treating human persons as a means to an end? Can it really be pragmatic, allowing 'one law for me and another for you'; can it really allow a poor example to be set or rely on secrecy as part of its own justification? Above all, Christian love always sees love at the centre of a person's life and love of God as being primary and Fletcher plays the latter down in the interests of making his theory as widely acceptable as possible.

Lack of Clear Guidance

Perhaps because of the lack of agreement over what love is, there is little agreement on what Situation Ethics is and what it may or may not justify in terms of action. This makes it difficult to follow Situation Ethics and easy for people to claim that their actions were motivated situationally, when they may actually have originated in misunderstanding or baser motives.

Bonhoeffer's ethic is very different from Fletcher's; it does not claim that love justifies the action, only that it makes not acting incompatible with being good. Bonhoeffer's ethic is probably the least practical version of Situation Ethics in terms of offering guidance, though it appeals to many Christians despite that.

Despite the fact that many people find Situation Ethics intuitively appealing, in practice it is impossible for any Church or society to permit it as a justification for action. Anglican bishops such as William Temple and even the controversial John Robinson highlighted the difference between acting on the motivation of love and jettisoning every rule, concluding that any situationalist must respect the law and prevailing values and must not descend into the antinomianism which some of Fletcher's more extreme examples suggest that he endorsed.[11]

Open to Abuse

Fletcher's insistence that situationists should follow the law of their community except *in extremis* is usually ignored. In practice, Situation Ethics is often used to justify doing what people feel inclined to do, rather than what may be right. It may be right to refuse to help a relative to die when they are suffering agonies and right to counsel a rape victim to keep a pregnancy – but few people are inclined to judge people who choose to assist suicide or terminate pregnancy in these circumstances. Bonhoeffer acknowledged that Situationism was open to abuse if people attempted to justify their own actions using it; he argued that people must leave it to God to judge.

Prediction

As with other forms of Utilitarianism, there will often be a difficulty in predicting outcomes and defining the limits of who might be affected. What may be loving for those immediately concerned may have bad consequences for others who may not be considered. Bonhoeffer rejected Consequentialism and seeing a loving motivation as any real justification because it is impossible to predict or define what leads to or comes out of actions.

Responsibility

Situation Ethics may well place too much moral responsibility on individuals, usually at moments of extreme stress when they may not be in the best position to assess the position dispassionately.

---

11 See Bishop John A. T. Robinson, *Christian Morals Today*, Philadelphia: Westminster Press, 1964.

Fletcher

In particular, Fletcher assumes that his readers are all like him, having a thorough Christian education and Christian values, while also having the humanist freedom to interpret the Bible and historical tradition liberally and dismiss any need for an authoritarian Church. As an academic discussion-point Fletcher's book *Situation Ethics: A New Morality* may have raised interesting questions (though its style and substance did not lend itself to this audience); however, as a populist paperback the book seemed to give licence to people to do what they want and still claim to be 'moral' or 'Christian'.

On the other hand, looking at Fletcher's broader contribution, it is clear that he had a valuable perspective on social ethics and bioethics in particular and he worked tirelessly to make Christianity engaged and relevant in a changing world. He wanted individuals to take their responsibility seriously – and could not see how they could without having the freedom to think and act for themselves.

Situation Ethics and Christianity

Situation Ethics has, of course, been rejected by the Roman Catholic Church. Pope Pius XII launched an aggressive attack on Situation Ethics in 1952, arguing that it confused the nature of the conscience, seeing it as a generative rather than an interpretive faculty. This means that if a person thinks that their conscience demands that the loving action is contrary to Natural Law it is the conscience that is at fault.[12] In 1956, the Sacred Congregation of the Holy Office banned Situation Ethics from being taught or approved in universities and other centres of Catholic learning or discussed and promoted in any other manner.

12 'Conscience' here is understood in the Catholic manner as *synderesis*, 'reason making right decisions' based on Natural Law; see Chapters 5 and 17.

Fletcher's Situation Ethics has also been rejected by the majority of Anglican leaders, though the teaching of many scholars, such as Richard Holloway, the former Bishop of Edinburgh, still reflects that of Temple. Writing on the Anglican Communion Francis Moss observed:

These are the days of Situation Theology, Situation Ethics and theological subjectivity ... all is negotiable, all is dispensable, nothing is actually definitive or binding at least in the sense of being enforceable ... It is unthinkable that officially anyone should be charged with heresy in the contemporary Church of England when it is a tenet of an accepted school of thought that there are no fixed criteria for the determination of theological truth and error.[13]

---

13 http://www.vision.org/visionmedia/article.aspx?id=729; quoted in http://www.churchsociety.org/churchman/documents/Cman_118_3_Atherstone.pdf.

10

Kantian Ethics

Immanuel Kant (1724–1804) was born in Königsberg in Prussia (now Kaliningrad in Russia). The son of a saddle maker, Kant was fortunate to receive a first-class education thanks to the generosity of a local philanthropist and the availability of scholarships. He was bright, but did not enjoy the hours of Lutheran religious instruction and classical languages that dominated the curriculum. He preferred maths – indeed history, geography, anything not to do with the Church. After years as a private tutor, he got a job at the university in Königsberg.

First, he worked as a private lecturer, paid directly by his students, and consequentially lectured on most subjects to make up the 20 hours a week he needed to make ends meet. Kant was a popular teacher, but his publications tended to be commercial, designed to win prizes or approval from the university authorities. Kant did not have tenure! Contrary to popular opinion, he enjoyed an active social life at this time, though like many men at the time he could not afford to marry.

Things changed when Kant was finally appointed Professor of Logic and Metaphysics at the University of Königsberg in 1770, at the age of 45. He was able to focus his energies on his chief interest, philosophy, and to spend time preparing more substantial works for publication. At this time Kant first really engaged with the work of David Hume, of which he said: 'I freely admit that it was the remembrance of David Hume which, many years ago, first interrupted my dogmatic slumber and gave my investigations in the field of speculative philosophy a completely different direction'.[1] Certainly Kant's philosophy changed once he settled down to sustained and focused research.

Kant did not share Hume's degree of scepticism, but he saw that he had a point. Doing traditional metaphysical philosophy was like building castles in the air; its claims were impressive, but had no foundations other than the authority of the writers who made them. Kant realized that for philosophy to get anywhere in this new 'age of enlightenment' it would have to go back to the beginning, to build strong foundations and build on them step by step, always referring back to what could be certainly known, through experience.

Kant's new system of thought was revealed in three parts – the *Critique of Pure Reason* in 1781 (2nd revised edition 1787), the *Critique of Practical Reason* in 1788 and the *Critique of Judgement* in 1793. These works are still of immense importance in philosophy and in establishing the foundations for related disciplines, from mathematics to architecture. They are still on university reading lists around the world.

Nevertheless, Kant could see potential problems with his system and explored these through essays and shorter works, which provoked discussion and refined his thinking. For example, Kant's moral philosophy was developed with reference to the *Groundwork for the Metaphysics of Morals* (1785) before being included in the *Critique of Practical Reason* (1788) and amplified in the *Metaphysics of Morals* (1797).

Towards the end of Kant's career, his approach to philosophy began to change again. He confronted a serious problem with his system in *Religion within the Boundaries of Reason Alone* (1793), a work which succeeded in alienating both the Prussian government and Kant's philosopher friends. He began to reformulate his system, making notes for a new master-work, but these were not finished at the time of his death in 1804. Some people

---

1 Immanuel Kant, *Prolegomena to Any Future Metaphysics*, Preface, 4:260. Unless otherwise noted references to Kant's works are to *The Cambridge Edition of the Works of Immanuel Kant*, trans. and ed. Paul Guyer and Allen W. Wood, Cambridge: Cambridge University Press, 1999.

said that he had lost his mind towards the end, but others still speculate on the form and argument that the final work would have taken.

There is no doubt that Kant's thinking changed western Philosophy; its effect has been described in terms of a 'Copernican Revolution'. Perhaps most importantly, Kant suggested that there is a limit to what we can know and that human understanding is inevitably coloured by perspective. This has caused a 'divide in the road' between those scholars who conclude that what cannot be known may as well not exist, that man really is the measure of all things, and those who accept that there is an unknowable Truth.[2] In this way, Kant was the father of Marxism and existentialism, Preference Utilitarianism, human rights theory and postmodernism.

What Can We Know?

The Critique of Pure Reason sets out the primacy of knowledge based on experience, **practical reason** as Kant called it. He later wrote that 'we cannot but observe with admiration how great an advantage the power of practical reason has over the theoretical in ordinary human understanding'.[3] However, he maintained that not all knowledge arises from sensory experience and it is perfectly valid to abstract from experience and use our understanding of the necessary relationships between things to predict how things will behave beyond it. Kant saw mathematics and logic as exercises in **pure reason**, explorations of relationships between concepts which are known independently of experience and which deepen our understanding of reality. Nevertheless, Kant famously said that 'thoughts without content are empty, intuitions without concepts are blind'.[4]

2 See Gordon Michalson, *Fallen Freedom: Kant on Radical Evil and Moral Regeneration*, Cambridge: Cambridge University Press, 1990.

3 Immanuel Kant, *Groundwork for the Metaphysics of Morals*, in *Works*, 4:404.

4 Immanuel Kant, *Critique of Pure Reason* A 51/B 75.

Kant believed that human experience is just that. What human beings can know, directly through practical reason or through pure reason, is limited by our senses as beings within time and space. Human knowledge is subjective; we do not know what it would be like to be a bacillus, a fly or a dog, to live in the last ice age or in the thirty-first century. Most importantly, we do not know what it would be like to look at the universe in its entirety, beyond the filters of time and space, to take a god's eye view and see things as they really are, objectively. Time and space are not concepts but *a priori* necessary conditions for any experience: that is, they are inescapable and filter everything we know. Human beings are trapped within the **phenomenal world** of time and space. Practical and even pure reason cannot take us into the **noumenal world** of things as they really are (***ding an sich***). This is highly relevant today as we understand more of the quantum world – we are effectively prisoners of our senses and we take reality to be what we perceive (the phenomenal world) but reality as it really is (the noumenal world) is necessarily inaccessible to us.

The closest human beings can get to understanding objective, noumenal Truth is through **judgement**. Kant noted that sometimes beauty and love, the highest forms of human experience, can take human beings beyond themselves and give them a glimpse of a greater truth. Unfortunately, they cannot communicate this to others because language can only refer to shared experience. The most they can do is to recommend that others see the same view or look at the same painting, listen to the same music or read the same book, in the hope that they may see the 'more' that lies beyond direct experience. Kant finally completed his philosophical system in 1790 with the ***Critique of Judgement***, a work in aesthetics which tried to pin down what it is in art, music and literature which inspires us. At the same time as he was writing this, Kant also wrote the essays which ended up in ***Religion within the Boundaries of Reason Alone*** (1793), in which he examined the importance of religious ideas in bringing human beings closer to the noumenal truth.

Kant, Plato and Aristotle

Kant's worldview was essentially Platonic but he was influenced by Hume's Aristotelian scepticism into rejecting philosophical discussions which extend beyond any possible experience. Like Plato, Kant saw reality in terms beyond just the physical, and like Plato he prized reason as the best route to Truth that human beings have, arguing that they should be guided by reason rather than by emotion or animal-instinct. Like Plato, he believed that reflecting on beautiful and good things can bring the reason closest to understanding the way things really are beyond time and space.

The Metaphysics of Morals

Kant criticized previous philosophers, from Leibniz to Hume, for failing to be clear about the grounds for knowledge. Whereas previous philosophers just distinguished between knowledge based on experience and knowledge based on concepts, Kant argued that within this distinction there are actually four different types of knowledge, not two.

- *A priori* judgements are independent of sensory experience. They apply universally, necessarily. Importantly, *a priori* judgements may or may not be consistent with experience – they just cannot be dependent on it. Kant argues that 'pure *a priori*' judgements exist in mathematics, but that other *a priori* judgements exist across other sciences and philosophy. A common example of an *a priori* is 'An unmarried man is a bachelor' – no experience is necessary to validate this statement.
- *A posteriori* judgements are dependent on sensory experience and are thus limited or contingent. An example of an *a posteriori* judgement would be, 'Given my experience, all blackbirds have yellow beaks' – it may or may not be true that all blackbirds, in all times and in all places, have yellow beaks. Scientific conclusions are known *a posteriori*. This gives rise to

the problem of induction in science: however many observed instances there may be, framing a general law based on these instances is always vulnerable to the next observation disproving the law. This happened when the first black swan was seen in Australia, which falsified the generally accepted principle that 'all swans are white'.

- **Analytic** judgements are those whose predicates are contained in their subjects and add no new knowledge. A proposition is analytically true if it contains no logical contradiction and denying it is contradictory. For example, the number 4 can be expressed as 2+2, so saying 2+2=4 is *non-contradictory*. Also, denying that 2+2=4 would contradict the evidence. However, 2+2=4 just explains the concepts '4', '2', '+' and '=' rather than telling us anything really new. For Kant, *all analytic judgements are known* a priori, *but not all* a priori *judgements are analytically true*.

- **Synthetic** judgements are those whose predicates are wholly distinct from their subjects, and are thus genuinely informative but require justification by reference to some outside principle. A proposition is synthetically true if it contains no logical contradiction and denying it does not entail a contradiction. Take 'This ball is red'. It is perfectly possible for there to be a red ball, whereas it would not be possible to have a square ball. Further, 'this' and 'red' give me information about the ball which I could not deduce from the concept of a ball; they tell me that a ball exists and it is red. This information is either true or false depending on whether the ball really exists and really is red, so it would need to be verified. For Kant, *all* a posteriori *judgements are synthetic, but not all synthetic judgements are* a posteriori.

Kant argued that:

- **Analytic** *a posteriori* **judgements** do not arise, since there is no need to appeal to experience when analysing an existing concept.

- **Synthetic *a posteriori* judgements** are common everyday knowledge based on experience – but Kant argues that they cannot tell us anything about God or morality.
- **Analytic *a priori* judgements** include all logical truths and definitions – but Kant argues that it is not possible to establish the existence of God or moral laws in this way.
- **Synthetic *a priori* judgements** are the only possibility for providing new information that is *necessarily* true. Controversially, Kant argued that synthetic *a priori* judgements provide the basis for much knowledge. It is this category of judgements that gives rise to many problems in Kant's philosophy.

For Kant, if metaphysics is going to be possible then it must be based on synthetic *a priori* judgements, since anything else would be either uninformative or unjustifiable.[5] These judgements are independent of experience and necessarily true (hence *a priori*) but provide new knowledge and are consistent with experience (hence synthetic). Kant argued that our knowledge of the moral law is a synthetic *a priori*.

Laying the *Groundwork*

Allen Wood wrote that 'many people's reaction to Kantian Ethics seems to resemble an allergic reaction, and for most of them … the *Groundwork* occasioned their first sneeze'.[6] Today many people make the mistake of seeing *The Groundwork for the Metaphysics of Morals* (1785)[7] as *the* statement of Kantian Ethics and neglect to explore the more developed accounts in

---

5 A fuller explanation of Kant's synthetic *a priori* may be found at http://consequently.org/papers/apriori.pdf pp. 1–7, accessed 14 April 2012.

6 Allen Wood, 'The Final Form of Kant's Practical Philosophy', in Mark Timmons (ed.) *Essays on Kant's Moral Philosophy,* New York: Cambridge University Press, 2000, p. 7. Available online at www.stanford.edu/~allenw/papers/Final.doc, accessed 14 April 2012.

7 The full text is available to download as a free pdf from http://www.earlymoderntexts.com/pdf/kantgrou.pdf, checked 14 April 2012.

his other works such as *The Critique of Practical Reason* or the *Metaphysics of Morals*. The *Groundwork* is only 55 pages and thus apparently more manageable than anything else Kant wrote, but if readers do not appreciate that this was part of a deliberate attempt to wake his contemporaries from their 'dogmatic slumbers', they could get a wrong impression of Kant's ethical system.

Nevertheless, the *Groundwork* does establish several important things about Kant's moral philosophy.

First, Kant's system cannot be accused of ethical naturalism: his morality cannot be reduced to any form of scientific analysis of what it is to be human. He saw his '"metaphysics of morals" as a system of moral principles, or even of moral duties, which would be entirely a priori, and hence could be spelled out entirely independently of any empirical knowledge of human nature',[8] though they would accord with experience in any case.

Second, the origin and standard of goodness is 'a good will'. The *Groundwork for the Metaphysics of Morals* begins with a significant claim: 'Nothing can possibly be conceived in the world, or even out of it, which can be called good without qualification, except a good will.'[9] Kant goes on to explain that a good will is inherently good, independently of what it produces, and is fostered by reason and dutiful (that is, rational, free) action. It is 'a concept that is already lodged in any natural and sound understanding, and doesn't need to be taught so much as to be brought to light'.[10]

A Good Will

To understand anything of Kant's moral philosophy, it is important to understand what Kant meant by the 'will'. Like Plato, Kant believed that human nature exists on three levels.

---

8 Wood, 'Final Form'.

9 Kant, *Works*, 4:393.

10 Kant, *Works*, 4:397. The Latin word for 'educate', *educare*, literally means 'to bring out'.

- **Universal Will** (*Wille*). On the highest level, human beings have the potential to be rational. Reason enables them to appreciate the inherent value in human life and the imperative to develop a 'good will' and do their duty, even when doing so does not serve their immediate happiness. Only when they act on the basis of the Universal Will are they fully human and *good*.

- **Free Character** (*Willkür*). On a normal level, human beings care about others; about relatives, friends, even countrymen. They are social and emotional, are made happy or sad by the situation of others, and can choose to act in ways which do not directly serve their own interests according to sentiment or reason. This faculty of choice gives them the potential to rise above social or biological ties and pragmatic concerns, to care about humanity for its own sake and act on principle, adopting the Universal Will as the basis for all their choices.

- **Instincts** (*Bestimmung*). On the most basic level, human beings are animals and are driven by the same mindless instincts to life, happiness and procreation. These instincts are positive in that they are essential to life and make them appreciate the value of their own life, which is the first step towards valuing the lives of others. Nevertheless, being driven by instinct is to fall short of the human potential to be rational and free. Doing things instinctively, for pleasure, ends up taking human beings further from true contentment; it reduces their ability to make rational choices and achieve a good will.

Kant assumed that human beings are free – this is an integral part of being human. They can choose to be selfish and base, to prefer their own group – or to be rational and respect all human life.

Like Aquinas, Kant saw self-preservation and acting for friends or family as good, just not as the real or total good to which human beings should aspire. Reason takes care 'not to let you subject your faculty of desire to weak and delusive guidance and to interfere with nature's purpose'.[11]

---

11 Kant, *Works*, 4:395.

Like Plato, Kant saw that rationality is the highest level of humanity and must be used to direct social, emotional and animal natures if it is to be preserved. Plato used the analogy of a charioteer in both *The Republic* and *Phaedrus* to make this point; in the latter he argues that only when the two horses of desire and emotion are driven by human reason will progress be made – if either horse were in charge there would be a crash.

Like Aristotle, Kant understood that a good person must fulfil their nature. Aristotle described human nature in terms of the functions of being human, arguing that a good person is a fully functioning person. Kant described the functions of being human more simply in terms of rationality and freedom, but he still argued that a good person is a fully functioning person. Whereas Aristotle's definition of a good life was rather prescriptive, Kant saw that listing the characteristics of fulfilled people just serves to undermine freedom and so makes people less likely to be good. Being good hinges on making decisions independently, even if those decisions turn out to be ones which others would have recommended in the first place. The difference between Aristotle and Kant lies in their definition of human functions (and how we come to know what they are) and in their attitude to habit.

Whereas Aristotle argued that cultivating the virtues is an essential part of being good, Kant saw that cultivating any form of behaviour (such as, courage or temperance) without putting it in the context of cultivating free rational behaviour may lead people to pursue the *apparent goods* of virtues for their own sake rather than prioritizing the *real good* of human fulfilment. He wrote: 'Some qualities are even conducive to this good will itself and can make its work much easier, but still have despite this no inner unconditioned worth.'[12] Against eudaemonists such as Rosalind Hursthouse, Kant would argue that mere possession of virtues does not make someone good. Cultivating the virtues encourages people to act out of habit, rather than thinking their actions through in every case, and acting out of habit is to be less than fully human. For Kant the only virtue or good habit should

---

12 Kant, *Works*, 4:393–4.

be acting freely and rationally: everything else follows from that.

Kant argues that human nature is to be **pathologically loving**. Rational human beings appreciate the equal value of all people but must use their reason and freedom to make equality real, to make love **practical**. A person is fully human and good when they act in respect of life naturally, out of duty, because doing so is an imperative for any free and rational person rather than because there is anything in it for them.

Like Aristotle and modern virtue ethicists, Kant believed that choices affect our character, that some actions diminish our ability to be fully human and good. If a person chooses to be selfish it then becomes harder to put another's interests first; if they choose to be nationalistic it then becomes harder to appreciate the equal value of all people, regardless of nationality or race. Character is formed by choices and, in the end, a person is judged on their total character. A good person must choose to act rationally on every occasion if they are to stay good; any flaw in the character will lead to irrational poor choices (and vice versa) and render someone probably unworthy of any reward after death. (Kant considered such reward essential if the universe was to be fair – as he assumed was the case – as quite clearly in this life good people are not treated well and, if this was the only life, then this would be unfair.)

Freedom

The importance of choice cannot be stressed strongly enough. Kantian Ethics is often wrongly portrayed as a system of mindless rule-following when in fact it is exactly the opposite. For Kant **freedom is an essential part of being human**. Individuals cannot fulfil their natures by suppressing freedom and becoming slaves to commandments. To be good they must choose anew in every minute to follow the demands of reason. Doing things out of habit or because somebody expects it, to create this or that image of oneself or to gain this or that personal advantage, is not good. So an instinctive act of kindness would not, for Kant, be a good act as it is not based on reason. Goodness comes from being fully human, having a free rational character. Being free and rational is not easy; being aware of and considering all the options before choosing the unselfish path every time places a heavy emphasis on individual moral responsibility.

Duty

Kantian Ethics are sometimes called 'duty ethics' or **deonto-logical**. This can be misleading because in English 'duties' are often seen as irksome and mindless tasks to be completed on some arbitrary rota. In Greek the root of the word *deontos* is the present participle of the verb *einai*, to be. *Deontos* literally means '*function of being*' in the way that flying could be seen as a function of being a seagull, or having rectangular poo the function of being a wombat. A human being who does not do their duty is less than human; they fall short and remain unfulfilled. In German *Pflicht* similarly means 'function of being'. For Kant it is our duty to fulfil our human nature, to be free and rational and to do what follows from that without regard for the immediate consequences. It might be said that it is a human being's duty to tell the truth and preserve life – yet this is because any rational person knows that deceit and murder diminish their humanity and thus chooses not to deceive and kill, not just because they follow any specific rule which says 'Thou shalt not ...'.

Hypothetical or Categorical?

In the *Groundwork* Kant argued that to be rational is to follow universal principles and thus that all rational people would choose to behave in the same way. He then tried to encapsulate the principle on which rational people would act.

Kant set out the difference between moral and non-moral situations. Essentially, to be moral a situation has to involve a free choice and has to concern human beings.

In a non-moral situation Kant argued that a rational person will adopt a **hypothetical imperative**. They will see the relationship between an action and its results and choose that which produces the desired end. Hypothetical imperatives, non-moral rational principles, can be recognized by the presence of '*if* ... *then* ...': for example, '*if* you want to catch the train *then* you should leave now'.

However, rational people will understand that when their choices affect their own or others' lives, it is not for them to decide on the desired end.[13] Rational people recognize the inherent and equal value of all people and must choose to act in respect of that value, to treat human beings as **ends in themselves**. The involvement of human persons makes the imperative that governs moral actions **categorical**, not hypothetical – there is no '*if* ... *then* ...'. Reason demands that the only desirable end is that personhood is respected, therefore the basic principle or maxim of moral actions will be the same regardless of the situation.

The Categorical Imperative

The 'Categorical Imperative' is a single rational moral principle – but Kant described it in several different forms of words in the *Groundwork* and elsewhere, which may be summarized into three principles of moral action.

1 **The principle of universalization** suggests that any rational person would '*always act so that the maxim of their action would become, through their will a universal law*'.[14] It is only reasonable to consider what would happen if everybody was allowed to do what you are doing.

---

13 See Christine M. Korsgaard, *Creating the Kingdom of Ends*, Cambridge: Cambridge University Press, 1996, p. 10 for a good explanation of this.

14 Kant, *Works*, 4:402.

A **maxim** is the basic principle underlying a moral action: for example, the principle of action behind both suicide and killing in war would be 'taking human life'. Kant is clear that it would be wrong to 'over-particularize the maxim', making the rule so specific that it could be universalized with ease. For example, the maxim suggested by voluntary euthanasia should be 'taking human life' and not 'helping a terminally ill person to die'.

2 **The principle of humanity as an end in itself** (sometimes called 'the Practical Imperative') suggests that a rational person would 'always treat humanity, whether in the person of themselves or another, always as an end in themselves and never as a means to an end'.[15] It is not reasonable to use people and it is rational to appreciate that everybody is equal and deserves the same respect by virtue of being human. It is unreasonable to treat yourself as if you were more important than others. Human beings are 'ends in themselves' and can never be a means to some wider end (this is a strong rejection of consequentialism).

3 **The principle of a kingdom of ends** suggests that a rational person would '*always act as a law-making member of a kingdom of ends*'.[16] There should not be 'one law for me and another for you'; everything a rational person does must stand up as a precedent and set an example worthy of being followed by other people.

A common mistake is to try to apply these principles separately, arguing that each would suggest a different response to a given situation and thus that Kant's system offers no clear guidance. **Kant never intended the principles to be used separately.** He considered that reflecting on all of them would focus the mind on its choices and on the demands of reason while avoiding any danger that they might be used like rules. Kant wrote:

15 Kant, *Works*, 4:429.
16 Kant, *Works*, 4:431.

The aforementioned three ways of representing the principle of morality are at bottom only so many formulas of the same law; one of them by itself contains a combination of the other two. Nevertheless there is a difference in them which is subjectively rather than objectively practical, viz, it is intended to bring an idea of reason closer to intuition [that is, to help people understand how a priori knowledge is mirrored in experience].[17]

It is easy to see how similar the three principles of moral action are, how Kant saw them reflecting a single rational principle, the Categorical Imperative.

Doing things mindlessly or out of habit is not the behaviour of a good will. Working out the options and choosing what to do is our human duty, the function of being fully human and a necessary condition of being good. A good action just done from habit and without reflection is not, for Kant, good.

Equality

At bottom, Kantian Ethics call on people to **make equality real**. All human beings are intrinsically valuable. Kant argued that this is *a priori* knowledge, independent of experience and necessarily true. What is more, all the major world religions and most atheists agree on this principle, which also underpins modern theories of **human rights**.

Despite seeing the distinctive qualities of humanity as rationality and freedom, which relatively few people possess, after reading Rousseau's *Emile* Kant argued that value does not depend on age, sex, race or ability. It follows that people are not more valuable if we know and like them, or less valuable because they are different or live a long way away; there is clear reason to treat all people equally, fairly, with justice. Equality demands that every person should realize that they are neither more nor less impor-

17 Kant, *Works*, 4:436–7.

tant than any other person and that any selfish or self-destructive action is irrational.

Both Nietzsche and Singer have disputed Kant's logic, arguing that one cannot move from saying that moral status is bound up in rationality and freedom to assigning equal moral status to anything with human characteristics.

Happiness

Kant wrote:

> [W]e find that the more a cultivated reason devotes itself to the aim of enjoying life and happiness, the further does man get away from true contentment ... existence has another and much more worthy purpose, for which, and not for happiness, reason is quite properly intended, and which must therefore be regarded as the supreme condition to which the private purpose of men must for the most part defer.[18]

Although Kantian Ethics are often derided for suggesting that people should act contrary to their own happiness, even while admitting that pursuing happiness is a natural instinct,[19] this passage is strikingly similar to passages in even John Stuart Mill's writings. The key is in the difference between short-term personal pleasures and the longer-term 'greater good'.

Kant's ethics are not impervious to ends and consequences. In *The Metaphysics of Morals*, *Religion within the Bounds of Reason Alone* and *Towards Perpetual Peace*, Kant argues that the only way of justifying moral behaviour is with reference to some greater good or *summum bonum* which will result from people deferring their own interests in the short term. He also postulates the existence of eternal life as a necessary feature of a fair universe which would make up for the obvious injustice

18 Kant, *Works*, 4:396.
19 Kant, *Works*, 4:395.

that follows from good people going unrewarded and evil people seeming to prosper.

God, Freedom and Immortality

Kant's ethics reflect his position as a philosopher of the Enlightenment. Enlightenment philosophy is strictly rational and does not presume the existence of God or rely on religious authority or custom. Yet Kant's entire worldview is deeply imbued with Christian values although these are generally implicit rather than explicit. Most philosophers believe that Kant's use of concepts such as God, heaven, hell, evil, grace and salvation was pragmatic rather than central to his system. This is a mistake.[20]

For Kant we simply have to accept certain **postulates** (that is, things which cannot be proved but which it makes no sense to deny), if any progress is to be made in philosophy; these are God, freedom and immortality. In order to believe that what reason suggests is true it is necessary to believe that the universe is fundamentally fair; in an unfair universe where things look one way and are actually another then no progress could be made. Reason suggests that we have the ability to choose and, in a fair universe, this means that we would have to be free. Reason suggests that in a fair universe good behaviour would not go unrewarded and evil behaviour unpunished – yet experience shows that bad things often happen to good people (and vice versa). This suggests that experience must not be everything and there must be a way of justice being done in an afterlife. Without these postulates there would be no hope for Kant's system. He cannot explain why the universe is fair without God and cannot argue that it is fair without freedom and immortality.

---

20 A. C. Grayling argues the case for Kant being an atheist in http://newhumanist.org.uk/996/reasonable-bounds, but the authors strongly dispute his conclusions.

Criticisms of Kant's Ethics

Kantian Ethics are often criticized but some criticisms seem fairer than others.

Inflexible and Unjust?

Both Joseph Fletcher and Alistair MacIntyre have accused Kantian Ethics of being too inflexible about individual actions; Henry Allison wrote that 'Kant's account of the moral life has struck many critics as both unduly harsh and incompatible with our moral intuitions'.[21] Textbooks sometimes even charge Kantian Ethics with leading to injustices.

On one level this is true. Kant will not allow that it could be rational to permit exceptions; if it is irrational to murder one person it must also be irrational to murder another. Yet it is this inflexibility, this lack of regard for particular situations which gives Kantian Ethics their greatest claim to produce justice. People are treated absolutely equally, given the same respect regardless of their circumstances. The terminally ill man, the disabled woman, the unwanted child, the criminal, the foreigner and the average person on the street all have the same human rights – as do the doctor, the carer, the mother and the prison-guard. Just as the vulnerable are protected, nobody can be required to do something irrational, even for another's benefit.

Justice must not be confused with popularity or happiness. Disraeli called justice 'truth in action' and Kant would certainly have agreed that the just choice is the rational choice, right for all people not just those immediately involved. Certainly the public may want to believe that assassinating a suspected paedophile is right, and a sick person may want to be allowed to commit suicide, yet Kant's system encourages people to look beyond their animal, social and emotional desires and see through cir-

---

21 Henry E. Allison, *Kant's Theory of Freedom*, Cambridge: Cambridge University Press, 1990, p. 148.

cumstance to people as equal human beings. It encourages everyone to consider the precedent that their choices establish and the longer-term effects on the world if they seem to accept 'one rule for me and another for you' or if they treat some people as less human than others.

Unloving

Kant's principle of treating humanity as an end in itself can be argued to be very close to the Christian idea of *agape* or unconditional love for others. Fletcher argues that it may be *loving* to kill a baby whose cries endanger a party of escaping refugees, that it may be *loving* to kill a terminally ill relative, yet Kant challenges this: respect for life must override desires and emotions! Although saving the lives of the group or stopping suffering seems like the most important thing, when one steps back it is possible to recognize that this situation is particular and temporary and thus that the enduring principle of life's sanctity is more important than any individual pain or even life.

The Spanish film *The Sea Inside*[22] shows a paralysed man who wants to die; one friend wants to kill him but, at the last, can't bring herself to do it. Most people understand that the consequences of devaluing life outweigh any particular gain. Philosophers like Singer argue that it is the result of millennia of religious indoctrination but Kant would argue that understanding that is pathological and known independently of experience. It is based on our common human rationality which goes to the heart of our human nature.

Rule-worship

MacIntyre accused Kant of being action-centred rather than agent-centred, of being too worried about the rights and wrongs

---

22 Alejandro Amenábar, 2004.

of little things and not worried enough about the broader moral character.[23] Someone can seem bad despite keeping the law and another can seem good despite having done something bad. Who was better, Anne Frank's neighbours who like good citizens turned the family over to the Gestapo, or Dietrich Bonhoeffer who risked everything in an assassination attempt on Hitler?

In fact, the broader Virtue Ethic that MacIntyre proposes is based on the ethic that Kant developed through *The Metaphysics of Morals*, *The Critique of Judgement* and *Towards Perpetual Peace*. As was said earlier, the *Groundwork* was just intended to get people asking the right questions. Kant had no easy answers to what people should do with their lives; for him it is for individuals to use their reason and their freedom to work out how to be good for themselves, by reflecting on their experience of other people's lives. He accepted that mistakes are bound to be made, and that regret would temper the satisfaction of even the best person, yet he never really despaired of the possibility of human beings living up to their natures and being good.

Kant was not obsessed with rules in the way that MacIntyre suggests; the *Groundwork*, which is used to support this view, aims to work out how a virtuous person would act, not to railroad anyone into following a code first and being human second. One important point to take from Kant into the discussion of Virtue Ethics is that the general moral character is built up of every choice it has made. Modern Virtue Ethics tends to shy away from offering definite advice about right and wrong and is unclear about the virtues to which one should aspire. In the confusion it would be easy to justify most behaviour. Kant is clearer and more demanding, not afraid to pin down his virtues of rationality and freedom or to describe how they would be enacted.

---

23 Alistair MacIntyre, *After Virtue: A Study in Moral Theory*, London: Duckworth, 1985.

One-dimensional

The German playwright Friedrich Schiller was the first to accuse Kant of prizing reason above other aspects of human nature to the extent that we may suppress our instincts and emotions, and thus be less than fully human. Certainly, as Iris Murdoch wrote, 'Kant's man stands alone, confronting the mountains and the sea and feels defiant pride in the free power of his reason';[24] yet Kant disputed the idea that following reason meant suppressing the instincts and emotions. Like Plato, he believed that all aspects of human nature pull in the same direction, provided they are being directed by reason. It is good to want to survive and reproduce, it is good to exercise freedom and to value others but it is best when love of life, freedom, empathy and sympathy are governed rationally, for the good of all. Emotions are part of what it means to be human – but emotions need rational direction.

Potentially Discriminatory

Some people suggest that the value Kant placed on reason as the defining feature of human nature would have made him unlikely to see those with no or less rational potential as fully human. Indeed, this quote from the *Groundwork* seems to confirm this view of Kant – at least for those who read no further:

> Now I say that ... every rational being exists as an end in himself and not merely as a means to be arbitrarily used by this or that will ... beings ... if they are not rational [have] only a relative value as means and are therefore called things.[25]

This might mean that Kant would accept the euthanasia of brain-damaged or intellectually sub-normal people – even of criminals. Certainly, some Nazis interpreted Kant's writings in this way. In

---

24 Iris Murdoch, 'The Sublime and the Beautiful Revisited', in *Existentialists and Mystics*, Harmondsworth: Penguin, 1999, p. 283.

25 Kant, *Works*, 4:428.

his early years this criticism would have been true to Kant (who as a man typical of his age thought that women and members of other races were less rational and thus only to be treated as human out of charity!), but his understanding of human value changed when he read the writings of Rousseau. He wrote to a friend:

> [T]here was a time when I believed that [reason] constituted the honour of humanity, and I despised the people who knew nothing. Rousseau set me right about this. This blinding prejudice disappeared. I learned to honour human beings ...[26]

Defining Personhood

Defining humanity, what makes a person a person, does cause a problem for Kant. Although under the influence of Rousseau Kant took a broad view of humanity, he was never precise about when human status begins or ends and modern science has only complicated the matter. For example, if a foetus is classed as a person then Kant would be absolutely against abortion, even to save the mother's life, and yet if it was not classed as a person he might support abortion in a variety of circumstances. However, this difficulty is not just limited to Kantian Ethics. A utilitarian or situational decision would be just as influenced by its particular definition of personhood; Peter Singer has spent his whole career exposing the fact that law-makers, churchmen and philosophers base their arguments on unsound definitions.

Unclear

Kantian Ethics, by offering three versions of the Categorical Imperative and failing to provide a robust definition of humanity, may be said to offer no clear guidance on complex moral issues.

26 Quoted in Allen E. Wood, *Kant's Ethical Thought*, Cambridge: Cambridge University Press, 1999, p. 5.

However, Kant would say that rather than this being a criticism, this was precisely his intention! For Kant, rules take away the sense of freedom and responsibility which is central to any action's being morally praiseworthy. It is true that it is often difficult to see beyond clashing duties to the right course of action but, for Kant, it is the business of engaging with the difficulty that enables human beings to develop reason, exercise their freedom and understand the extent of their human moral responsibility.

Atomistic

Bernard Williams accused Kantian ethics of being '**atomistic**', of making people selfishly concerned with their own goodness and refusing to accept that sometimes it could be right to do a wrong thing.[27] Certainly Kant encourages people to be concerned with their own moral character, to do what is right not just for others but for their own sake.

According to Kant, people should 'always treat humanity, **whether in the person of themselves or another**, always as an end in themselves and never as a means to an end'. Doing the wrong thing to protect somebody else would be to sentence oneself to hell on their behalf, to use oneself as a means to an end of their happiness. Kant's approach may be valid for a Christian, but for an atheist who refuses to accept God, heaven and hell as postulates, it may seem difficult to argue that the damage to an individual moral character caused by lying to a Gestapo officer outweighs the good which may result from the action.

Again, Kant would argue that a rational person would see beyond the circumstance to the essential humanity of the Gestapo officer, and would understand that the precedent set by making their right to honesty conditional would be more corrosive than the damage the officer may choose to do with the information.

---

27 Jonathan Lear and Bernard Williams, *Ethics and the Limits of Philosophy*, London: Fontana, 1985.

Further, Kant notes that all consequentialist systems rely on being able to predict outcomes, despite the fact that predictions are often flawed and sometimes impossible. Also, by becoming actively involved in a situation, people become responsible for its outcomes.

However much one may believe that the man in the Nazi uniform will use information for ill, this cannot be known for certain, nor can one know that the information supplied in place of the truth will not cause suffering in its own way. For Kant, we should not meddle but rather do what we know to be objectively right, leaving all blame to be attached to those who choose to act immorally. This could, however, leave the Kantian looking like Pilate washing his hands.

Unrealistic

Kantian Ethics are accused of being **unrealistic** in their demands. Few, if any, human beings attain the heights of dispassionate rationality and sustain their sense of moral freedom as well. This criticism is perhaps the most powerful; Kant himself struggled with it and never answered it satisfactorily. The real difficulty lay in Kant's belief that every action affects the status of the moral character and that a good will cannot have acted out of habit or irrationally at any time. Given the inescapable fact that human beings spend close to 20 years growing up, during which time they will not fulfil their human potential to be both free and rational, it is difficult to see how anybody can really be good.

Unnatural

In seeming to reject happiness as an end, Kantian Ethics are sometimes seen to work against human nature. Yet to argue that Kant was not concerned with ends and happiness is misguided. In both *Religion within the Bounds of Reason Alone* and *Towards Perpetual Peace* Kant referred to the long-term happiness, the greater good or **summum bonum** as the only end worth acting for. No rational person could be satisfied with achieving their own happiness, knowing that they did nothing to relieve the misery of others. Although it is a cliché to wish for world peace and an end to poverty, people still do because they know that they cannot be personally fulfilled while war goes on and children starve.

Kant's thinking starts with thinking; he establishes the basis for his philosophy *a priori* and does not in the end rely on experience. If Kant's claims began with experience then technically he would not be able to move from the particular to universal claims[28] and realistically he could not move from the real world to arguing that it is fundamentally fair and ordered. Kant starts with the huge assumption that the universe is the ordered, predictable place he would like it to be – and this, perhaps, is the single greatest area of vulnerability to an ethical system that otherwise has much to recommend it.

Modern Kantian Ethics

Many books imply that Kantian Ethics started and finished with Kant's own thinking. This is misleading. There have been and are many moral philosophers who use versions of Kant's system. Naturally enough, they do not agree with every point Kant made, but their work is still recognizably Kantian. Some of these are dealt with below.

---

28 His moral principles would be subject to criticism for relying on the 'Naturalistic Fallacy', moving from saying that some people think and behave like this to saying everybody should think and behave like this. See Korsgaard, *Creating the Kingdom of Ends*, pp. 24f. for a good account of this.

Prima Facie Duties

W. D. Ross (1877–1971) criticized Kantian Ethics for three main reasons.[29] Building on the intuitionism of G. E. Moore (see page 12), he disputed whether reason dictates that moral acceptability relates to the universalizability of maxims, that the only good motive is to do duty for its own sake and that moral rules must be absolute and inflexible. Ross tried to do justice to the complexity of life. He suggested that there are several intrinsic goods, not just a good will, and that there are many different moral requirements, not just the Categorical Imperative. Things can't just be simplified and formalized to a single moral principle.

Ross agrees with Kant that human beings have at least five *prima facie* duties or responsibilities:

- non-maleficence (not to harm others), which is the most important
- fidelity (honesty)
- reparation (to right past wrongs)
- gratitude
- and the duty to promote the greater good.

However, Ross did not see these duties as either absolute *a prioris* or pragmatic. Rather, they present themselves *prima facie*, as evidence which seems sufficient to prove a case unless or until it is rebutted; all our experience points to the reality of these duties regardless of the immediate consequences of following them, so it is reasonable to say that they exist unless a convincing case is made to the contrary. In this way, Ross developed a version of deontological ethics which evaded the standard criticisms of utilitarians.

Ross went on to argue that Kant is wrong to ignore the special duties that people have to family, friends, compatriots or

---

29 W. D. Ross, *The Foundations of Ethics*, Oxford: Oxford University Press, 1939 and *Kant's Ethical Theory*, Oxford: Oxford University Press, 1954.

those with whom they have contracted promises. Whereas Kant argues that we should treat all human beings equally, admitting no preferences, Ross argues that this is unrealistic and would really require people to cut themselves off from society. The fact is that if we are a good citizen, if we marry[30] or have children, if we have friends or take out a mortgage we have obligations or special duties towards some people.

A Theory of Justice

John Rawls (1921–2002) was also inspired by Kant. He suggested that people should derive moral principles from an Original Position, from imagining themselves in a situation where 'no one knows his place in society, his class position or social status; nor does he know his fortune in the distribution of natural assets and abilities, his intelligence and strength, and the like'.[31] In this way people would be able to consider what principles would serve the interests of anybody without being influenced by specific personal interests. Rawls does not suggest that we can derive moral principles from synthetic *a priori* judgements, but tries to use reason to eliminate as many of the possible shortcomings of Ethical Naturalism as possible.

Like Kant, Rawls holds that 'each person possesses an inviolability founded on justice that even the welfare of society as a whole cannot override'. He argues that from this follow certain principles of justice, including liberty and equality. Like Kant, Rawls maintains that a negative right trumps a positive one; that is to say, somebody's right to be left alone and not interfered with

---

30 Kant saw the difficulty in reconciling marriage and moral integrity. On one level the marriage promise is just a reiteration of aspects of the general duty to others that Kantians recognize – that is, to honour, protect, be honest, etc. – but on another level it is a promise to behave irrationally and a choice to limit one's freedom – that is, forsaking all others, as long as we both shall live.

31 *A Theory of Justice* is available to download free at http://www.ebook3000.com/politics/A-Theory-of-Justice_131390.html.

is primary and comes before any right that they may have to positive assistance. Yet human beings still have duties to others; it is in everybody's interests to guarantee equality of opportunity, which may entail providing such things as democratic rights, shelter, healthcare and education to those who cannot provide for themselves. This will lead to a fairer, even just, society in which more people will flourish – not unlike the Kantian *summum bonum*.

Korsgaard, Kant and Sex

Professor **Christine Korsgaard** (b. 1952) of Harvard University is probably the best-known Kantian at work today. In 1996 she published *Creating the Kingdom of Ends*, which showed how Kant's philosophy is coherent and can be used to respond to contemporary issues.

In this book, Korsgaard considered the issue of human relationships, noting that in both *Lectures on Ethics* and *The Metaphysics of Morals* 'Kant gives inarticulate voice to the view that there is something morally troublesome, even potentially degrading, about sexual relations'.[32] She explains that his concern is not because sex involves using another person as a means to an end of getting pleasure, because that is not necessarily the case, but rather because 'sexual desire takes another person for its object'.[33] It is difficult to see how actions which take another person as their object are compatible with a good will, which must always take duty as its object.

Korsgaard explained that this difficulty is not insurmountable, but is resolved through sexual acts being undertaken reciprocally. Kant concludes that 'in this way the two persons become a unity of will'.[34] Somehow the will desiring another will that equally desires it fuses the two into one with genuine reciprocity, which

32 Korsgaard, *Creating the Kingdom of Ends*, p. 194.

33 See Immanuel Kant, *Lectures on Ethics*, trans. Louis Infield, London: Methuen, 1979, pp. 162–3.

34 Kant, *Lectures on Ethics*, p. 167.

is good. Kant argued that sex outside marriage is wrong, because in his world (and even today?) women had fewer rights over men than men had over women and this meant that an extramarital affair could not be one between free equals. Kant is also scathing about most marriages, indeed how the institution of marriage has been used to subjugate women,[35] and yet it is still marriage which Kant thinks offers the only possible context for right sexual relations. Ideally marriage provides the opportunity to consider feelings rationally and make commitments in a clear and explicit way so that there is less opportunity for misunderstandings. For Kant, love is based not on emotion (which is transitory) but on rationality. Korsgaard sees that Kant's thinking contains something valuable that could be the basis for a modern sexual ethic. She wrote: 'I believe that this view of responsibility is implicit in our actual practices, and therefore that, on this point at least, Kant's account can make us more transparent to ourselves.'[36]

O'Neill, Justice and Bioethics

Baroness **Onora O'Neill** (b. 1941) is the best-known British Kantian moral philosopher. She made her name defending the metaphysical foundations of Kant's approach and argues that theoretical and practical reason is unified in Kant's thinking, which implies that he was advancing towards a single 'theory of everything'. She wrote:

Kant has argued that the Categorical Imperative is the supreme principle of practical reason, and that practical reason has primacy over theoretical reason. It follows, therefore, that the Categorical Imperative is the supreme principle of reason.[37]

---

35 *The Metaphysics of Morals*, in Kant, *Works*, 6:278–9.

36 Christine M. Korsgaard, *The Sources of Normativity*, Cambridge: Cambridge University Press, 1996, p. 197.

37 Quoted from Garrath Williams, 'Kant's Account of Reason', *The Stanford Encyclopedia of Philosophy* (Summer 2009 edition), ed. Edward N.

O'Neill argues that Kant offers a real alternative to three flawed alternatives, pragmatism, cultural relativism and non-naturalism. For her, reason is not just convenient: it can speak beyond cultural boundaries and it is not composed of arbitrary ideas; it offers moral philosophers the possibility of speaking meaningfully about issues which affect us all while retaining a grip on the limitations of the human perspective. From these foundations, O'Neill has developed responses to major issues in justice and bioethics.

In response to a question on famine-relief O'Neill argued, against Peter Singer, that although not treating other people as mere means is a clear requirement of Kantian ethics, beneficent treatment of other people is not a requirement. Singer argues that charitable action is an obligation; O'Neill argues that in a famine-stricken population, people are obliged not to cheat any rationing policy and to fulfil their promises and contracts, including those made with dependants. Outside the famine-zone, people are obliged not to take advantage of the unfortunate (for example, through exploitative business practices or unfair policies) but are not obligated to assist.

In *Autonomy and Trust in Bioethics* (2002) O'Neill argued that Kant's non-individualistic view of autonomy provides a basis for a practical approach to issues in medicine and biotechnology. Her arguments are illustrated with reference to questions raised by the use of genetic information by insurance companies, research using human tissues and the use of new reproductive technologies. For example, against common utilitarian arguments on the 'right to a child' she argues:

> Recent debates on reproductive or procreative autonomy have not shown that individual or personal autonomy can be the sole, or even the central, ethical consideration in reproductive decisions. Reproduction is intrinsically not an individual proj-

Zalta, available online at http://plato.stanford.edu/archives/sum2009/entries/kant-reason/. See Onora O'Neill, *Constructions of Reason*, Cambridge: Cambridge University Press, 1989, Chapter 1.

ect ... Avoidance of harm is not a sufficiently robust constraint on individual autonomy in procreative decisions.[38]

Conclusion

Kantian Ethics are, in basic terms, fairly straightforward. Kant holds that being human is really to be rational; when people fail to act according to reason, then they cannot act well. Kant has more in common with the Natural Law approach to ethics than is often supposed. He takes a clear and single definition of human nature and argues that goodness lies in actions which fulfil it. One of the principal difficulties with Kantian Ethics is to work out just what reason requires human beings to do; although the Categorical Imperative provides some guidance, there can be disagreement about the nature of the rational demand and the work of modern Kantian philosophers tends to be focused on the practical application of Kant's theory.

38 Onora O'Neill, *Autonomy and Trust in Bioethics*, Cambridge: Cambridge University Press, 2002, pp. 65–6.

11

Two Roads Diverge

Kant relied on his argument that there are synthetic *a priori* foundations for moral philosophy; that the moral law appeals directly to reason and is supported by experience. This is more controversial than any other aspect of Kantian Ethics. Although the German Idealists and Romantics accepted Kant's point, by the end of the eighteenth century both the concept of synthetic *a priori* and Kant's wider epistemology were being widely criticized. Gordon Michaelson Jr has argued that this issue caused a 'divide in the road' in philosophy with one group of philosophers choosing to abandon Kant's faith in universal 'real' foundations for philosophy and moving towards relativism and the other group retaining the faith in 'real' foundations but losing confidence in philosophy as a means of exposing and exploring them.[1]

The First Alternative

Hegel and the Road to Relativism

Georg Hegel (1770–1831) moved from Kant's position, that human knowledge is necessarily subjective and that we cannot know the *Ding an sich* (truth in itself), to arguing that truth depends on human beings, that it develops with society over time through a **dialectical process**. Two accounts are put forward

---

1 Gordon Michaelson, *Fallen Freedom*, Cambridge: Cambridge University Press, 1990.

which oppose each other – a thesis and anti-thesis – and these are seen as irreconcilable; but, over time, a synthesis emerges which brings the apparently irreconcilable together. This forms a new thesis and a new antithesis emerges. So, Hegel claims, truth (including truth in ethics) develops through history. Human society is dynamic and continually struggling towards greater truth and understanding.

Hegel's heirs tended to interpret his thinking to mean that 'man is the measure of all things' and that truth is relative to human perception, thus doubting the very existence of a separate objective truth as well as its ability to be known. This was to have a direct effect on future discussion of ethics. Once the noumenal world is rejected and human beings become the measure of everything then human perspectives and human interests become central and the search for other foundations for ethics is at an end.

Karl Marx (1818–83)

Marx took Hegel's development of Kant even further, suggesting that there is no need to speculate about metaphysics when we can assert an account of human nature and make following its demands (even contrary to individual interests) an act of will justified by progress and the greater good of humanity. Marx's approach implied that metaphysical objective truth is not just unknowable; it is irrelevant and may as well not exist; truth is whatever it is convenient to believe in order to produce the progress of humanity. Marx's thinking opened the door to the sacrifice of individuals in favour of what is perceived to be 'the greater good' of society. Stalin's and Pol Pot's death camps arose from a version of this philosophy. The irreducible importance of each individual was radically eroded.

Arthur Schopenhauer (1788–1860)

Schopenhauer questioned Kant's faith in a fair and ordered universe, arguing that neither reason nor experience supports this. Schopenhauer argued that the universe is fundamentally irrational and that the Will is a blind force in nature, which does appeal to human beings but which influences them negatively rather than positively. Drawing on Chinese philosophy, both Confucianism and Buddhism, Schopenhauer argued that life is a struggle against the will, which inevitably causes us to suffer.

For Schopenhauer, it does not make sense to say that we know that the *Ding an sich* exists and is the cause of all our knowledge, when it is independent of both mind and experience and we cannot know what it is. He concluded that there is no noumenal truth which is beyond and yet causes human knowledge, rather that the Will is just a different way of looking at the phenomenal world that we experience.[2]

Friedrich Nietzsche (1844–1900)

Like Schopenhauer, Nietzsche criticized Kant for failing to engage with the real world. He started from the inconsistencies within Kant's own system, which had mostly been suggested by Kant himself. Nietzsche saw circularity within Kant's concept of synthetic *a priori* judgements. The law appeals directly to reason from experience, yet Kant argues that experience is not a necessary foundation for knowing what the law is. This might suggest that Kant's ethics are built on shaky foundations.

Nietzsche also pointed out inconsistencies between Kant's insistence that knowledge is limited by perspective and his confidence in his own ability to develop a single universal system of philosophy. He wrote that '[s]ystematisers ... practice a kind of play-acting: in as much as they want to fill out a system and round off its horizon'. He also saw inconsistencies between Kant's claim

---

2 Arthur Schopenhauer, *The World as Will and Representation* (1819).

that human beings cannot know the *ding an sich* and his claim that people can act on the Categorical Imperative. He wrote that 'old Kant obtained the "thing in itself" by stealth and was punished when the "categorical imperative" crept stealthily into his heart and led him astray'.[3] Like Schopenhauer, Nietzsche accused Kant of having it both ways, both arguing that the objective Truth or *ding an sich* is beyond knowledge and that it causes us to think and act in a particular way.

Nietzsche, therefore, rejects metaphysics and all conventional ethics: the man of exemplary strength and character will live in a world beyond conventional categories, responsible to himself alone and living life to the full in a Dionysian manner. He provides one of the most profound challenges to any idea of 'ethics' in any conventional sense.

Pragmatism

In *Pragmatism: A New Name for an Old Way of Thinking* (1907) **William James** (1842–1910) identified a fundamental tension between two approaches to philosophy, *'tough minded'* empiricism (that is, science) and *'tender minded'* rationalism (including religion). James suggested that both approaches are inadequate and proposed a new *pragmatic* middle way forward, 'a philosophy that is both empiricist in its adherence to facts yet finds room for ideals and religious belief'.[4] James argued that moral theories are just instruments; they are pragmatic. We might postulate the existence of moral laws (even very much like those described by Kant) and even the truth of religious dogmas, but we do so if and because doing so is useful and produces greater happiness. In this way, James' pragmatism may be compared with early twentieth-

---

3 Friedrich Nietzsche, *The Gay Science* and *Anti-Christ*, quoted by Bernard Williams in 'Nietzsche's response to Kant's Morality', *The Philosophical Forum* 30:3 (1999). Article first published online in 2002 at http://online library.wiley.com/doi/10.1111/0031-806X.00014/pdf, checked 9 April 2012.

4 Christopher Hookway in http://plato.stanford.edu/entries/pragmatism/.

century theories of Rule Utilitarianism, which have superficial similarities with Kantian Ethics but which do not rely on the same epistemological foundations.

Ethics and the Limits of Morality

Bernard Williams (1929–2003) observed that by the mid twentieth century philosophers had abandoned moral philosophy altogether. He quipped that 'contemporary moral philosophy has found an original way of being boring ... by not discussing moral issues at all'.[5] Moral philosophy, according to Williams, had responded to the lack of firm foundations for moral discussions by abandoning them altogether and turning to limited codes of ethics and their application.

Doctors agree on a pragmatic code of professional ethics and discuss issues such as abortion or euthanasia within the rules of medical ethics; business people agree on their own code of ethics and consider whether certain practices do or do not conform to it; and sportspeople agree on the rules of sportsmanship and argue about whether diving for the ball, using drugs or wearing the latest full-body swimsuits is compatible with them.

In 1951, in the essay 'Two Dogmas of Empiricism', **W. V. Quine** (1908–2000) had convincingly rejected Kant's argument for synthetic *a priori* judgements. As Sullivan has commented, 'Quine goes so far as to refer to the notion of a priori knowledge as a "metaphysical article of faith".'[6] He concluded that all knowledge depends on experience – and this fuelled the shift towards emotivism, radical relativism and the rejection of any objective truth in moral philosophy which was described in Chapter 3 of this book.

---

5 Bernard Williams, *Morality: An Introduction to Ethics*, Cambridge: Cambridge University Press, 1972, p. 9.

6 http://evans-experientialism.freewebspace.com/sullivan.htm.

Human Rights and International Law

On one level developing theories of human rights and systems of international law were a response to this mid-twentieth-century despair with finding solid foundations for moral philosophy, a despair which can be traced back to Kant. Kant himself suggested that, although political philosophy should be based on moral philosophy, there is a difference between what the state can do (in terms of imposing laws, punishing and even coercing people) and what individuals can reconcile with their desire to develop a good will. The state has to be pragmatic in creating a framework which protects individual liberty and thus allows people to be good.[7] Kant was ahead of his time, recommending that all states should become republics and form a 'league of nations' within which individuals would be 'citizens of the world' whose right to liberty (and consequent rights to property, equality before the law and equality of opportunity) would be respected.[8] Of course Kant believed that these rights appeal directly to reason but, in the light of Quine's criticism, people began to found theories of rights pragmatically rather than epistemologically.

As an example, **Richard Rorty** (1931–2007) built on Quine's critique to conclude that there is no objective truth, that the mind is not a 'mirror of nature' and that how we see the world may not be how it really is. If truth is just what people agree is the case then ethics needs to be constructed for the benefit of society and philosophers should not waste time discussing the epistemological foundations for morality. Rorty's argument for human rights denied that there is any natural foundation for rights, but suggested that (for whatever reason) most people have moral sentiments[9] and that it makes sense to build on these in order to protect vulnerable minorities and resist power-politics which

---

7 See Immanuel Kant, Part One of *Metaphysics of Morals*, 'The Doctrine of Right'.

8 See Immanuel Kant, *Towards Perpetual Peace* and Brian Orend, *War and International Justice: A Kantian Perspective*, Toronto: Wilfrid Laurier University Press, 2000.

9 Like Hume, see note 3 on p. 81 and also Chapter 16.

tries to label some groups as sub-human and of less moral status.

The rationale behind many countries accepting international law is similar. People do not agree on the origin of moral ideas or even that everybody has them – but it makes sense to use them as the basis for rules which serve the greater good. The problem with this rationale is that when the usefulness of the law is not apparent, when it is profoundly unpopular to uphold the human rights of a terrorist or a notorious paedophile, it is difficult to argue that the law or human rights should be universally applied. The standard response is that if exceptions are allowed to the rule then international laws or human rights cease to deliver the benefit which justifies their existence. If a terrorist is extradited from Britain to a country which permits torture, then the right not to be tortured becomes meaningless. Talk of rights then comes down to popular opinion and we are a step away from being like Germany in the 1930s.

The Second Alternative

Kierkegaard and the Road to Individualism

Søren Kierkegaard (1813–55) reacted strongly against Hegel's interpretation of Kantian philosophy. Whereas Hegel saw truth as limited to what human beings can know, perhaps even originating in humanity, Kierkegaard saw truth as absolute and independent. Human knowledge is *either* correct *or* incorrect. He was, therefore, a philosophic realist (see pages 8–16).

Both Kierkegaard and Kant begin with human experience as free, rational agents. They both appreciate the enormity of human moral responsibility and the sense in which everyone lives in a state of 'fear and trembling'. Kierkegaard wanted to awaken individuals from their slumbers, to confront them with the importance of making a decision about their lives, knowing that the stakes are immense and there can be no certainty about the existence of God or meaning in the universe. For Kierkegaard and

Kant doing what is right is not doing what is easy or what produces personal happiness: we must act in relation to the Truth, the Absolute, even God. (Although, for Kierkegaard as for Kant, there is no way of showing that God exists although Kierkegaard firmly believed in God – he was a philosopher, theologian and psychologist.)

The major difference between the two thinkers is over the role of reason. Kant believed that human beings can use reason to uncover universal moral laws and therefore it would be impossible for somebody to act irrationally, against accepted moral laws, and still be doing the right thing. Kierkegaard disagreed and argued that a personal relationship with God could call an individual beyond ethics. He argued for the possibility of the teleological suspension of the ethical, using the example of Abraham when he offered up his son as a sacrifice: he did what was rationally, ethically and personally unthinkable but was right before God.

Kierkegaard had a passionate commitment to the importance of each individual (in this he was similar to Kant) and wanted to force individuals to stake their lives on the choices they made. He thought that most people drifted through lives like drunken peasants asleep in a cart. As such, the closest they came to ethics was conformity with what was accepted within their society and Kierkegaard hoped his reader would come to realize that this was not an adequate basis for a human life. Like Bonhoeffer, he called individuals to stake their lives on a commitment to absolute Truth, even though this could not be established by reason. He argued that 'as you have lived, so have you believed': the best indication of a person's ethics was not what they said or wrote but how they had lived. In this sense he could be seen as the father of later existentialism, although he was a realist in the Aristotelian tradition.

Kierkegaard suggested a new approach to the search for wisdom, **indirect communication**. For Kierkegaard, as for Kant, knowledge is necessarily subjective but truth is real. Human beings cannot get outside their own perspective but, as individuals, they can at least try to use imagination to get outside the confines of their own experience. Kierkegaard's philosophy was developed through a series of pseudonyms, characters which represented particular types of people and which explored reality from their different perspectives. No one account contains the truth but they each point to the truth. In this way Kierkegaard's approach relates to Kant's concept of Judgement, his argument that it is possible to gain a sense of the noumenal truth through literature or art or beauty, but this cannot be communicated directly to others.[10] The best that can be done is to encourage people to share our experience and hope they will respond as we do. This approach also seems to lie behind the postmodern ethic of Levinas.

Ludwig Wittgenstein (1889–1951)

Wittgenstein was influenced by Kant but accepted the criticisms of his approach which suggested that we can have even less metaphysical certainty than Kant supposed. He was also influenced by Kierkegaard's approach, which saw access to truth limited by perspective (he described Kierkegaard as the greatest philosopher of the nineteenth century – and a saint!). Wittgenstein concluded that 'of that which we cannot speak we must be silent'. Meaning can only be established subjectively, in relation to what people accept and agree. However, and importantly, for Wittgenstein that does not mean that the objective truth is irrelevant or does not exist (see pages 17–18).

Postmodern Engagement

The term 'postmodernist' was used by Arnold Toynbee to describe the world forged by the First World War, where nineteenth-

---

10 See Ronald M. Green, *Kierkegaard and Kant: The Hidden Debt*, Albany: State University of New York Press, 1992.

century certainty, its faith in reason, progress and humanity, had been destroyed. The term has, therefore, been used to describe an era as well as a broad set of ideas and this has led to considerable confusion about what postmodernism is and to very different philosophies being labelled as 'postmodernist'.

Walter Anderson describes four separate strands within 'post-modernism',[11] including

1 'Postmodern-ironist': truth is a social construction and only meaningful relative to a particular culture.
2 'Social-traditional': truth is to be found in the heritage of American and/or western civilization.
3 'Scientific-rational': truth may be found through systematic enquiry.
4 'Neo-romantic': truth may be found through harmony with nature and/or exploration of the inner self.

It would be wrong to say that all postmodernist thinkers reject the existence of objective truth. There is a strand within post-modernism which sees ethics in terms of individuals engaging with the truth (whatever this may be), not following moral rules but taking their autonomy and responsibility seriously and trying in themselves to live in relation to something ultimate.

In 1926, the Anglo-Catholic theologian **Bernard Iddings Bell** (1886–1958) used the term 'postmodernism'[12] to describe both a new era and an intelligent alternative to liberalism (relativism) and totalitarianism (absolutism). For Bell both approaches share 'a faith in mankind's ability to discover the underlying principles that govern nature and societies through right use of reason',[13] which he disputed, believing that this faith actually impover-

---

11 Walter T. Anderson, *The Fontana Postmodernism Reader*, London: Fontana, 1996.

12 Bernard Iddings Bell, *Postmodernism and Other Essays*, London: Morehouse, 1926.

13 Michael Drolet, *The Postmodernism Reader: Foundational Texts*, London: Routledge, 2004, p. 5.

ishes humanity. Peter Vardy makes a similar point in *What is Truth?*, using Yeats' poem 'The Second Coming' to suggest that, although 'The best lack all conviction, while the worst are full of passionate intensity', there is a way of living in relation to truth without claiming to possess it.[14]

In his famous book *Nineteen Eighty-Four*, George Orwell warned against 'a boot eternally trampling a human face', and, for Bell postmodernism is a reaction against 'the boot' (totalitarian certainty) and a reorientation of philosophy to begin with the transcendent experience of being human (what Levinas later called 'the face'). Michael Drolet argues that Bell's critique of modernism has a parallel in the work of Augustine, who judged that the philosophies of Plato and Aristotle 'led man to ignorance and spiritual isolation'. For Bell, the postmodern individual is 'intellectually humble and spiritually hungry' and even 'longs to fall upon his knees and worship a comprehending Absolute' though he/she knows that this longing will never be fulfilled.[15]

Whether philosophers claim that they *possess* the objective truth or that they *know* that truth is subjective, they are claiming to be able to describe the way things really are and conclude various things from that. For Bell, the hallmark of postmodernity is scepticism about such claims, what Lyotard later called 'incredulity towards metanarratives',[16] and in a way this can be traced back through the work of Wittgenstein to Kierkegaard and the late Kant.

Although postmodernism has been dominated by its criticism of other approaches, by the 1990s some postmodernists started to consider being constructive and providing a positive response to the experience of being human. They have drawn inspiration from postmodern writers such as **Jacques Derrida** (1930–2004),

---

14 Peter Vardy, *What is Truth?*, Sydney: University of New South Wales Press, 1999, Part Three.

15 Drolet, *Postmodernism Reader*, p. 5.

16 Jean-François Lyotard, 'Introduction to *The Postmodern Condition: A Report on Knowledge*', available online at http://www.idehist.uu.se/distans/ilmh/pm/lyotard-introd.htm, accessed 21 April 2012.

Emmanuel Levinas (1906–95) and Jean-François Lyotard (1924–98), who all saw discourse, literature or art as a means of engaging with social issues, helping people to engage with concepts of right and wrong when more direct forms of ethical discussion had been discredited.

The Swiss writer Max Frisch quipped, 'We can now do what we want, and the only question is what do we want? At the end of our progress we stand where Adam and Eve once stood: all we are faced with now is the moral question'; and Robert Eaglestone claimed that 'postmodernism, implicitly or explicitly, is about ethics before it is about anything else'.[17]

Levinas and 'the Other'

Derrida pointed out that 'Levinas does not want to propose laws or moral rules ... it is a matter of [writing] an ethics of ethics'.[18] Unlike Kant or Bentham, Levinas' morality does not begin with reason but with the experience of 'the Other'; responsibility begins in 'the affective, immediate experience of "transcendence" and "fraternity"'.[19] Ethics begins in experience, but this is not sense-data or observation of the world as for Aristotle or Hume. Experience is the realization of being human and the responsibility that entails. As Zygmunt Bauman (b. 1925) wrote:

> morality means being-for ... the Other. To take a moral stance means to assume responsibility for the Other; to act on the assumption that the well-being of the Other is a precious thing calling for my effort to preserve and enhance it, that whatever I do or do not do affects it, that if I have not done it, it might

17 Quoted by Steven Connor in *The Cambridge Companion to Postmodernism*, Cambridge: Cambridge University Press, 2004.

18 Jacques Derrida, 'Violence and Metaphysics', in *Writing and Difference*, trans. Alan Bass, Chicago: University of Chicago Press, 1980; first published in 1967.

19 Bettina Bergo, 'Emmanuel Levinas' at http://plato.stanford.edu/entries/levinas/.

not have been done at all, and that even if others do or can do it this does not cancel my responsibility for doing it myself ... And this being for is unconditional (that is, if it is to be moral, not merely contractual) – it does not depend on what the Other is, or does, whether s/he deserves my care or repays in kind.[20]

Taking the Road Less Travelled

It seems that the dominant approaches to normative ethics discussed so far, Natural Law and Virtue Ethics, Utilitarianism and Situation Ethics, Kantian Ethics and Postmodern Ethics, all struggle to provide moral guidance which both has a claim to applying universally and is clear and useful.

* Natural Law offers clear guidance which arguably leads to the common good, but seems to rely on flawed reasoning, moving from a necessarily partial experience of the world to universal claims about morality.
* Virtue Ethics tries to avoid the flawed reasoning but in doing so loses the clarity of guidance.
* Utilitarianism mostly relies on the same naturalistic reasoning as Natural Law but also results in guidance which is unclear. Applying utilitarian calculations in every situation is impractical and open to abuse but developing rules on utilitarian grounds either collapses into Act Utilitarianism anyway or ends up conflicting with the basic principle of serving the greatest happiness for the greatest number.
* Situation Ethics takes love and not happiness as its aim and, although it does not rely on naturalistic reasoning but takes love positively or as an article of faith, ends up in much the same situation as Utilitarianism in being either impractical or

20 Zygmunt Bauman, *Ethics After Certainty*, London: Demos, p. 15. Available online at http://www.demos.co.uk/files/aloneagain.pdf?1240939425, accessed 21 April 2012.

supporting rules even when they contradict the basic principle of Situationism.

- Kantian Ethics tries to argue from 'synthetic *a prioris*' to a universal moral law, but these foundations are widely criticized and the conclusions Kant draws from them are nothing if not controversial.
- Postmodern Ethics starts with the experience of being human and encourages people to take their autonomy and responsibility seriously – but offers no real guidance on how to behave at all.

Where does this leave moral philosophy? It seems that a choice must be made between three possible approaches:

1 One can accept one of the normative systems, for all the probable flaws, and try to refine it so as to make it more robust and useful.
2 One can accept relativism and construct code(s) of ethics which serve the needs of a particular society, always accepting that these may be subject to change and that they can say little that is absolute or comment meaningfully about matters outside their jurisdiction. We will examine what this option might entail in the following chapters on applied ethics.
3 One can confront the dilemma that being human places each one of us in, accepting the postmodernist challenge and starting by sharing the experience of 'the Other' and seeing where that leads. We will return to this option in the final chapter of this book.

PART THREE

Applied Ethics

12

Abortion, IVF, PGD, Germ-line Therapy and Embryonic Stem-Cell Research

Having considered meta-ethical foundations and possible normative systems and frameworks, it is necessary to turn to the practical application of ethical theories in relation to contemporary issues. Clearly not all issues can be covered, so we have chosen to focus on those which are perennially in the news and which highlight some of the key philosophic questions.

One of the aims of philosophy is to examine the underlying assumptions of any argument. Many people base their views on opinions they have received from their parents or the media, but philosophy trains the mind not to accept the obvious. It goes back to first principles, analyses existing arguments and seeks to construct stronger ones.

Abortion

Abortion is one of the most controversial ethical issues today. People tend to have strong views, but few people are clear on the intellectual basis for them. Those who reject abortion usually do so because it is considered to be equivalent to murder. This assumes that the embryo or foetus is a person, having the same moral status as the mother or any other human being. Those who argue that abortion should be allowed usually do so because they assume that the embryo or foetus is not a person, or is less of a person, than the mother, whose rights are seen to be more important.

Abortion is increasingly common; about 42,000,000 women have an abortion each year.[1] In 2008, there were 1,210,000 legal abortions in the USA, representing 22 per cent of all pregnancies. About 25 per cent of these took place prior to nine weeks' gestation using the 'abortion pill' Mifepristone (which causes a miscarriage), while 5.3 per cent took place after the sixteenth week[2] and would have involved a saline injection into the amniotic sac and induced labour. Of course, it is the 64,130 dead fully formed foetuses which excite most public concern and which are the focus of pro-life campaign literature. Of those American women who had abortions in 2008 54 per cent became pregnant despite using contraception,[3] and it is estimated that nearly half of all pregnancies in the USA occur accidentally.

Abortion is legal in many – but by no means all – countries, either 'on demand' or for medical reasons and usually up to a given number of weeks of gestation. For example, in the UK abortion is legal before 24 weeks, if two doctors agree that there is a sound medical reason or existing children will suffer from an addition to their family,[4] and in New Zealand before 20 weeks under similar conditions.[5] However, it is illegal except to save a woman's life in Somalia and the Republic of Ireland where traditional religious attitudes prevail.[6]

---

1 http://www.cbc.ca/news/world/story/2010/04/27/f-map-legal-status-abortions.html, accessed 16 April 2012.

2 The most recent statistics from the Guttmacher Institute, published January 2011: http://www.guttmacher.org/pubs/fb_induced_abortion.pdf, accessed 16 April 2012.

3 Guttmacher Institute statistics.

4 Under the terms of the 1967 Abortion Act, modified by the 1991 Human Fertilisation and Embryology Act. In practice there are many doctors who 'sign off' on abortions which may not meet the spirit of the legal criteria.

5 The Contraception, Sterilisation and Abortion Act 1977.

6 See note 1.

Ethical Concerns

Ethical concerns over abortion spill over into a number of related issues.

The use of some contraceptives may allow an egg to be fertilized but prevents pregnancy from becoming established; progesterone-only pills, implants and injections, the IUD/IUS and emergency 'morning after' contraceptives such as Levonelle and ellaOne are potentially abortifacient and some people object to them on ethical grounds.

In-vitro fertilization (IVF) is a well-established technique[7] which enables many infertile couples to have a baby which may be biologically related to one or both of them. An increasing number of young people in the western world are infertile.[8] This may be due to sexually transmitted diseases or to a lowering of the male sperm count which has thus far not been adequately explained.[9] Traditionally, if a woman has viable eggs then she is given drugs to cause 'super-ovulation' before eggs are harvested and screened. The newer technique of IVM enables eggs to be taken directly from the ovaries. If a woman has no viable eggs then she may choose to use those of a donor, who will have her eggs harvested in the same way. In both cases, the eggs are fertilized with sperm from the partner (if viable) or a donor (if not) in a petri dish.

If successful, a number of embryos are created which are increasingly carefully screened using a technique known as **preimplantation genetic diagnosis** (PGD). Scientists believe that, in time, it will become possible to correct defects in these embryos or even to import certain genes to impart advantages. This is known as **germ-line therapy**. Currently, the most they can do is to select

---

7 The first successful IVF birth was that of Louise Brown, in 1978.

8 http://news.bbc.co.uk/2/hi/health/4112450.stm, accessed 15 April 2012.

9 http://www.ispub.com/journal/the-internet-journal-of-urology/volume-2-number-1/the-sperm-count-has-been-decreasing-steadily-for-many-years-in-western-industrialized-countries-is-there-an-endocrine-basis-for-this-decrease.html, accessed 15 April 2012.

embryos which are healthy and which have desirable character-istics – such as gender or freedom from certain genetic defects. Embryos are either implanted straight away or frozen for later use or research. They remain viable for several years; in western Australia the TV news reported that a couple conceived two gift-ed children using embryos they had created and frozen ten years before.[10] Frozen embryos may in some countries be donated to other couples. Defective or surplus embryos are destroyed, along with embryos used for research as soon as they approach 14 days after conception. In most western countries the number of em-bryos that may be implanted at any one time is limited to 2–3, which reduces the incidence of multiple pregnancy and later mis-carriage. Rates of pregnancy following IVF or IVM depend on the health of the parents and the skill of the clinic; they vary widely but are generally not high, meaning that couples usually have to undergo more than one cycle of treatment.

Research on 'spare' embryos created during IVF has opened up a new world of **stem-cell research** and related treatments. Stem cells are not specialized and have the potential to become different types of tissue. They are found in early-stage embryos and in some parts of the adult body, for example bone-marrow. Research on embryonic stem cells is controversial because it can involve the destruction of early-stage embryos to harvest the cells, though this form of research still offers the best hope of new treatments for major spinal damage. Most actual research today focuses on adult stem cells.

Context

A normal female has over a million eggs in each ovary – these are in place by the time a foetus is 15 weeks old and, after puberty, eggs ripen and about 400 are discharged from the ovaries at a rate of 1–3 every 28 days until about 25,000 eggs remain and

---

10 Nine Network News, 14 April 2012.

the menopause begins[11] at an average age of 52 years. A huge number of eggs are unreleased, most that are released are unfertilized and most that are fertilized fail to develop into a foetus.[12] In the western world a normal male ejaculation contains at least 39 million sperm[13] and generally several hundred million; average sperm counts have been falling by 1–2 per cent per year for a number of years.[14]

The embryo/foetus goes through a gradual process of development and there is no clear point, after conception and before birth, when it 'comes alive' or acquires a particular capability. Once fertilization has taken place, all the genetic material for the new person is present – the fertilized egg is clearly human tissue and is alive – but whether it is a person at this stage is controversial. There are various stages that are important in considering this issue:

1 when sperm enters egg;
2 when implantation occurs and a pregnancy is established, 6–10 days after fertilization;
3 when 'twinning' (that is, the embryo splitting and becoming two or more identical individuals) is no longer possible, 14 days after fertilization;
4 by 30 days, just two weeks past the mother's first missed period, when the embryo has the beginnings of a brain, eyes, ears, mouth, kidneys, liver, an umbilical cord and a heart;
5 when the mother can first feel the movement of the foetus, about 15 weeks;
6 when the foetus can feel pain, about 17 weeks;
7 when the baby is viable or could survive (this depends on the medical technology available – in the very best hospitals this

11 http://www.babycentre.co.uk/preconception/activelytrying/howbabiesaremade/.

12 Some research suggests that up to 70 per cent of fertilized eggs do not end up as full-term foetuses. See http://miscarriage.about.com/od/pregnancyafterloss/qt/miscarriage-rates.htm.

13 Lower parameter according to the WHO, 2010.

14 See note 9.

could be 22–23 weeks but if there are no medical facilities
available it could be around 35 weeks);
8   when the baby is born and takes its first breath.

Medical research means that our understanding of the process
of development is improving all the time. Doctors used to believe
that the heart did not start beating until 16 weeks and that the
foetus could not feel pain until 28 weeks. The point of potential
viability is also getting earlier and earlier as neonatal intensive
care units get better – no baby could survive before about 28
weeks in the 1960s, but today a 22-week baby has a 1 per cent
chance of being discharged from hospital in the UK[15] and by 25
weeks that improves to 44 per cent.

The Status of the Embryo

At the heart of all of these discussions is the status of the embryo.
Is a human embryo like the embryo of an orangutan or a mouse
or does it have particular moral status? Can an embryo or foetus
be regarded as a person and, if so, on what basis? These questions go to the heart of the debate but often people who hold
strong opinions have not thought through the issues.

Souls and Bodies

Plato was a dualist; he believed that human beings are not just
matter like animals but have a 'soul'. If Plato was right and human
beings are not like other animals then the grounds for objection
to abortion and related issues become stronger. **Dualism** is not a
popular philosophic position today but it nevertheless has a very
long history, has been supported by many major philosophers
in the past and is held by many ordinary people today who may

---

15 http://www.bma.org.uk/ethics/reproduction_genetics/AbortionTime
Limits.jsp?page=6.

consider that, after death, the soul survives. However, if one is a dualist then it is necessary to consider what a 'soul' is, what evidence there could be to support its existence and at what stage the soul is implanted.

Christian and Muslim philosophers wanted to affirm that there was an essential *ontological* difference between animals and human beings. Like Plato, they associated this difference with the human 'soul'. They argued that God created only human beings in God's own image and so God must implant a 'soul' at some point before birth, marking the beginning of personhood and moral status.[16]

Augustine and Aquinas argued that a human person was not formed until a soul was implanted at 40 days after conception in the case of a male and 90 days after conception in the case of a female. Augustine argued that if someone causes a miscarriage very early in pregnancy he would not be guilty of murder because there was no soul present and a person had not yet been formed.

The Qur'an was not clear about intentional abortion. It forbade the killing of children, which was common in poorer families in pre-Muslim times,[17] but scholars did not agree on whether early-stage abortion was the same as killing children. The Prophet never ruled on a case of intentional abortion, but did impose a lesser fine[18] in respect of the foetus on somebody who intentionally killed a pregnant woman.[19] When did the embryo or foetus become a person? Both the 22nd and the 23rd Surah described the unborn child going through several stages of development prior to being created as a person. Al Ghazali (1058–1111) argued that ensoulment occurs at conception, at the moment that a new being

16 The early Christian Church proclaimed it to be a heresy (called Traducianism) to hold that a man and woman could make love and produce another human being without God's action in implanting a soul.

17 See for example Qur'an, Surah 6, verses 137 and 151.

18 About ½o of full blood-money.

19 M. H. Katz, 'The Problem of Abortion in Classical Sunni fiqh', in Jonathan E. Brockopp (ed.), *Islamic Ethics of Life: Abortion, War, and Euthanasia*, Columbia, SC: University of South Carolina Press, p. 27.

is created,[20] but Ibn Hazm (994–1064) taught that ensoulment occurs at 120 days after conception. There was no consensus on ensoulment and this ambiguity gave rise to a variety of teachings on abortion and related issues in different schools of Islam.

Since the Enlightenment, the Roman Catholic Church has been reluctant to say exactly when ensoulment occurs. Nevertheless, the Declaration on Procured Abortion (1974) states: 'Life must be safeguarded with extreme care from conception; abortion and infanticide are abominable crimes.' *Evangelium Vitae* (1995) teaches that,

> even if the presence of a spiritual soul cannot be ascertained by empirical data, the results themselves of scientific research on the human embryo provide a valuable indication for discerning by the use of reason a personal presence at the moment of the first appearance of a human life: How could a human individual not be a human person?

Catholic teaching against abortion or any measure which destroys a conception is clear; nevertheless, the reasoning behind it is sophisticated. The Church holds that as one cannot be certain when life begins it is right to treat embryos as if personhood begins from conception (note the reference to a 'personal presence' above), because if it does then destruction of the embryo would be equivalent to murder.

The Roman Catholic Church also forbids the use of IVF/IVM and abortifacient contraceptives as they involve the destruction of early-stage embryos. The Church discourages embryonic stem-cell research, arguing that research on adult stem cells may be as productive.

Other Christian denominations hold different views on when a person is formed but all agree that the human embryo deserves respect. Anglicans argue that this respect does not necessarily rule out the use of abortifacient contraceptives or abortion in extreme cases, because it must be balanced against respect for the

---

20 Katz, 'Problem of Abortion', pp. 40ff.

life and health of the mother. Anglicans are not usually against IVF/IVM and tolerate stem-cell research.[21]

Mainstream Islam insists that abortifacient contraceptives and abortion should only be used for clear medical reasons, to save the life of the mother or protect her from serious harm. Today, most Sunni Muslims (and therefore the majority of Muslims worldwide) maintain that God implants a soul at 120 days after conception and this changes the status of the embryo: it becomes a 'new creature' according to the Qur'an.[22] Nevertheless, as Katz observes, contemporary scholars can learn from the 'high level of tolerance for ambiguity and complexity'[23] which characterizes Islamic discussion of these issues. IVF/IVM is only permissible if the eggs come from the wife and the sperm from the husband, because of the central importance of the family in Islam. Some Muslim countries (such as Egypt) are open to embryonic stem-cell research, using 'spare embryos' from IVF.

Following the scientific enlightenment fewer philosophers accepted the existence of a separate soul. Looking back to Aristotle, many argued that human beings are simply animals who have the ability to use reason – they are entirely made up of matter and do not have a separable soul. This is **Monism** which holds that humans are made from a single substance, matter.

From a monist position there are fewer grounds for arguing against abortion and other measures which cause the destruction of embryos. Nevertheless, even without a soul, most monists accept that human beings have special moral status and so monists have to decide when 'personhood' begins. There is no agreement

---

21 Since 1967 at least. A helpful summary of different church teachings may be found at http://www.bbc.co.uk/religion/religions/christianity/christianethics/abortion_1.shtml, accessed 15 April 2012.

22 Qur'an, Surah 23, verses 12–14 (Sahih International Version: 'And certainly did We create man from an extract of clay. Then We placed him as a sperm-drop in a firm lodging. Then We made the sperm-drop into a clinging clot, and We made the clot into a lump of flesh, and We made from the lump, bones, and We covered the bones with flesh; then We developed him into another creation. So blessed is Allah, the best of creators.'

23 Katz, 'Problem of Abortion', p. 45.

and this explains many of the differences of opinion in bioethics. If it is held that a person is not formed until some time after conception, then it is likely that a reasonably relaxed attitude will be taken to the treatment of the embryo. If, by contrast, a person is formed at conception, then abortion or the destruction of or experimentation on the embryo may be completely unacceptable.

Following Kant, discussion of what makes human beings different from animals and persons with moral status focused on capabilities rather than the particular faculty of a soul. Kant argued that human beings are uniquely free and rational, but this immediately raised a question over the status of humans who lack one or both of these attributes and particularly over the status of humans who do not even have the potential to develop them. As we have seen, prior to reading Rousseau Kant suggested that assigning moral status to women and members of other races might be charitable rather than deserved. **Peter Singer** (b. 1946) has argued for this position and maintains that Christian and Muslim attitudes, as well as the attitudes of many philosophers, are irrationally speciest. He sees no essential difference between human beings and animals except that most human beings have a higher level of intelligence and consciousness than most animals. For Singer, moral status should depend on sentience and be assigned wherever sentience exists – whether in human or ape form – and denied wherever sentience is lacking. He has no problem with abortion, or with related issues, providing it is in the best interests of those concerned.

Consent

One argument in favour of legal abortion which makes no claims about the status of the embryo has been developed by **Judith Jarvis Thomson** (b. 1929).[24] Thomson uses an analogy to make her point.

---

24 Judith Jarvis Thomson, 'A Defense of Abortion', *Philosophy and Public Affairs* 1:1 (1971). Available online at http://spot.colorado.edu/~heathwoo/Phil160,Fall02/thomson.htm, accessed 5 May 2012.

Imagine that you are involved in an accident and wake up in intensive care to be told that while you were unconscious another person, in fact a world-renowned violinist, was also involved in an accident and the only way to save him was to use you as a life support-system. He will need you to remain in the hospital, keeping him alive, for nine months, after which you can have an operation (carrying some risk) to separate you. You might protest that you never consented to this and that it is unreasonable for one human being to expect another to put their life on hold, experience discomfort and take risks on their behalf. You might get angry and demand that the operation is carried out straight away, regardless of what happens to the violinist. How would you feel if the doctors replied that that would be illegal: seeing as you happened to be around in the emergency room when the violinist came in you have no choice over what happens now?[25]

Thomson's argument is clear. It does not matter what the moral status of the unborn child may or may not be; if the mother did not specifically consent to become pregnant then it is unreasonable to expect her to carry and give birth to it.

Opponents argued that consenting to sex constitutes consent to pregnancy, but Thomson and her supporters disputed this arguing that in cases of rape this is obviously not the case. Further, many would argue that it is not reasonable to claim that sex may only be used as a means of procreation in the modern world. If a woman uses contraception which she believes will prevent pregnancy and if that contraception fails, then Thomson would maintain that the woman's right to terminate the pregnancy is clear. It is significant that 54 per cent of American women who had abortions in 2008 had used contraception.

Opponents continue to argue that mothers have special obligations to their offspring (which people do not have to strangers) and that abortion actively and intentionally kills the embryo/foetus and is not equivalent to unplugging the violinist and letting him die as a side-effect. Nevertheless, Thomson's argument was influential and seems broadly consistent with the ruling made in

---

25 Thomson, 'Defense of Abortion', pp. 48–9.

the famous and controversial Roe vs. Wade judgement, which made abortion on demand to the point of viability legal in the USA in 1973.

Rosalind Hursthouse, now Professor of Philosophy at the University of Auckland, made her name by applying Virtue Ethics to the issue of abortion.[26] Like Thomson, Hursthouse argues that the important issue is not the moral status of the unborn child but rather the meaning of the woman's rights in the situation. If Thomson argues that a woman's right to autonomy means that she should be able to request an abortion at any stage in pregnancy, Hursthouse argues that having a right does not mean that one is justified in exercising it. Hursthouse notes that abortion also involves another person, the doctor, conferring on her or him the obligation to carry out a termination. She asks whether one person's right can ever oblige another to do something which they feel may be wrong.

Pre-Implantation Genetic Diagnosis

For couples where one or both has a family history of a medical condition with clear genetic markers it may be desirable for them to use IVF and PGD to choose only embryos without those genetic markers, thus avoiding the possibility of having a child or even several children with a genetic condition, even if they would not otherwise have needed IVF treatment to get pregnant.

PGD is used to identify embryos that will be susceptible to developing monogenic disorders (this means that the condition is due to a single gene only, whether an autosomal recessive, autosomal dominant or X-linked disorder, or due to a chromosomal structural aberration). The most frequently diagnosed autosomal recessive disorders are cystic fibrosis, beta-thalassemia, sickle cell disease and spinal muscular atrophy type 1. The most common autosomal dominant diseases are myotonic dystrophy, Hunting-

26 Rosalind Hursthouse, 'Virtue Theory and Abortion', *Philosophy and Public Affairs*, 20 (1990–1).

ton's disease and Charcot-Marie-Tooth disease; and in the case of the X-linked diseases, most of the cycles are performed for fragile X syndrome, haemophilia A or Duchenne muscular dystrophy. PGD helps couples who know they are at risk of having a baby with one of these conditions to identify and use embryos which are free of risk, thus avoiding the difficult choice of abortion later on in pregnancy or having a child with severe abnormalities.

PGD for such medical reasons is perfectly legal in many countries, including the UK, although not in Germany since 1990, where there is a natural sensitivity to allowing anything which could be interpreted as eugenics. Nevertheless, some of the more recent advances in PGD have caused people to ask questions about the ethical acceptability of allowing doctors to continue offering some options to patients.

One of the early applications of PGD was to select embryos to become **saviour siblings**. In these cases an embryo is chosen because it has the right tissue-type to donate an organ or bone-marrow to a family member, usually a brother or sister.[27] Ethical concerns centre on the idea of using one person as a means to an end of saving another and the psychological and relational implications of such treatment for the family. This use of PGD is legal in many countries, but remains controversial.

It has also become possible to use PGD to test for a number of conditions which do not develop until later in life, usually in or after someone's forties. Also, PGD can now be used to identify genetic markers which do not diagnose a condition, that is, which do not relate to a monogenic condition, but which just indicate an elevated risk of a condition which is related to a number of genetic and non-genetic factors. One such example is the gene BRCA1, which reliably indicates a high probability of developing a particular form of breast cancer.

Another recent development in this field involves people with Huntington's disease, a neurodegenerative genetic disorder that affects muscle co-ordination and leads to cognitive decline and dementia. The disease is caused by an autosomal dominant

---

27 http://www.bbc.co.uk/news/health-12055034, accessed 16 April 2012.

mutation on either of an individual's two copies of a gene called 'Huntingtin',[28] which means any child of an affected parent has a 50 per cent risk of inheriting the disease. In rare situations where both parents have an affected copy this risk increases to 75 per cent, and when either parent has two affected copies, the risk is 100 per cent (all children will be affected). Physical symptoms of Huntington's disease can begin at any age from infancy to old age. PGD offers couples from families affected by Huntington's disease the chance of having unaffected children. Normally the procedure would identify if one or both parents are carriers and how many copies of huntingtin each affected parent carries.

Some people just do not want to know what genetic defects they carry, nor do they want formal test results to exist because then they would have to disclose them to employers, insurance companies and the like. In order to get round this problem the European Society of Human Reproduction and Embryology (ESHRE) has a code of ethics which recommends that clinics use *exclusion testing* by default, which avoids the need to detect the mutation itself. Nevertheless this raises questions in itself about whether it is right for policy to restrict information available to insurers, thus unnecessarily raising premiums for the vast majority of unaffected patients.

Nearly half of clinics offering PGD offer to allow couples to choose the sex of their children. This issue is controversial as choosing embryos of one gender is sometimes done as a simple way of avoiding the risk of a child developing a genetic condition such as haemophilia. Most of the time, however, gender selection is done for non-medical reasons (because, culturally, in some societies boys are valued more highly than girls) and many people feel that it is wrong. On the other hand, it does avoid the relatively common problem of couples, at least in some cultures, seeking termination of a pregnancy once the gender of the foetus becomes apparent. There seems no ethical basis for such a choice unless relativism is accepted; then, if abortion of female foetuses is acceptable in a society, this can be endorsed.

---

28 http://ghr.nlm.nih.gov/gene/HTT, accessed 26 April 2012.

In the future, PGD may also be used to screen for other perceived genetic advantages. Scientists believe that, in time, germline therapy will become possible, which will enable embryos to be altered at the genetic level in order to, for instance, improve intelligence or other physical attributes.

James Watson's Argument

In 1953, James Watson shared with Francis Crick a Nobel prize for the discovery of the DNA double helix. He has called for a campaign to use genetic research to rid society of genetic defects. In praise of experimental germ-line therapy he wrote: 'To my knowledge, not one illness, much less fatality, has been caused by a genetically manipulated organism. Never postpone experiments that have clearly defined future benefits for fear of dangers that cannot be quantified.'[29] Watson claims there are two main arguments against germ-line gene therapy:

1 Scientists should not interfere in the human genetic code for fear of unknown consequences. This is the 'risk against reward' argument.
2 Allowing any germ-line therapy is the slippery slope to eugenics. Once we allow the removal of 'bad' genes, the next step will be the insertion of 'good' ones. Once any alterations to embryos are permitted then soon we will be having 'designer babies', engineering for intelligence, etc. ...

Watson rejects both arguments. He points out that no one would question that, if a baby has birth defects, then the best medical attention should be applied to rectify this. Logically, therefore, if there are defects in an embryo there would seem to be no sound ethical reason why defects should not also be eliminated.

---

29 http://www.gmwatch.org/latest-listing/1-news-items/8382-major-uk-paper-promotes-human-germline-engineering April 2001, accessed 15 April 2012.

He also wrote, 'I strongly favour controlling our children's genetic destinies. Working intelligently and wisely to see that good genes dominate as many lives as possible is the truly moral way for us to proceed.' Watson is effectively arguing that it is ethically irresponsible to continue to reproduce in the old-fashioned way and that, instead, humans should be breeding for genetic advantage. In practice this involves the selection of embryos rather than their alteration. Of course, we all 'select' characteristics to pass on to our children by selecting our partners; for Watson PGD offers people a more precise and effective means of ensuring advantage for their offspring. In terms of the commercialization of the process, Watson argues that buying genetic advantage is no different from buying other sorts of advantage in life. All are not equal and genetics can provide further advantages to an individual that they ought to be allowed to enjoy.

Theory and Practice

In the first part of this book various normative theories were outlined, each of which will influence discussions about abortion and related issues in particular ways.

1 Traditional Natural Law holds that certain actions are 'intrinsically evil' and absolutely wrong. If the embryo is regarded as a person from the moment of conception, then it can never be right to abort, to use the morning-after pill or to use IVF/IVM or PGD. This position underpins the official teaching of the Catholic Church. If 'personhood' is assigned later, as in most schools of Islam, then IVF/IVM, PGD and abortifacient contraceptives may be allowed.

2 Proportionalism is a variety of Natural Law which holds that sometimes, in truly exceptional circumstances, abortion may be permissible.

3 Situation Ethics would approach issues in a similar way, acknowledging the sanctity of life and the fact that destroying

potential or actual people is not usually loving, but accepting that in certain situations the consequences would justify unusual measures. It is important to note that Situation Ethics would demand that the effects of any moral decision on the wider society should be considered. For instance, freely available abortion might be argued to damage the fabric of society by devaluing the importance of human life. One of the greatest problems with Situation Ethics is that five different people may arrive at five different answers concerning the most loving action.

4 Utilitarianism takes various forms. It is often crudely caricatured as the ethical system that promotes happiness, but much depends on how the 'greater good' or the 'greater happiness' is defined. It is certainly a mistake to think purely in the short term. Mill and many modern utilitarians aim for wider human fulfilment rather than happiness as such. Applying Utilitarianism to bioethical issues is therefore not straightforward. Many factors need to be taken into account including:

a What will the long-term effect be for the individual concerned? When a girl is accidentally pregnant her immediate reaction may be that this is a disaster and that only an abortion can secure her happiness, but when she looks back on the decision over a number of years it may become more complex. Ten years later, the abortion may be bitterly regretted – or, of course, it may be seen as being by far the best decision for the individual.

b Utilitarianism demands that all those whose interests are in question should be considered – this means that the father's as well as the mother's interests must be taken into account as well as the wider family. This is frequently ignored and the girl or woman will take a decision based on what she sees as her immediate happiness or convenience.

c If the embryo is seen to be a person then its interests need to be taken into account. Since it can be argued that it might be better for the embryo to be able to exist than not to exist (even if this means that he or she is given up for adoption after birth), Utilitarianism may well regard this as being a strong argument against abortion.

d   The interests of the community as a whole need to be considered, especially by rule utilitarians. Is a society that permits abortion on demand a better or a worse society than one that does not? The difficulty of determining answers to such questions should be obvious.

5   Kantian Ethics argues that every human being is of irreducible worth and may never be used as a means to an end. At surface level this might seem therefore to involve rejecting the killing of any embryo whether in abortion or IVF/IVM but, of course, much will depend on whether or not the embryo is a person. If the embryo is regarded as a person, then Kant's position would indeed be clear, but Kant did not address the issue with any clarity and so followers of Kant would first have to determine whether or not an embryo is a person. The issue, therefore, of how Kant would respond to abortion and related issues is open and subject to divergent views.

Each position maintains that there is an ethical truth to be sought regarding abortion. They may differ as to how this truth should be arrived at, but they agree that truth is 'out there'. This is in marked contrast to a culturally relativist view which rejects any claim to truth in ethics.

In the case of genetic selection or improvement the issues become more complex.

1   Natural Law considers that each person should be measured in relation to a single human nature. A person who is blind, suffering from Down's Syndrome or homosexually inclined is suffering from a defect. Once the language of 'defect' is used, then it logically leads to talk of 'correction of defects' and, where possible, any measures taken to bring somebody

closer to 'normality' would be morally justifiable. However, the more we learn about genetics the more questionable the assumption of a common human nature becomes.

Would enhancing athletic ability or intelligence at a genetic level be permissible? On strict Natural Law grounds, there seem to be few arguments against this. It is often at this point that the debate becomes confused, with some thinkers suggesting that God creates each individual with his or her own potential and that interfering with this would be wrong. God is not a necessary feature of Natural Law ethics and it is not philosophically easy to defend the idea that God determines an individual's genetic makeup.

2 Utilitarianism could argue that fostering genetic perfection through the elimination of defects or even enhancement would maximize the happiness of all concerned. Nobody enjoys being ill or limited, or seeing those they love ill or limited. An economic argument could be employed, maintaining that children born free of defects would be more economically productive and place less strain on healthcare resources. Most utilitarians would also be in favour of saviour sibling treatments, as more people are likely to benefit from this than would potentially suffer.

Rule utilitarians might raise questions about whether an emphasis on physical perfection is really conducive to the good of society as a whole. Already it is clear from the United States, where PGD is increasingly common and where eggs and sperm or even surrogate mothers can be ordered online (with prices set according to their physical, intellectual and social attributes), that the commercialization of reproduction may have a worrying effect on the relationships between parents and children and on the children's psychological wellbeing. This would not be a popular argument to promote but it is, at the least, an arguable position. It may follow that a society that values physical perfection and where physical perfection was more common would be less tolerant of the disabled, the sick or the less perfect who would then feel marginalized or, in some way, 'sub-human'. The film *Gattaca* raises these issues with considerable effect.

3   Situation ethicists could argue that, taking account of all those involved, minimizing genetic defects and maximizing intelligence and athletic ability, for example, would often be a good thing, provided that there are no adverse side-effects. Alternatively, the more human reproduction becomes a matter for the laboratory then the more the 'unitive' side of love-making and the special unconditional relationship between parent and child could be undermined. If this could be shown to be the case then genetic selection and genetic manipulation might often be rejected.

4   Immanuel Kant does not, of course, address these issues directly. However, it is quite clear that creating a 'saviour sibling' would be against the principle of humanity as an end in itself as the new child is being used as a means towards some wider end. It might be argued that the more a person can allow reason to control his or her life the better, and if physical defects are likely to impede rational development or if certain genes are likely to increase rational capabilities, then measures taken to change genetic makeup would be positive. Nevertheless, it would be necessary to prove that removing defects or altering genes really would have this effect on rationality; clearly, there have been many geniuses who have suffered physical defects. The inter-relationship between different genetic sequences is far from being fully understood and the consequences of genetic manipulation are almost impossible to predict. Kant himself was very short and it is not usually the case that philosophy departments are populated by athletic bionic people.

13

Euthanasia

In his *Utopia*, the sixteenth-century Catholic Thomas More en-
visaged a society in which those whose lives had become burdensome as a result of 'torturing and lingering pain' would be helped
to die with dignity. It is only in recent years, however, that the
euthanasia debate has moved to being something that may soon
affect legislation round the world. Most people in the western
world say they support euthanasia but many of these are not
aware of the philosophic issues. Various distinctions need to be
made at the outset:

1 **Involuntary euthanasia** is where a person is killed without
   their consent. This might apply if a patient is in a coma and
   has no hope of recovery, yet the term has also been applied
   to the killing of so-called undesirables. For example, the term
   was applied to the murder of disabled people during the Holocaust.
2 **Voluntary euthanasia** is where a person is killed at their request or with their consent. This might apply when someone
   is terminally ill and is suffering.
3 **Assisted suicide** occurs where a person is given the means to
   kill themselves.

It is also worth distinguishing between **active euthanasia** or
assisted suicide, which involves administering a lethal drug or
otherwise killing somebody by an act of commission, and **passive
euthanasia**, which involves allowing somebody to die by an act of

omission, of treatment or even food or water. The line between acts of commission and acts of omission is blurred when it comes to, for instance, switching off life-support machines. Generally patients are allowed to refuse treatment and ask for such machines to be switched off if they are able to communicate and are in sound mind at the time. However, 'advance directives' are not necessarily legally binding and where they go against the wishes of family members they are sometimes not acted upon where life-support is already in place.

In cases like that of Tony Bland, one of the victims of the British Hillsborough Stadium disaster in 1989, a comatose patient is unable to give a view on whether life-support should continue despite there being no hope of improvement and the patient may remain in intensive care for months or years. In 1993 the British Law Lords famously ruled that it would be acceptable for the Airedale NHS Trust to withdraw the treatment from Tony without his consent, because his life was effectively a burden to him and, without hope of improvement, the means being used to sustain it were officious. Both Peter Singer and John Finnis have highlighted this case as a significant change in legal thinking.[1] It goes to the heart of many cases in modern medicine where doctors and ethics committees need to distinguish between **ordinary means** and **extraordinary means** of keeping somebody alive. The law and most moral codes make the former obligatory, but it seems reasonable to most people that doctors should not use extraordinary and heroic measures to save a life which will be burdensome.

In practice, many terminally ill people are allowed to die at their own request or at the request of a next of kin. Doctors usually advise people when treatment offers no hope of improvement and when prolonging life will just mean prolonging suffering. Patients (or their next of kin) may then choose to terminate a

---

1 The full decision is available online at http://www.bailii.org/uk/cases/ UKHL/1992/5.html. See J. M. Finnis, 'Bland: Crossing the Rubicon', *Law Quarterly Review* 109 (July 1993), pp. 329–37 and Peter Singer, *Rethinking Life and Death: The Collapse of Our Traditional Ethics*, London: Macmillan, 1996, Chapter 4.

course of treatment and patients may even refuse to be fed and/or hydrated. This is not a quick or particularly pleasant death, but may seem preferable to the slower and more painful alternative.

The use of morphine to relieve pain and 'make them comfortable' during the end stages of terminal disease may also have the side-effect of shortening life by depressing breathing. The law in most countries permits doctors to use morphine provided the dose is not unreasonable in relation to the end of relieving pain and providing that death does not result immediately and as a direct result of the administration of the drug. In this way the law reflects the **Principle of Double Effect** which emerged out of Natural Law.

The Contemporary Debate

The contemporary euthanasia debate only concerns voluntary euthanasia and assisted suicide. People generally agree that it is wrong to actively kill someone without their consent, even when it seems that doing so would be in their best interests. They also agree that the person making the request should be of sound mind when making the request and that care should be taken to avoid hasty uninformed decisions or decisions which are unduly influenced by others. This is directly linked to the Principle of Autonomy in medical ethics. It is also widely agreed that appropriate medical safeguards are necessary, for instance by the approval of two independent doctors, although another key principle in medical ethics – the Principle of Non-Maleficence – calls on doctors never to harm patients and killing a patient, whatever the circumstances, might fall under this heading.

Various arguments are used to support legalized assisted suicide and/or voluntary active euthanasia.

- Suicide is legal and therefore not allowing elderly, sick and disabled people to commit suicide seems to discriminate against them.

- A right to life implies a right to choose the manner of one's own death.
- Personal autonomy means nothing if individuals are not allowed to make meaningful decisions about their own lives and deaths.
- If death is inevitable then it is nonsensical to force people to suffer pain and indignity when they have the means to give themselves a quick death of their choosing.
- Animals are 'put out of their misery' and, indeed, owners would be criticized for allowing an animal to continue to suffer when in considerable pain as some human beings are – vets manage to deliver humane deaths sensibly every day.
- Increasingly, medical advances mean that people experience a prolonged and undignified death where they might in the past have died of heart-attack, stroke, pneumonia, infection or influenza. It is both unfair to expect people to suffer more than they might have done without medical intervention and unsustainable from an economic point of view to place the burden of managing prolonged deaths on the medical establishment.

One of the significant differences of opinion relating to voluntary active euthanasia or assisted suicide concerns whether these should be made available to those who are not in the final stages of terminal illness. Should it, for instance, be available to someone who has become a quadriplegic as a result of an accident or even to someone who is profoundly depressed and has 'lost the will to live'? In the Netherlands, where voluntary active euthanasia has been legal for many years, loss of independence rather than terminal illness is the main reason for people seeking to die.

Various arguments are used against the legalization of voluntary active euthanasia or assisted suicide.

- Murder is absolutely wrong. Suicide is wrong and not to be encouraged or seen as a right. In the UK, it was decriminalized, not legalized as such, in 1961.

- There is no right to choose the manner of one's own death, especially when this confers upon others an obligation to be involved in causing a death.
- Doctors and nurses undertake to preserve life (the Principle of Non-Maleficence). Legalizing voluntary active euthanasia or assisted suicide would put them in an impossible position (although doctors who objected on moral grounds would not be required to participate in such procedures).
- Elderly or frail patients may feel undue pressure to opt for death for economic reasons or to ease the burden on their families.
- Experience in the Netherlands suggests that legalization is the beginning of a 'slippery slope' into the more widespread killing of vulnerable people.
- It would be difficult to regulate and therefore wide open to abuse.
- Advance directives cannot represent the informed will of the patient at the point of death. People often change their minds when it comes to the point.
- There may be value in suffering, both for the patient and those close to them.
- Modern palliative care means that no one need die in agony. There are ways of making people comfortable without intentionally killing them. Interestingly there are almost no hospices in the Netherlands.

Natural Law

Germain Grisez and Joseph Boyle[2] reject any consequentialist position in ethics, any suggestion that consequences determine the rightness or wrongness of human actions. They challenge the assumption that there is a distinction between bodily life and personal life. They reject both the view that one can cease to be a

2 Germain Grisez and Joseph Boyle, *Life and Death with Liberty and Justice: Contribution to the Euthanasia Debate*, South Bend: University of Notre Dame Press, 1979, pp. 336–439.

person and yet still be bodily alive and the view that there is a distinctively human component which is not yet present in the unborn or newly born and which is lost in the irreversibly comatose. Because of this, Grisez and Boyle (cf. Chapter 6) reject any distinction between being 'dead as a person' and 'dead as a body' which some supporters of euthanasia argue for as they hold some may be 'dead as a person' but still bodily alive. They argue that the human being is one and bodily life is a good in itself.

The basic premise of Grisez and Boyle's argument is that there are certain basic human goods constitutive of human wellbeing, including life, and these cannot be measured against one another in order to establish any form of hierarchy (see pages 62–5). These basic human goods provide motives for moral action and are the source of the moral obligation to promote human wellbeing; it can never be right to act against one of these basic goods. If this argument is accepted, then euthanasia would be absolutely prohibited because it turns against one or more basic goods. Euthanasia wrongly assumes that the choice for death over life can be morally right, because it serves higher goods of freedom, integrity or dignity (conspicuously absent from Grisez's list) which are somehow more important than basic goods such as life. However, according to Grisez and Boyle, human goods cannot be compared or made subservient to each other in this way. They therefore argue for an absolute prohibition against euthanasia.

Proportionalism

Daniel Maguire[3] is a Roman Catholic but holds that life is a basic but not an absolute good and that therefore one is bound to respect it, but not to prolong it in every circumstance. Maguire argues that the special task of ethics is to bring sensitivity, reflection and method to the way people decide on the sort of persons

3 Daniel Maguire, *Death by Choice*, New York: Doubleday, 1974; see also *Ethics: A Complete Guide to Moral Choice*, Minneapolis: Augsburg Fortress, 2009.

they ought to be and the sort of actions they ought to perform. Issues such as euthanasia can only be discussed adequately within the context of a complete ethical theory.

When considering an issue such as euthanasia, the first step is to clear the ground, establish the facts and discover the 'moral objective'. This is done by asking reality-revealing questions such as what, why, how, who, where, when, what if and what else. Only when this is done can proper evaluations be undertaken.

Maguire argues that the central questions in a case of euthanasia are as follows (and he gives his own answers to these):

1 'Can it be moral and should it be legal to take direct action to terminate life in certain circumstances?' Maguire answers 'Yes'.
2 'Must we in all cases await the good pleasure of biochemical and organic factors and allow these to determine the time and manner of death?' Answer: 'No'.
3 'Can the will of God regarding a person's death be manifested only through the collapse of sick or wounded organs?' Answer: 'No'.
4 'Can the will of God be discovered through human sensitivity and reasoning?' Answer: 'Yes'.
5 'Could there be circumstances when it would be reasonable and therefore moral to terminate life through either positive action or calculated benign neglect?' Answer: 'Yes'.

Maguire rejects the idea of a kind of fatalistic theism which forbids expanding the human dominion over dying because the time of death is organized by God alone. This would imply that human beings are God's property and it follows that no interference should be allowed in God's plan. All medicine would then be immoral. Maguire argues that from this perspective there is no essential difference between ending and preserving life. He argues that the human dominion over life and death has been underestimated. Human beings now have the ability and responsibility to discover the good and choose it, even when the good in question is death.

Maguire challenges the 'absolute' character often given to the principle 'Thou shalt not kill'. Against traditional advocates of Natural Law he argues that terminating life may be good so long as a greater good than physical life is being served (Grisez and Boyle, of course, argue that this is not possible). He defends his position, arguing that the principle 'no direct killing of innocent life' is valid most of the time, but in specific circumstances the principle may not apply and would yield to a greater good. Maguire argues that unless someone holds that continued living in any condition is always preferable, (s)he will have to enter into the weighing of proportional values. He accepts that making such a judgement is not easy, may be mistaken and must always be undertaken very seriously.

Charles Curran is another Catholic theologian who is a proportionalist (see page 69). He argues that the sanctity of life is a basic principle and respect for life is a moral imperative, but since the dying process indicates that life has reached its limit, he does not see euthanasia as contrary to respect for life. [4] He gives a qualified acceptance to euthanasia, in more strictly limited circumstances than Maguire.

Curran argues that the value of life is more than a person's achievements, possessions or capacities, but warns against too great a stress on life as a gift, as this can undermine human responsibility. Curran's fundamental position is as follows:

I agree with the traditional argument against euthanasia, that man [sic] does not have full dominion over his life and, therefore, cannot positively interfere to take his life ... Man does have some dominion over the dying process because he can as a matter of fact shorten the time of his dying by not using or discontinuing even readily available means to prolong life. [5]

---

4 Charles Curran, *Ongoing Revision: Studies in Moral Theology*, Notre Dame: Fides Publishers Inc., 1975, pp. 145–209.

5 Richard M. Gula, *What Are They Saying About Euthanasia?*, Mahwah, NJ: Paulist Press, 1986, p. 77.

Curran finds in the Catholic tradition that respect for life is not the only criterion for making judgements involving human life; quality of life and other values also claim attention.[6] He distinguishes the theoretical basis for respecting life from practical exceptions which are usually allowed. As an example, in a conflict one may legitimately take a human life when one's own life is at stake. He concludes that life is not totally sacrosanct.

Curran challenges the adequacy of traditional Catholic teaching which prohibits using direct means to achieve what may be accepted if achieved indirectly, as in the Principle of Double Effect. Curran sees human actions more broadly and disputes whether a direct and an indirect action which have the same effect are really different; the moral significance of the distinction between an act and an omission dissolves when the dying process overtakes a person. Unlike Grisez and Boyle, Curran would allow one to act directly against some basic good in order to save other proportionate goods, but, unlike Maguire, only when the dying process has begun.

Both Maguire and Curran advocate proportionalist positions. They recognize that values come into conflict in life or death situations and try to determine the morality of an action on the basis of its total meaning, not just the action in itself or just the consequences. Their position does include consequences (and is therefore sometimes referred to as a 'moderate' or 'mixed' consequentialist position) but it is not entirely consequentialist as it does maintain that certain actions are right or wrong in themselves.

Situation Ethics

Like Proportionalism, Situation Ethics acknowledges the validity of traditional Christian values such as respect for life and, like Proportionalism, Situation Ethics recognizes the complexity of real-life situations, such as those involving questions about

6 See 'Declaration on Euthanasia' for example, available online at http://www.newadvent.org/library/docs_df8oeu.htm.

euthanasia, and weighs consequences against principles in considering what is best and most loving for those concerned. Like Proportionalism, Situation Ethics is rejected by traditional advocates of Natural Law such as Grisez and Boyle.

Fletcher maintained that there is more to being human than just being alive and that a key feature of humanity is rationality, which may be used to make a free choice to die when life becomes burdensome. For a situationist, each case must be taken on its own merits and judgements concerning what are the most loving actions must recognize the effects on the family and the wider community as well as the interests of the dying person.

Situation Ethics has often been criticized for offering little clear guidance and therefore for placing too much responsibility on the shoulders of people who are likely to be stressed and confused and potentially for providing a cloak for self-interest. Being clear on one's own motives is never easy, particularly when it comes to the death of a close relative.

Kantian Ethics

Kant emphasizes rationality and also the intrinsic worth of every human being. He is clear that it can never be right to use a human being as a means to some wider end. In relation to euthanasia, this would rule out suicide or asking somebody for help to die and it would rule out killing somebody to satisfy personal feelings or economic or political imperatives. Kant's position on suicide is clear. He says:

> Firstly, under the head of necessary duty to oneself: He who contemplates suicide should ask himself whether his action can be consistent with the idea of humanity as an end in itself. If he destroys himself in order to escape from painful circumstances, he uses a person merely as a means to maintain a tolerable condition up to the end of life.[7]

7 Immanuel Kant, *Groundwork for the Metaphysics of Morals* in *The*

Nevertheless, Kant is also clear that there is a difference between an act and an omission; though one may be obligated not to do something evil one may not be obligated to help somebody else when doing so is not consistent with reason. This might suggest that doctors would be justified in withholding treatment or even nutrition from dying patients, even against that patient's wishes, if they are certain that treating or nourishing them will just prolong agony.

Some people try to argue that, using the versions of the Categorical Imperative separately, it might be possible to universalize a principle allowing voluntary euthanasia for the terminally ill. However, there is no doubt that this would be against the spirit of Kant's moral philosophy; he never intended the versions to be used separately. Also, Kant warned against 'over-particularizing the maxim'. It is clear that if one made the maxim extremely specific just about any action could be justified using the principle of universalization – but then the maxim is not really a maxim, which is by definition a *general* law of action.

Utilitarianism

Many arguments for euthanasia are justified on utilitarian grounds. On the most basic level voluntary euthanasia is designed to alleviate suffering and therefore causes 'the greatest happiness for the greatest number'. Also, many utilitarian thinkers have seen liberty and autonomy as integral to meaningful happiness; respecting a person's right to die and to decide the manner of their own death is a clear affirmation of their liberty and worth.

These arguments may not, however, recognize the complexity of analyses that some versions of Utilitarianism demand. Will euthanasia really bring the individual, those helping him or her as well as the wider community closer or further away from

Cambridge Edition of the Works of Immanuel Kant, trans. and ed. Paul Guyer and Allen W. Wood, Cambridge: Cambridge University Press, 1999, 4:422.

fulfilment? On one level killing somebody cancels out any future happiness they might have experienced, for example from being with their family. Also, confusing physical pain with suffering is an elementary mistake. If effective palliative care is available then this might make the decision to die less justifiable on utilitarian grounds. A rule utilitarian may well reject the legalization of assisted suicide and voluntary active euthanasia, because the few cases in which it brings more happiness than pain are more than offset by the negative effects on society and the medical profession, the probable abuses and the energy spent trying to prevent a slippery slope into more widespread killings.

For a rule utilitarian, the argument in favour of devoting resources to palliative care and hospices would be very strong. Anyone who visits a hospice will generally find these are places of light which help people to take joy in the process of living. People with severe disabilities and long-term degenerative diseases can go on to live 'useful' lives (in the utilitarian sense, lives full of happiness).

Stephen Hawking is an example of this. He suffers from motor neurone disease and was told that he would probably die of asphyxiation before the age of 30. Although he is paralysed and many would consider his condition to be intolerable, he has become one of the greatest scientists in the world, has had three wives, children and grandchildren and, at the age of 70, still lives a full and enjoyable life. He said 'Although there was a cloud hanging over my future, I found to my surprise that I was enjoying life in the present more than before.'

A Final Thought

One final point should be considered (although it is not one that many philosophers have been willing to address). The cost of caring for people in the final years of their lives is rising; by far the largest part of the healthcare budget of most countries is spent on people in the last three years of their lives. Whether this is a good use of medical resources must be, at least, debatable, particularly as the quality of life of individuals in the final years may not be high. The population is growing, people are surviving for longer in old age and the basic costs of providing an acceptable standard of accommodation and healthcare are rising. In times of economic hardship difficult choices have to be made about the use of resources. This will inevitably lead to a discussion of whether people in this position who wish to die should be allowed to do so. This will be a painful and difficult discussion but it is one that is badly needed.

Conclusion

Being sick or old is not necessarily a bad thing. It can sometimes be during such infirmity that lessons about life can be learnt which people who are healthy and well do not consider. As Tolstoy said of his character Ivan Ilyich:

> He wept on account of his helplessness, his terrible loneliness, the cruelty of man, the cruelty of God, and the absence of God. 'Why hast Thou done all this? Why hast Thou brought me here? Why, why dost Thou torment me so terribly?' He did not expect an answer and yet wept because there was no answer and could be none. The pain again grew more acute, but he did not stir and did not call. He said to himself: 'Go on! Strike me! But what is it for? What have I done to Thee? What is it for?' Then he grew quiet and not only ceased weeping but even held his breath and became all attention. It was as though he were listening not to an audible voice but to the voice of his soul, to the current of thoughts arising within him. 'What is it you want?' was the first clear conception capable of expression in words that he heard. 'What do you want? What do you want?' he repeated to himself. 'What do I want? To live and not to suffer,' he answered. And again he listened with such concentrated attention that even his pain did not distract him. 'To

live? How?' asked his inner voice. 'Why, to live as I used to – well and pleasantly.' 'As you lived before, well and pleasantly?' the voice repeated. And in imagination he began to recall the best moments of his pleasant life. But strange to say none of those best moments of his pleasant life now seemed at all what they had then seemed.

This goes back to the issue of the purpose of life which both Plato and Aristotle discussed and which has always been a central part of ethical analysis. The religious perspective holds that there is life after death, caring for one's soul is vital and pleasure is not the main purpose of life. In this case pain and suffering during the dying process may be an integral part of the human journey and opting out of life merely because it is not pleasant may be a mistake. It was in his dying that Ivan Ilyich first began to realize this and the superficiality of his life was laid bare. A religious perspective on life can, therefore, change one's attitude to central issues in medical ethics.

14

Business Ethics

The Circle of Concern

At the most basic level businesses exist to make money for their **owners**. Some businesses are very small and some are international conglomerates, extending across many countries and working in nearly every country in the world, but whether they are owned by a single individual, a small group of partners or much larger numbers of shareholders, the primary beneficiaries will always be the owners.

Where businesses have **employees**, they pay them wages or a regular salary; employees have defined roles within the business and benefit so long as it continues to trade and they perform satisfactorily, whether or not it is profitable. Employees take no personal risk; their work earns defined rewards and, providing they behave responsibly, they are not held accountable for the success or failure of the business. Employees rarely share in success, however. Their rewards remain the same whether or not the business makes a profit, unless there is a defined bonus scheme in place, designed to incentivize employees to generate more profits.

Businesses also rely on other businesses to be **suppliers**. Each business affects many others in this way, with one failure leading to loss of trade, layoffs and even bankruptcies in many other businesses. Businesses are therefore interested in the credit-worthiness of other businesses and will try to minimize risk by only trading with those with a good credit rating. Ratings agencies have an important part to play in regulating business; they provide information which enables businesses to manage risk and trade effectively.

Businesses also rely on their **customers**. Without people to buy products or use services they would fail. Responsibility to customers tends to be transactional. However, it makes sense for businesses to produce quality products or treat customers well, because customers are more likely to return if they do. The truth of the contingent nature of this relationship can be experienced where businesses have a 'captive audience' and do not operate in a competitive environment. If there is no competition, prices are likely to be higher and service may well be of a lower quality.

Business activities also affect **other people**; people who do not own shares, earn wages or buy products. People who have never had a Big Mac will be affected by the deforestation of the Amazon, and people who have never had a mortgage will be affected by the banking crisis. Conversely, the whole of society may benefit from economic success driven by business, even if not everybody is directly involved. Business practices are therefore a matter for government regulations, which aim to maximize the benefits while ensuring that they do not cause undue harm; however, now that many businesses operate across national boundaries these regulations are not necessarily effective.

The **environment** is also likely to be affected by business. Many businesses make money by using finite resources, or their work is likely to harm animals or their habitats, or produce emissions, pollutants and waste. The concept of 'externalities' is an important one – these are all those factors (such as pollution, global warming and disposal of waste) which are part of the manufacturing or distribution process but which generally do not have to be paid for by businesses. Nevertheless they affect the wider community. By ignoring the 'externalities' businesses can increase their own profits because they are not accountable for these costs.

There have been many examples of businesses causing harm to individuals, communities, landscapes or even the world as a whole:

- the Bhopal disaster in India
- the BP Gulf of Mexico oil spill
- the effects of tobacco on health or of leaded petrol on health and forests
- the effects of manufacturing and building using asbestos
- the pollution of water supplies by fracking for shale-gas in the USA and, increasingly, elsewhere
- the destruction of half a million acres of Australian farmland by irresponsible irrigation[1]
- the destruction of historic sites caused by dams in Egypt and China
- miners left to die below ground for want of safety procedures
- the personal tragedies of workers forced to suicide by workplace bullying.

The harm done by business activities is immense. On the other hand, the wealth created by business is perhaps even more important.

Liability

One of the most important legislative advances (in 1855 in the UK) was to authorize 'limited liability companies'[2] as vehicles for doing business. This allowed businesses to be seen as legally independent entities; **'limited liability companies'** allowed businesses to issue shares and thus generate the capital needed for their operations, to share ownership between hundreds or thousands of people. The crucial factor is that a limited liability company is a separate legal entity which can own property, trade, employ people and incur obligations as if it were a person. The liability of those who invest in the company is limited (hence the name 'limited liability') to the amount of their investment – if the company

---

1 Douglas L. Johnson, *Land Degradation: Creation and Destruction*, Lanham, MD: Rowman & Littlefield, p. 198.

2 Known as 'corporations' in the USA.

fails, the shareholders may lose their investment but they have no other liability. However, shareholders may also feel sufficiently distant from their investment that they do not have any direct moral responsibility for the company's behaviour.

Limited liability companies encouraged ordinary people to invest in shares and so generated a great deal of capital and economic activity. The downside was that, more than ever before, business activity was motivated by owners' profits without thought for how those profits might affect others, let alone the environment. The sole criterion by which those who ran companies were (and generally are) judged was profit.

Before the mid nineteenth century (and the introduction of limited liability) business was often conducted with a high level of social responsibility; owners were directly liable for the activities of their businesses, and this served as a powerful incentive for them to remain interested in what was going on and make sure that it would reflect well on their reputation. Banks such as Lloyds Bank and Barclays Bank or businesses such as Lever Bros, Rowntree and Cadbury were founded by people with strong convictions. Business leaders often donated a substantial proportion of their wealth to charities or other philanthropic enterprises (such as galleries, museums, hospitals, schools or colleges) and became famous by association with these projects.

Not all entrepreneurs behaved well in the past, but there was a general expectation that those running companies felt that they had an ethical responsibility to use their wealth for the benefit of society. This persists to some extent in the United States with some of the wealthiest individuals, such as Bill Gates and Warren Buffett, giving away billions of dollars to help the Third World and even moderately wealthy people giving to charitable causes as a matter of course. However, in other parts of the world the sense of social responsibility which used to come with wealth has diminished. Wealth is often made up of a portfolio of shares (often managed by stockbrokers or hedge-fund managers) which generates income but carries with it no liability. If people make a great deal of money from investing in a company they generally do not care too much about the moral consequences of business operations.

In practice, most of the shareholders in large companies are actually pension funds. Ordinary people invest a percentage of their salaries in return for a pension in old age. So the owners of a business are removed by a considerable distance from its actual operations – most people who have a pension do not even know in which companies their pension funds are invested. This raises a central issue: limited companies are treated as people from a legal point of view, but they are not people. The whole idea of moral accountability is, therefore, problematic. If the real owners of a business do not even know that they are the owners, if directors are judged on performance and profit is central, then where does moral responsibility lie?

The Wealth of Nations

The Wealth of Nations (1776) by **Adam Smith** (1723–90) is probably the most influential book on economics ever written. It set out the advantages of competition in driving down costs and advocated 'free trade'. It argued that if countries and businesses can trade freely (without taxes being imposed on imports and exports) then the 'invisible hand' of the market will increase efficiency as those companies able to produce goods and services at the lowest cost combined with good quality will prosper and inefficient companies will fail through 'market forces'. In many ways, *The Wealth of Nations* underpins capitalism, which has now been embraced in most countries. There are more billionaires in newly capitalist China than anywhere else.

Adam Smith did not consider *The Wealth of Nations* to be his most important work. His earlier book *The Theory of Moral Sentiments* set out the philosophical context within which he believed *The Wealth of Nations* should be understood. Smith was a pupil of the early utilitarian Francis Hutcheson (see page 81) in Glasgow and took from him a passion for liberty and reason and the belief that human beings have an innate moral sense built on sympathy for others, which we all have. Human beings, Smith argued, gain happiness from acting in a way which would impress an 'impartial observer'[3] and do not feel satisfied when they profit from behaviour of which they feel ashamed.

When the Chinese Premier visited the United Kingdom in February 2009, he was asked which book influenced him more than any other. His answer might be surprising, given that China has been widely criticized for buying into an extreme form of capitalism. Wen Jiabao said that he always carries *The Theory of Moral Sentiments* with him on his travels. He said, 'Adam Smith wrote that in a society if all the wealth is concentrated and owned by only a small number of people, it will not be stable.'[4] Perhaps, if more politicians and economists put their reading of *The Wealth of Nations* in context like this, the worst excesses of capitalism might be avoided, but this has rarely happened. Adam Smith also said in this book that those who run businesses are, or should be, motivated by altruism and acting as if before an independent observer of their conduct. Sadly, these ideas have been largely lost, and with them the idea of an ethical imperative in much of modern business. The introduction of limited companies has also contributed to the decline in any sense of individual moral responsibility for the way a business is conducted.

Although Adam Smith thought he was describing human motivation, he seems to have been mistaken. It is clear that most people do not seem to consider those outside their immediate circle, either because they do not think about the wider effects of their actions or because they simply do not care. Many people in business ignore the effects of their work on others and focus entirely on personal benefits and what they will facilitate in terms of lifestyle. Smith's insights still have great value, however. If people's actions were more widely known, if they were motivated

---

3 Compare with a similar idea in the philosophy of R. M. Hare or John Rawls.

4 http://adamsmithslostlegacy.blogspot.com/2009/02/premier-speaks-quoting-moral-sentiments.html, accessed 3 October 2011.

by altruism and if they did feel that their actions were being observed by an independent observer, then they might well modify their decision-making.

Ethical Criteria in Business

Peter Henriot SJ, who since 1990 has been director of the Jesuit Centre for Theological Reflection in Zambia, argues that at the heart of the ethical issue of globalization is the question of what the ethical criteria are by which globalization can be judged. In *Opting for the Poor: The Challenge for the Twenty-First Century*,[5] he argues that in practice there are competing criteria:

1 a neo-liberal economic ideology, which gives market operations and profit margins the major priority and consequently values globalization in terms of the individualism, competitiveness, consumerism and profits it produces;
2 an ideology which takes human dignity, rights and duties, promoted within a communitarian context, as its foundation and judges globalization in terms of community, solidarity, social sustainability and the common good.

Henriot argues that the neo-liberal ideology dominates, but he criticizes it for overlooking the fact that economic systems are made up of interactions between human beings and have the basic purpose of benefiting them. Business values need to be interrogated as to whether they are really benefiting humanity or simply making profits for the few.

Business Ethics in Practice

The core of business ethics is in the need to 'widen the circle of ethical concern' so that those who own, direct and manage

5 Center of Concern, 2004.

businesses feel accountable for the effects of the business on customers, suppliers, workers and the environment as well as being concerned with profitability. It is the neglect of a wider sense of ethical concern that is the major contributor to any lack of ethical concern in business today. 'Whistle-blowers' who are prepared to stand up against ethical wrongdoing and report this to more senior levels of management need encouragement and protection: too often the price of speaking out against moral wrongdoing is for the individual who does so to lose their job or to lose any hope of advancement, and where this occurs it is a reliable sign of an unethical business.

In spite of the priority given to financial success, there are individuals and businesses who do care about ethics in business. There are ways in which the issue of business ethics has been and is being addressed and some of these are considered below.

Co-operatives

Originating in the eighteenth century, the idea of a co-operative society was to use the bulk-buying power of consumers to obtain the best prices for them directly. Rather than individuals or companies making profits out of people's need to buy food, pay for funerals or insure their homes, by joining a co-operative people could share in the profits, both by paying lower prices and through dividends paid by the society to its members. A good example of an early co-operative is given in Elizabeth Gaskell's novel *North and South*, where mill-workers are encouraged to club together to buy food in bulk and so make savings.

Traditionally, building societies operated on this model (they are sometimes referred to as 'mutuals'), having no shareholders but rather distributing profits made on lending for mortgages directly to people who invested in them. Saving in a building society typically paid a lower rate of interest but was seen as a safe investment; societies were run by members for members and had an incentive only to lend to people who were sure to repay the loans.

In the UK, in the late 1980s, legislation was passed which encouraged building societies to 'demutualize' and become banks with shareholders. This was one factor which changed the climate in banking, leading to the Global Financial Crisis of 2008/09 – those who ran the newly privatized building societies became preoccupied with profit rather than the best interests of their savers and customers and many of the newly privatized companies went into liquidation or had to be taken over because greed had overcome prudence. The drive for profit can have many negative effects if it is allowed to dominate other factors.

Employee-Owned Businesses

Businesses such as the John Lewis Partnership, a British retail concern which turned over £8.73 billion in 2011/12, are owned by their employees who become 'partners' in the business. John Lewis is owned by its 81,000 employees and administered by a trust on their behalf. The trust uses profits to fund leisure activities, a generous pension scheme, life insurance and sabbaticals for partners. In addition, employees receive an annual bonus determined by profits that year; in 2010 this was 15 per cent of earnings.

John Lewis has been held up as a model for ethical business, being typically:

- more efficient: employees work harder and are happy to take lower salaries, when they are rewarded with the possibility of sharing in profits. Employees also stay in their jobs for longer, meaning that costs of training and carrying inexperienced staff are lower than in other businesses;
- more responsible: employees are shareholders (and typically have a large proportion of their wealth tied up in the business) and so are concerned to find out about what is going on and have a say in decision-making.

It is probably not a coincidence that John Lewis has long traded on its reputation for quality and value for money ('never knowingly undersold') and was a pioneer in offering organic and Fair Trade products and ethical investments.

Being run by partners and for partners gives John Lewis the incentive to make longer-term decisions. Employee-managers have a responsibility to make the maximum profit, but tend to interpret this in the short term. Most bonus schemes actually add to this tendency, giving employees an incentive to maximize profits in the current financial year without much concern for longer-term results, which will emerge after the bonus has been paid and possibly after the employee has moved on. Having a big stake in the business, and perhaps particularly having your pension depend upon its success, influences partner-managers' decision-making processes.

Fair Trade

Originating in the 1950s, the Fair Trade movement aimed to redistribute the benefits of business, ensuring that those who do most of the work receive most of the benefit thus addressing the inequality between the First and Third Worlds. The slogan 'Trade not Aid' gained recognition in 1968 when it was adopted by the United Nations Conference on Trade and Development. Today many development charities (such as Oxfam) operate Fair Trade schemes and the value of this business exceeds 5 billion dollars. Fair Trade relies on consumers making 'ethical' choices, choosing to pay a little more or buy a less expensively marketed product because of the values it represents.

Pressure from Consumers

Customers are a vital part of pressurizing a business to take ethical responsibilities more seriously. Nike was forced by customer pressure to stop their suppliers using child labour and is now a leading advocate of careful monitoring of the way suppliers behave. Similarly McDonald's now takes much more seriously the health content of its food and the ethical ways in which beef can be produced, because of pressure from customers. Body Shop led the world in producing cosmetics that were not tested on animals and made this a central plank of its marketing strategy. Apple has been pressurized by consumer groups because of the high suicide rates among workers at its Chinese suppliers and in 2012 moved to force suppliers to address the conditions of workers because of consumer pressure. There is a real sense in which pressure from customers can be one of the most effective ways of bringing about ethical change in business but this requires customers to know about the ethical abuses that sometimes take place so that they can respond.

Ethical Investments

Socially Responsible Investments (SRIs) are designed to consider the common good, rather than just profitability. Inspired by responsible investment practices encouraged by religious groups such as the Society of Friends (Quakers) and Methodists, SRIs promise not to invest in ethically questionable businesses including those which make money out of

- oil
- tobacco
- arms dealing and manufacturing
- gambling
- animal testing
- environmental pollution
- human rights abuses.[6]

---

6 A useful table of such investments, what they do and don't invest in, may be found at http://en.wikipedia.org/wiki/Ethical_investment.

Ethical investors choose to invest in SRIs because they wish to avoid investment in certain industries but this is a crude way of measuring ethical concern. Arms are needed for defensive purposes and to keep the peace; the world depends on oil for much of its energy needs; and some essential treatments, for instance for cancer, need to be tested on animals before being used on patients. Possibly the way a business is conducted is more important than simply the type of business. Nevertheless, SRI funds have been able to exert some pressure on businesses to address issues such as equality, labour relations, giving back to the community and increasing 'shareholder advocacy' (that is, shareholders being aware of business practices and having a say in them).

Islamic Finance

Islam has long had a commitment to ethical business practices.[7] Islamic finance has developed to be compliant with sharia law (based on the Qur'an and Hadith) and has been hailed, by the Vatican as well as by journalists and politicians, as a possible remedy for the abuse of ethical standards by financial institutions.[8] Sharia emphasizes justice and partnership and this translates into a ban on speculation (*gharar*) and the charging of interest (*riba*), though Muslim jurists differ on how these terms are interpreted and therefore on which financial instruments may or may not be Islamic. In practice, this means that Muslim banks and individuals cannot invest in companies which make money from tobacco, alcohol, drugs or gambling (this may mean not investing in companies which are over-borrowed or which invest money at interest) and they cannot charge interest (as such) on their loans.

---

7 http://www.islamic-finance.com/ is a useful site, listing books and articles relating to this field.

8 http://www.worldbulletin.net/index.php?aType=haberArchive&Article ID=37814.

Mortgages and business finance are typically arranged via a *sukuk*, an Islamic bond, which involves the setting up of a new entity in which the borrower and the lender(s) both have interests. As the borrower repays the debt, the ownership of the new entity gradually transfers from the lender(s) to them. The lender(s) have security, as they are partial owners of the business, property or other asset until the loan is repaid. Any increase in value is shared between the lender and the borrower.

For example, if Lucy, a single freelance journalist, borrows $100,000 to buy a house from a western bank, she will be charged interest on the loan of maybe 6 per cent. Over 25 years she will repay $193,290, being charged a fee or 'interest' of $93,290 for the privilege of borrowing the money and to offset the risk taken by the lender.[9] On the other hand, after Lucy repays the mortgage any increase in the property's value is Lucy's, and she may use this to upsize to a bigger property or to save for her retirement.

Given the housing market in recent years, people have expected that property will increase in value by more than it costs them to take out a mortgage. Property has been a very good investment. If someone bought an average house in Britain in 1987, it would have cost £43,000, but the same house would cost £162,000 in 2012,[10] meaning that the asset value has increased by more than 350 per cent – far in excess of the mortgage interest cost. The buyer takes most of the risk and enjoys most of the rewards and the bank makes a profit most of the time (it retains the deeds of the house until the last repayment is made and can usually repossess a house and sell it if somebody stops paying). Western banks have not, therefore, had much of an incentive to check whether people are being wise in taking on a mortgage (for example by going through Lucy's stated earnings carefully to ensure she could repay the loan and manage the interest) and this contributed substantially to the recent crisis.

---

9 Check the figures at http://math.about.com/library/blcompoundinter est.htm.

10 http://www.housepricecrash.co.uk/indices-nationwide-national-infla tion.php.

Under Islamic finance Lucy would have to arrange a *sukuk*, in which she would invest her deposit and the bank would invest the rest of the purchase price in a new company, which then buys the house. Every time Lucy makes a repayment (which is based on the current value of the company and, therefore, of her house), her share in the new company increases; when she owns the whole company, she owns the whole house. As the value of the house increases, so the value of her repayments increases, so the cost of buying the remaining share rises. If the value of the house decreases, then the value of the company decreases and she pays less to increase her share. Lucy and the bank share the risks of the investment and the rewards.

Although the possibility of making a large profit on property investment is smaller under Islamic finance, the bank has an interest in lending only to people who are responsible and the downside risks for the homeowner are considerably less. Sadly, however, some Islamic bankers have been unwilling to do business with women at all, let alone freelance journalists, which may present Lucy with a problem.

Islamic finance is big business. At the end of 2011, it was valued at $1.3 trillion[11] and Islamic financial instruments are increasingly sophisticated, being used for a wide variety of business transactions; nevertheless, Islamic finance still accounts for only around 1 per cent of the world's financial transactions while 20 per cent of the world's population is Muslim.

Triple Bottom-Line Accounting

Present accounting methods measure business success solely in financial terms. It is easy to ignore the effects of the business on people and on the environment as well as the ethical dimension of business generally. One of the major shortcomings in business ethics has been the inability to measure business performance in

---

11 http://www.economist.com/blogs/graphicdetail/2012/04/focus-2.

ways that are not just financial but which are also meaningful and consistent.

Triple bottom-line accounting grew out of **The Balanced Scorecard**, a business philosophy popularized by Robert Kaplan in the 1990s.[12] It began with Kelvin's principle that 'if you cannot measure it, you cannot improve it'. Kaplan reasoned that if you measure only financial performance, you can hope only for improvement in financial performance, but if you take a wider view and measure things from other perspectives, then you stand a chance of achieving broader goals. He recommended that businesses should consider their performance from different points of view: the customer's perspective, the company's internal perspective and that of innovation and improvement. Boardrooms embraced The Balanced Scorecard with enthusiasm as it enabled them to think longer-term and defend themselves against shareholders demanding short-term financial profits. Nevertheless, it did not explicitly deal with how businesses behave with respect to the broader community and the environment.

The phrase 'the triple bottom line' (TBL) was first coined in 1994 by John Elkington, the founder of a British consultancy called SustainAbility.[13] His argument was that company accounts should detail three separate bottom lines. In addition to the traditional, financial, profit and loss account, Elkington proposed a 'people account' (a measure of how socially responsible an organization has been) and a 'planet account' (a measure of how environmentally responsible it has been).

TBL was ratified by the UN in 2007 and is now the standard for measuring the 'full cost' of public projects and consequently it is used by some companies which claim to be socially responsible in one form or another. Supporters of TBL do not deny the importance of profit but they argue that profit cannot be considered

---

12 R. S. Kaplan and D. P. Norton, 'The Balanced Scorecard – Measures that Drive Performance', *Harvard Business Review* 70 (January–February 1992), pp. 71–9.

13 See John Elkington, *Cannibals with Forks: The Triple Bottom Line of 21st Century Business*, Bloomington, MN: Capstone, 1997.

in isolation from other factors. Yet, as Moses Pava has observed, 'one of the major limitations of the business ethics movement, to date, has been the inability to measure and track social and environmental performance in a meaningful, consistent, and comparable way'.[14] Utilitarianism is also criticized for trying to place a numerical value on complex effects and, like Utilitarianism, TBL suffers from being open to abuse, potentially justifying or covering-up shoddy behaviour.[15]

A good example of this is the tobacco company Brown and Williamson which, in 2003, claimed that it used TBL and that its practices could be judged successful on all three accounts, concluding that 'balancing responsibility to ensure the long-term sustainability of our company with our responsibilities as a good corporate citizen is not a dilemma'.[16] This, coming from a tobacco company, is highly implausible! TBL may be unduly influenced by perspective. It presumes a high level of transparency and that information about the effects of practices is both plentiful and accurate. In the real world businesses rarely operate in such an environment; the effects of business practices are often unknown even to the managers who authorize them, let alone to company accountants and directors, and in any case they may not become apparent until many years later.

Very few business leaders oppose TBL in principle although doubts about its implementation remain. Perhaps it is best to see that 'triple bottom line reporting is a metaphor to remind us that corporate performance is multi-dimensional',[17] rather than placing too much hope in its rigor and usefulness as a method of accounting.

---

14 See http://isites.harvard.edu/fs/docs/icb.topic732868.files/Supplemental per cent20Reading per cent20for per cent20Week per cent205/pava_2007_response_to_norman_macdonald_3BL.pdf p4.

15 An excellent, if controversial, critique of TBL may be found at http://isites.harvard.edu/fs/docs/icb.topic549945.files/Canadian per cent20Paper.pdf.

16 Quoted by Moses Pava in 'A Response to Getting to the Bottom of Triple Bottom Line', *Business Ethics Quarterly* 17:1 (2007), p. 105.

17 See note 14.

Conclusion

Perhaps Adam Smith was right and the key to business ethics lies in altruism combined with acting as if being observed by an impartial arbiter – it is interesting that none of the traditional ethical theories can easily be applied to the business environment. Persuading business leaders and others to take altruism seriously, however, is far from easy when society, friends, peers, the media and everyone else values financial success above everything. This may be partially because of an educational failure in schools which do not always communicate to young people the ethical responsibilities they should have when entering the workplace.

15

Environmental Ethics

Ethical concerns over the environment are not new. In the nine-teenth century, John Stuart Mill warned of 'a world from which solitude is extirpated' and in which 'every rood of land is brought under cultivation ... every flowery waste or pasture ploughed up, all quadrupeds or birds which are not domesticated for man's use exterminated as his rivals for food'.[1] He argued for the creation of National Parks, seeing that green spaces and natural beauty are essential to human wellbeing, and wrote:

> [I]f the earth must lose that great portion of its pleasantness which it owes to things that the unlimited increase of wealth and population would extirpate from it, for the mere purpose of enabling it to support a larger but not necessarily better or happier population, I sincerely hope, for the sake of posterity, that they will be content to be stationary, long before necessity compels them to it.[2]

The Use of Resources

The use of the world's resources is of fundamental ethical con-cern. Most resources are finite; we must decide how it is appro-priate to use them, when and for whose benefit. For example,

---

1 J. S. Mill, 'Principles of Political Economy' in *Collected Works Vol. III*, London: Routledge, 1965, p. 756.
2 Mill, 'Principles of Political Economy', p. 756.

during the industrial revolution huge amounts of wood, coal and iron ore were extracted from the British countryside and turned into products which have since been discarded. The scars on the landscape remain; woods and forests disappeared, green valleys were turned into industrial wastelands, rivers were polluted and the air turned to smog which turned the buildings black and killed wildlife. Huge cities sprang up to support industry, and people were drawn away from farms and traditional communities and housed in slums where disease was rife and social breakdown gradually took hold.

In 1842–44 Friedrich Engels, a close associate of Marx, observed conditions in Manchester and concluded that capitalist industrialization had actually reduced living standards and life expectancies for the poor. Engels argued that the people doing most of the work were clearly not benefiting – the benefit went to those who controlled the factories and the workers received almost nothing in return. Things have not really changed in many parts of the world. From China to Bangladesh industrialization brings with it social breakdown, disease, pollution and unrest. Profits make a few people very wealthy, usually a long way from the factories. Factory work might pay better than farming, but the increased cost of food and accommodation near factories more than offsets this. People who hope for a better life often end up as wage-slaves.

This, then, is an important question for environmental ethics to address. How should natural resources be used? How can they be managed sustainably and for the benefit of as many people as possible, particularly those whose lives will be affected by the changes brought about by resource-depletion? Obviously, environmental ethics and business ethics are closely related on this point.

Climate Change

The use of resources has, in more recent times, brought with it an even bigger concern. Scientific evidence in favour of climate change and global warming is overwhelming. The destruction of rainforests, the lungs of the planet, combined with CO_2 and 'greenhouse gas' emissions have led to depletion in the ozone layer and an increase in temperature around the world. Polar ice caps and glaciers are melting and sea levels are rising, extreme weather events are becoming more common and large areas of land are becoming unusable due to flooding or desertification.[3] The population continues to rise, and it seems inevitable that conflict will arise as competition for space and even basic resources such as water becomes fiercer. Some scientists believe that concerted action by individuals and governments could slow the rate of climate change and reduce its effects, though there is little consensus over how much can be achieved.

A second question for environmental ethics must therefore concern action to combat climate change. What should be done, by whom and when? Suggestions have varied:

- Educate ordinary people to 'reduce, reuse and recycle': to use the car less frequently, take holidays at home, insulate houses and become more energy-efficient. If education by itself doesn't work then use fiscal policy as a stick to persuade people!
- Tax carbon-emissions, waste produced and pollution incidents caused by businesses, thus encouraging them to 'clean up their acts'.
- Make regulations governing big business tougher and really hold managers to account for corporate manslaughter and causing environmental disasters.
- Get national governments to sign up to emission-reduction targets and threaten them with huge fines if they fail to de-

3 A good summary of the most popular arguments in favour of climate change is made in Al Gore's film *An Inconvenient Truth* (2006).

velop comprehensive and effective policies for reducing emissions.

- Organize countries to act together to enforce shared policies, worked out at international conferences such as Kyoto or Copenhagen. Accept creative, practical solutions to reducing emissions such as carbon-trading schemes whereby wealthy developed countries pay undeveloped countries not to industrialize.

In practice a combination of all of these measures will probably be needed to achieve any significant reduction in emissions, and this may well be too little too late.

Environmental Fatigue

Sadly, a lack of leadership on environmental issues has led to 'environmental fatigue' in some quarters with increasing scepticism of climate change, or at least the human ability to respond to it, a feature in many western countries. Reports of disagreements between scientists over the causes, scope and future of climate change have not helped.

In 2009 emails between scientists at the University of East Anglia were leaked to the press. In November of that year, the *Guardian* newspaper reported:

Climate change sceptics who have studied the emails allege they provide 'smoking gun' evidence that some of the climatologists colluded in manipulating data to support the widely held view that climate change is real, and is being largely caused by the actions of mankind.

The same year (according to Gallup), 41 per cent of Americans thought that claims about global warming were 'exaggerated'. In January 2010, only 28 per cent of Americans thought that dealing with global warming should be a top political priority, down from 38 per cent in 2007; and in February 2010 a Populus poll for the BBC showed that 25 per cent of British people said that global warming is not taking place. In this respect environmental ethics may link to media ethics.

Conservation

A third issue related to environmental ethics concerns the extent to which human beings have a moral responsibility to conserve animals and plants. This is a wide-ranging issue, relating to a number of discussions:

- Resource-depletion and climate change often lead to a loss of habitats which can lead to animal and plant species becoming threatened or extinct. Do animals and plants have any rights and is there any obligation on human beings to care for their interests?
- Industrialization and population-growth create pressure for food and water. This has led to an agricultural revolution, with intensive farming becoming integral to sustaining life. Selective breeding and, more recently, genetic modification creates new strains of animals and plants which (though they may bring many benefits to health and wealth) may threaten 'natural' species. Do human beings have an obligation to constrain such activity or to restrict the possibility of competition between GM and 'natural' strains?
- Do animals or plants have any moral status and is there an obligation to ensure that their interests are considered in any moral decision? For example, is the quality of life of farm-animals a necessary factor to consider in deciding how to farm?

Discussions relating to these matters and to environmental ethics are influenced by two different basic positions.

Shallow Ecology

This approach is anthropocentric, centred on human concerns, and is fostered by most versions of Natural Law, Utilitarianism and Kantian Ethics as well as by some versions of Christianity and Islam. The basic premise behind shallow ecology is that only human beings have moral status and therefore that moral decisions must only consider the interests of human beings. The only value given to animals, plants, habitats or even the world as a whole is instrumental, that is, in terms of the benefit they offer to people. Care of the environment is essentially a pragmatic affair; human beings need to look after the environment, because it is in their best interests to do so. It would only be wrong for any individual or group to act in ways which damage the environment if it could be shown to diminish the happiness of other human beings.

Shallow ecology does not necessarily lead to the exploitation of nature. Human dependence on the natural world is undeniable. Food, health, material wellbeing and personal fulfilment are all dependent on the biosphere. Enlightened human self-interest could provide strong arguments for action to preserve the environment but there would be few arguments to prevent the destruction of wildernesses or plant or animal species, providing that people did not suffer. Christian statements on the environment, such as that made in 1997 by the Roman Catholic Bishops of New Zealand, underline this point:

> Use of mineral, vegetable and animal resources cannot be divorced from respect for moral imperatives. The integrity of the ecosystem within which human life exists is vital to our very survival, to the well-being of future generations, and to respect for the work of God. Creation itself provides the primary source from which all life flows. Within creation all life forms are interconnected.

Peter Singer describes such a human-centred approach as 'speciest'. He notes how widespread it is and blames it on the

legacy of the Abrahamic religions which place human beings in a
different category from the rest of creation.

Deep Ecology

Deep ecology is a position traditionally taken by Indic religions,
which see all aspects of the world as interdependent and deny
the special status of human beings. For many Hindus and Sikhs,
people go through many lives, each influenced by choices made
in previous incarnations. Only some of these lives are human
and other forms of life may be far preferable to inhabit because
they pass more quickly and offer fewer possibilities for negative
choices. Jain monks take their belief in the value of all nature
so far as to be vegan, wear a mask against inhaling insects and
carry a broom to sweep ants away from being stepped on. Cows
are venerated in much of India because they represent the interdependence of nature: cows eat grass, produce milk and work
the land; their dung is fuel and fertilizer which helps grow more
grass. Cows are not killed or eaten – who would destroy a being
on which so much depends for the sake of steak and chips?

For some Indian thinkers, the western approach to environmental ethics is flawed because it fails to acknowledge the essential moral value of non-human beings and the planet as a whole.
Satish Kumar, an environmental activist who was once a Jain
monk,

> is in no doubt about the nature of the problem affecting hu-
> manity, that is, a lack of reverence and compassion for nature.
> This important element, once seen as crucial to the environ-
> mental debate, seems to have been left by the wayside in all
> the talk of emissions targets, carbon footprints and impending
> doom.[4]

---

4 http://www.guardian.co.uk/environment/ethicallivingblog/2008/jan/16/
whatpartdoesspiritualitypl.

Within the western tradition of moral philosophy the Norwegian utilitarian **Arne Naess** (1912–2009) is most associated with the development of deep ecology as an ethical position.[5] Naess argued that people should live simply, 'touch their earth lightly', seek to reduce the human population and accept that animals, plants and the environment as a whole have rights. Building on Mill's harm principle (that is, that actions should be allowed except where they cause harm to others), he suggested that a full human being recognizes their own place as part of a complex web of interdependence, which incorporates plants, animals and landscapes (particularly mountains, which Naess as an ex-mountaineer saw to be important) as well as other people. People should choose to act only in those ways that they know will cause minimal harm and choose to refrain from acting if the consequences of acting are negative or profoundly uncertain. Naess argued that Aristotle would have supported deep ecology as he saw the integrated unity of the whole planet, and every part of the planet, as contributing to the good of the whole. Deep ecology argues for a persuasive view of the world which sees human beings as part of the complex whole, sometimes referred to as 'Gaia' (the Greek goddess of the earth).[6]

The film *Avatar*[7] illustrates the difference between shallow and deep ecology effectively. Human beings came to the planet intent only on exploiting it for valuable minerals; they had no appreciation of the value of the planet as a whole. The indigenous people lived in harmony with the planet and valued it for itself. They regarded every part of the planet as sacred (there are many parallels with Australian aboriginal approaches). Comparisons can also be drawn between situations around the world and the basic concept behind the film. Perhaps this is why the film was initially banned in China because of the government's concern that indig-

---

5 See Arne Naess, *Ecology, Community and Lifestyle*, Cambridge: Cambridge University Press, 1989.

6 After James Lovelock.

7 James Cameron, 2009.

enous Chinese people might identify the central government with the exploitative humans in the film.

What may be significant today is that shallow and deep ecology seem to be coming together, seeing caring for the environment as a high priority regardless of its motivation.

Natural Law, Virtue Ethics and the Environment

Natural Law assumes that every species of animal and plant is good when it fulfils its nature. It is, of course, difficult for anything to be fulfilled when it is dead and therefore Natural Law would discourage killing even animals and plants unnecessarily, in a way that does not contribute to human survival. Recently this reasoning has been used by various Christian churches in making statements stressing the interconnectedness of things and the need for human beings to consider the whole impact of their actions if humanity is to flourish.

Roger Scruton (b. 1944) has argued that since human beings are the highest species on the planet, they fulfil their nature when they safeguard the environment and animals and do not simply use them for their own ends.[8] This is a form of Virtue Ethics and rests on a particular understanding of human nature. It could be counter-argued that human nature is not fulfilled by safeguarding the environment; a more conventional interpretation is that human beings are fulfilled when they survive and prosper and safeguarding the environment is not always compatible with this. Nevertheless, Scruton argues that the way a person treats an animal is important for the person's character. If killing an animal is enjoyed it makes a person callous, encourages vice and diminishes the person. In practical terms, Scruton might support a decision to erect a dam in order to produce cheap and clean electricity, even if the habitat of many animals will be destroyed,

---

8 Roger Scruton, *Green Philosophy: How to Think Seriously About the Planet*, New York: Atlantic, 2012.

providing that damage is minimized and it is done with a feeling of regret.

Christian Environmental Ethics

There is no single Christian view on environmental ethics. There is a tension between two opposed positions:

1 The first position sees the natural world as created for the benefit of human beings and, therefore, favours shallow ecology. This is reinforced by the creation story in Genesis (Genesis 1.26–29) with human beings having dominion or control over the natural world.
2 The second position sees human beings as custodians of God's creation. This is the more common Christian view today and is reinforced by figures like Francis of Assisi. The world is seen as God's creation and humans as having a responsibility to God for its preservation.

For Aquinas, God created the world and determined its purpose. The way human beings use the environment must glorify God. This is a theocentric and not anthropocentric view of creation. The problem is to work out which actions glorify God and which do not. What will be the criteria? From Genesis 1—3, Aquinas concludes that animals are not equal to humans, they are not made in 'the image of God'. Aquinas would reject inflicting unnecessary pain or suffering on animals but would consider that animals are there for use by human beings. He provides a good example of the position that Peter Singer rejects – namely that human beings are in a different order from the rest of creation.

Because there is no single Christian position on environmental ethics, much will depend on other assumptions that may be applied to the debate rather than an appeal to any single Christian view – although the idea of being responsible to God for human actions is one that Muslims, Christians and Jews would all share.

Confucianism and Environmental Ethics

Confucianism has had great influence in China, Korea, Japan, Vietnam and many surrounding countries. It is distinguished by its concern for the cultivation of human relations towards a harmonious society rather than one's relations with any transcendent or supernatural world. However, Confucianism is not purely humanistic; it is a philosophy which is concerned with harmony between heaven, earth and the human order. It is impossible to ignore the responsibilities both to the natural world (earth) and to the transcendent world (heaven) as these are part of the traditional Chinese trinity which are necessary for harmony. Relations between people and the natural world are therefore of intrinsic interest to those who profess Confucian ethics: human beings are embedded in a web of relationships that need to be properly maintained for harmony to be preserved and these relationship include the natural order.

Mary Tucker has described this as 'organic holism'. [9] She has written that:

> the universe is seen as unified, interconnected, and interpenetrating. Everything interacts and affects everything else, which is why the notion of microcosm and macrocosm is so essential to Chinese cosmology. The elaboration of the interconnectedness of reality can be seen in the correspondence of the five elements with seasons, directions, colours, and even virtues. This type of classification began in the third millennium BCE and resulted in texts such as the I Ching (Book of Changes). This sense of holism is characterized by the view that there is no Creator God behind the universe. Chinese thought is less concerned with theories of origin or with concepts of a personal

---

9 Mary Tucker, *Confucianism and Ecology: The Interrelation of Heaven, Earth and Humans*, Cambridge, MA: Harvard University Press, 1998.

God than with the perception of an on-going reality of a self-generating, interconnected universe described by Tu Weiming as a 'continuity of being'.[10]

She continues:

Western traditions tend to underscore the importance of the individual, highlighting her/his rights and freedoms. The Confucian tradition stresses the importance of cooperative group effort so that individual concerns are sublimated to a larger sense of the common good. In this view, self-interest and altruism for a common cause are not mutually exclusive, and responsibilities rather than rights are stressed. Such a communitarian value system may be indispensable for fostering sustainable communities.[11]

Actually applying this rather general insight to specific environmental problems is, as with most ethical theories, rather more difficult.

Utilitarianism

Peter Singer raises the question of how far our 'circle of ethical interest' should extend in utilitarian calculations. Should it be extended to all human beings? Should it include advanced animals? Should it include all animals? Should the interests of the wider environment be included? On Singer's analysis Preference Utilitarianism is the best way of approaching environmental ethics, but the preferences to be taken into account must not be confined to human beings. He can therefore be seen as supporting a version of deep ecology whereas, barring the Utilitarianism of Arne Naess, most twentieth-century versions of Utilitarianism as well

---

10 See Mary Evelyn Tucker, 'The Relevance of Chinese Neo-Confucianism for the Reverence of Nature', *Environmental History Review* 15:2, Special Issue: The Moral Sense of Nature (Summer 1991), pp. 55–69.

11 Tucker, 'The Relevance of Chinese Neo-Confucianism'.

as Classical Utilitarianism have been anthropocentric and supportive of shallow ecology.

Kantian Ethics

Kant is of limited use in relation to environmental issues except insofar as people are concerned – he did not address wider issues. The Principle of Universalization (see page 144ff.) would rule out any wanton destruction of animals, plants or landscapes and the Principle of Humanity would rule out selfish actions which directly damage the interests and wellbeing of other people. Scruton's Virtue Ethic is influenced by Kantian Ethics as well as by Natural Law and may demonstrate how the influence of Kant is used in environmental ethics today.

Conclusion

The contrast between deep and shallow ecology and the question as to how wide the circle of ethical concern should extend are the most important philosophical issues to be addressed in relation to environmental ethics. In a world with an increasing human population and an ever growing demand for resources it seems likely that shallow ecology will continue to dominate, although understanding of how human wellbeing depends on the wider environment is growing.

One significant insight generated by our recent environmental experience is how difficult it is to predict the consequences of our actions. Thomas Midgely Jr (1889–1944) has been described as 'the unluckiest inventor'. He invented both leaded petrol and CFCs and inadvertently caused many of the devastating environmental problems we face today. A decision which seems harmless today may go on to cause chaos and this presents moral philosophers, particularly but not exclusively consequentialists, with a real challenge.

16

The Ethics of Warfare

Lord Paddy Ashdown, a former British foreign secretary and high representative for the United Nations in Bosnia, is also a former member of Britain's elite Special Boat Service (SBS). His book *Swords and Ploughshares* reflects on war in the modern world and acknowledges that the basis for any discussion of justice in war goes back to Thomas Aquinas and Augustine of Hippo.[1]

Augustine (354–430) differentiated between two issues, when it is right to go to war (*jus ad bellum*), and what constitutes right conduct in war (*jus in bello*).

Jus ad Bellum

Augustine set out two major criteria:

1 The war has to be authorized by a legitimate authority. Augustine was writing shortly after the Roman Empire had become Christian. The emperor's authority was absolute; he had been anointed by God. Through history Christian kings, queens and emperors have claimed a 'divine right' to rule – and part of this is the ability to declare a 'just war'.

---

1 Paddy Ashdown, *Swords and Ploughshares: Bringing Peace in the Twenty-First Century*, London: Weidenfeld & Nicholson, 2007. http://www.just wartheory.com/ is a useful resource, bringing together a short introduction to the history and principles of JWT with recent articles and book-reviews on related topics.

2 There must be a just cause in going to war. War should aim to restore justice and peace.

Both of these criteria are problematic in the modern world.

Thomas Aquinas (1225–74) developed Augustine's thinking, perhaps drawing on the ideas of contemporary Christian and Muslim scholars and on the recent experience of the Crusades. Aquinas' theory formed the basis for Catholic thinking on Just War. In 1993, the Catholic Bishops in the United States set out six principles which should govern when to go to war and these are all based on the approach of Thomas Aquinas. They may be regarded as representative of Just War thinking today.

1 There has to be a legitimate authority.
2 There has to be a just cause.
3 There has to be comparative justice: the claims of the party that goes to war must significantly outweigh any claims to justice by the other party.
4 There has to be a significant reason and a right intention in going to war – there cannot be some hidden agenda.
5 There has to be proportionality between the benefits to be achieved by war and the suffering that war will cause.
6 There must be a reasonable probability of success.
7 War must be a last resort.

All these principles are controversial, and they need to be evaluated in turn.

Legitimate Authority

Many people feel that the only legitimate authority in the modern world should be the United Nations; the governments of nation states rarely have an undisputed mandate. However, within the UN five permanent members of the Security Council hold a veto. If any one of these five – China, Russia, the USA, France or Britain – vote 'no' to a resolution supporting the justice of a war then it cannot pass. For example, in the case of Kosovo the UN could not support NATO action against Serbia as just because of threatened vetoes by Russia and China. In the case of Libya, the UN resolution was watered down because of Russian and Chinese pressure so that international forces were restricted to providing air-cover, which arguably prolonged the conflict. Increasingly, the UN is seen as the only legitimate authority but the weaknesses of the UN need to be recognized.

Just Cause

Justice is hard to define and evaluate. Arguably the only just cause for war is in response to aggression. This is too simple, however. What is aggression? Invasion is not the only form of provocation. One country may undermine another by inciting a minority to rebel, by appropriating its resources or by exerting economic pressure. It is not easy to decide which, if any, of these are acts of aggression.

Both sides in a conflict will tend to see their own position as the one that is just; judgements are therefore likely to be subjective. Merely because the media of a country and the national government proclaim that a country's position is 'just' does not mean that it is. Evaluating the justice of both sides of a dispute is never easy but unless it is possible to make a dispassionate assessment, then any proposed war cannot be regarded as just.

This principle was developed most clearly in the work of **Francisco de Vitoria** (c. 1492–1546) who declared that 'difference of religion is not a cause for war'.[2] Interestingly, he also condemned the use of force by Spanish armies to take away the sovereign territory of rulers in South America (such as the Incas).

---

2 Quoted in John Macquarrie and James Childress, *A New Dictionary of Christian Ethics*, London: SCM Press, 1966, p. 328.

Comparative Justice

It is also difficult to judge where the balance of justice lies. This is one reason why the role of the UN is so important, but it is also why questions over the objectivity of UN decisions are so problematic: global politics often plays a major part in the UN decision-making process and this is not always conducive to justice.

Right Intention

Aquinas' criterion of 'right intention'[3] has often not been given the attention it deserves. There must be a genuinely significant reason for going to war. Aquinas opened the door for individuals to challenge the state's decision to go to war if they considered the war was being conducted for a base motive. It would be easy to assume that if there is a just cause there must be a right intention, but sometimes a government may have a 'hidden agenda' which is never disclosed to the public and will loudly proclaim the justice of its cause when its real motives are rather different.

There have been suggestions that this applied in the case of the British and United States intervention in Iraq. The reasons given for the war (the claimed existence of weapons of mass destruction) appeared to support the justice of the conflict but many commentators felt that the real intention behind the war was other than what was being proclaimed (the need for a revenge attack after the 'twin towers' attack in New York and the wish to gain access to Iraqi oil). Paskins and Dockrill wrote:

[W]ars fought in defence of national honour must be viewed with suspicion as if one weighs the value of human beings against national honour, the former should always have priority. It is always important to maintain a clear view of one's own and one's enemies' humanity.[4]

---

3 Gratian (in his 'Decretum') as well as Peter of Paris also emphasized 'right intention'.

4 Barrie Paskins and Michael L. Dockrill, *The Ethics of War*, London: Duckworth, 1979.

'Right intention' is one of the most problematic criteria as it is so difficult for most people to have anything approaching the full picture of a potential conflict which might enable them to assess the real intentions of the parties. Nevertheless it is an important part of the jigsaw of Just War thinking.

Proportionality

War is an evil. In some cases it may be the lesser of two evils, however. John Stuart Mill once wrote:

> I cannot join cause with those who cry 'Peace, Peace!'... War, in a good cause, is not the greatest evil a nation can suffer. War is an ugly thing, but not the ugliest of things: the decayed and degraded state of moral and patriotic feeling which think nothing is worth a war is worse.[5]

The principle of proportionality recognizes the enormous suffering and damage caused and tries to balance it against the aims and achievements of a war. Without consideration of proportionality the human cost of war may be ignored. Casualties and suffering on all sides of a war must be taken into account before it is embarked on. It is easy for countries to be biased in their assessment of a war, tending to ignore suffering and damage inflicted on opponents, but this is a moral failure.

It is significant to recognize that proportionality is rejected by the Catholic Church when it comes to issues such as sexual and personal morality but held to be central in the ethics of warfare. There seems to be an inconsistency here.

---

5 Quoted in Richard Reeves, *John Stuart Mill: Victorian Firebrand*, New York: Atlantic, 2007, p. 337.

Probability of Success

This may seem a surprising factor yet, as Aquinas recognized, it is important. To go to war when there is little or no chance of success means inflicting great suffering for no likely benefit and cannot, therefore, be justified.[6] The principle does have weaknesses. It can lead to an arms race, with countries building up armaments in order to ensure a reasonable chance of success in any forthcoming conflict. At best this criterion may avoid a needless loss of life but in reality few countries are likely to lie down and accept defeat if it seems likely that their opponent will win, even if they feel they are the victim of unjust aggression. Churchill said 'We will fight them on the beaches,' not 'They will probably win so let's cut our losses and negotiate.' Was he unreasonable? Probably! But this did not make the war against Nazism unjust.

Last Resort

This is possibly the most important of all the criteria. It is important to recognize that there are many alternatives available before military means are adopted, including:

1 **UN arbitration** (or that of a regional body such as the African Union, Association of Southeast Asian Nations (ASEAN) or Arab League), possibly followed up by a resolution and/or peace-plan.
2 **Sanctions,** including the suspension of diplomatic, sporting or economic relationships. These measures can make it impossible for the government of a country to function and this can apply immense pressure without the need for military intervention (though they can hurt the poor even more than they hurt the government). Recently 'smart sanctions' have been applied which freeze the financial assets of key figures of an oppressive regime and this can be highly effective.

---

6 This principle originated most clearly in the work of Francisco de Vitoria in the early sixteenth century.

3 **The International Criminal Court,** which may issue an arrest warrant for individuals held responsible for crimes against international law. Most countries round the world recognize the ICC (this does not include North Korea, Sudan, Somalia and the USA). If the ICC issues an arrest warrant for a general or even the leader of a nation, as it recently did for Charles Taylor, the former president of Liberia,[7] it makes it hard for them to travel and undermines their political position. The prospect of a very long prison term for tyrants can be a real inducement for them to cease their aggressive behaviour. Sometimes even the threat of such action can be enough to make a tyrant abdicate and seek asylum a long way away.

4 **A no fly zone** to prevent an aggressor from carrying out surveillance or attacking people on the ground, though few countries have the capacity to enforce one.

All these options need to be considered and/or exhausted before war is initiated and it is the task of diplomacy to seek peace, being prepared to pressurize an aggressive regime in some or all of these ways.

Human Rights

There is one final issue which has surfaced in recent years and which traditional writers on just war thinking have not addressed. This is whether it is ever permissible to intervene in the internal affairs of a sovereign country because of human rights abuses within the country.

The traditional answer to this is 'no' – the United Nations' charter says it is never right to intervene in the internal affairs of a sovereign state. However, this principle has recently been challenged by events in Kosovo, Rwanda, Libya, Syria and elsewhere; increasingly the world community, through the United Nations,

---

7 See http://theliberiantimes.com/?p=8051, accessed 26 April 2012.

is willing to take action if there are clear and sustained abuses of human rights within a country.

This is highly significant. In the past, as Augustine argued, the 'legitimate authority' had to be the nation state. This is now being challenged: the ultimate authority is increasingly seen to be the United Nations and if a particular government is guilty of clear, severe and prolonged violations of human rights, if the effects of these human rights abuses are likely to spread beyond the country's borders and if significant loss of life is likely, then modern Just War thinking allows for the possibility of intervention either through one or more of the five methods set out above or, ultimately, through the exercise of armed force. This is the single greatest development in thinking about the justice of warfare in modern times. The nation state is no longer necessarily supreme – although it must be recognized that the most powerful nations on earth (particularly the United States, China and Russia) can exercise a veto to prevent international action against themselves or their interests and this must be recognized as lessening the sense in which the United Nations can be regarded as the ultimate authority.

Some countries have argued for the right to a 'pre-emptive strike' – in other words for the right to take military action to stop what they perceive as a possible threat from another country that may emerge in the future (the USA and UK argued this when they invaded Iraq and Israel has argued it to justify an attack on Iran). There is no basis in international law for such a right – war cannot be undertaken to stop what might happen in the future.

Jus in Bello

There have been various attempts to rule out certain weapons, ranging from crossbows to chemical weapons, biological agents to nuclear bombs, on the grounds that they are inherently unjust, usually because they do not discriminate between combatants and non-combatants.

In 1054, at the Council of Narbonne, the Church sought to lay down certain days on which fighting could not take place. In 1139, the Second Lateran Council banned crossbows, bows and arrows and siege machines as unethical: however, these restrictions only applied to warfare between Christians; between Christians and Muslims there were no restrictions. These attempts to legislate for the means of war had limited success.

Today the **Geneva Convention** (which has been signed by almost every country in the world) lays down certain rules for how wars should be conducted and how prisoners should be treated. Other international treaties have sought to ban certain weapons, for instance landmines, as these fail to discriminate.

Augustine argued that the means used to fight a war must take into account the suffering likely to be caused and must be proportional to the end to be achieved, and that there must be a clear separation between combatants and non-combatants. Augustine's principles of proportionality in war and protection of the innocent are still of central importance, though they have become more difficult to apply in recent years. Arguably opting for 'shock and awe' through using overwhelming force to quell an enemy shortens the conflict and saves lives; however, the principle of proportionality needs to be invoked and questions asked as to whether the casualties caused by the use of overwhelming force can be outweighed by the lives saved as a result of the war being shortened.

In the 2003 Iraq conflict, disproportionate means were used to overwhelm the Iraqi forces, but the result was a long-term insurgency which claimed the lives of hundreds of thousands of Iraqis. No real attempt was made even to count how many Iraqis died, let alone to record injuries, though every single allied death was recorded on national news and afforded ceremonial repatriation ceremonies.[8]

---

8 Watch http://video.pbs.org/video/1082076175, an Emmy award-winning documentary which explores the reality of the 'rules of engagement'. There is also a quiz which you can take to test your understanding of *jus in bello*.

Everyone would agree that war should target 'the guilty' and protect 'innocents', but the line between combatants and non-combatants is not easy to draw. Combatants may well be conscripted and may be punished if they do not fight (they may even be child soldiers) while some insurgents dress as women and primary school teachers sometimes strap explosives to themselves in order to kill shoppers. Women often take part in fighting and are always a crucial part of supporting the war effort.

Hugo Grotius (1583–1645) maintained that if State A is just in fighting against State B, then all those in State A are guiltless and all those in State B are guilty. However, this is far too simplistic. Wars are waged by a small minority in power and there can be no assumption of meaningful consent (that is, to the detailed means by which a war is fought) by a whole population. For example, it is true that Hitler was democratically elected, but that did not mean that the individual citizens of Dresden were complicit in the Blitz or Final Solution.

Richard Holmes (1946–2011) divided people into categories, dependent on their degree of involvement in a war:

1 initiators of wrongdoing – the government leaders;
2 agents of wrongdoing – military commanders and combatants;
3 contributors to war efforts (by means of armament manufacture, military research, propaganda and the like);
4 tacit approvers of the war;
5 those who neither contribute to nor support the war such as children and the insane.

On this basis, munitions workers or civilians driving trains loaded with military supplies would be proper targets, but this might ignore the fact that, in war, many people are forced to contribute to the war effort who do not approve of it. Tens of thousands of Jews were forced to manufacture armaments for the Third Reich and nobody would suggest that they voted Nazi. They contributed to the war effort but were also innocent.

Deciding on legitimate targets is not straightforward and the issue is further complicated by the likelihood of causing 'collateral damage'. For example, air strikes against factories are likely to damage nearby houses and kill or injure people inside.

The Principle of Double Effect

The Principle of Double Effect is often used to determine the justice of such actions in war. If the military target is significant, relatively certain to be destroyed, and efforts are taken to distinguish between combatants and non-combatants and reduce the probability of collateral damage (such as by timing the raid so that people are likely to be at work or school), then, it is argued, the military action is justified even if innocent civilians die as a side-effect provided there was no reasonable alternative.

Two examples of the possible abuse of the Principle of Double Effect in war are as follows.

When the United States was at war with the Vietcong in Vietnam, it would spray napalm (burning petroleum jelly) across villages which would literally vaporize all those living there. Their argument was that Vietcong soldiers were sheltering in the villages and that the local population often aided the Vietcong so the killing of innocent people in the villages (including children and the elderly) was justified as this was collateral damage. This is a misapplication of the principle as no attempt was made to discriminate between combatants and non-combatants or to reduce collateral damage.

A more recent example is the use of depleted uranium (DU) in Iraq. DU is used in the manufacture of shells, enabling them to pierce armour and so destroy opposing tanks. However, when these shells explode they leave behind radioactive dust which (it is alleged) contaminates the ground and causes cancer and the most appalling birth defects for several generations. DU seems to offend both the Principle of Proportionality and the Principle of Discrimination and cannot be justified by Double Effect. Since conventional armour-piercing shells would penetrate the armour of almost all Iraqi tanks, there was no compelling reason to use depleted uranium shells.

Anthony Kenny (b. 1931) argues that 'wars may be waged not in order to destroy an enemy society but to force the enemy to desist from the wrong in which he is engaged or about to engage'.[9] This is important because the idea of not 'destroying society' takes the discrimination clause much further than not killing 'innocents'; it may involve not bombing infrastructure unless there are proportionate reasons to do so. After the First World War, German society was systematically dismantled. Factories were stripped of equipment and rails torn out of the ground and sent to be melted for scrap. This led to the economic destitution of Weimar Germany, which in turn fostered the rise of National Socialism. After the Second World War, the allies were careful not to make the same mistake. American loans actually enabled Germany to rebuild faster than England, but they also prevented extremists from taking over a chaotic country.

Nuclear Weapons and Weapons of Mass Destruction

The USA used nuclear bombs against Hiroshima and Nagasaki in 1945 and this was credited with bringing the war in Asia to a swift and relatively bloodless conclusion – at the cost of about 200,000 lives, many of them women and children.[10] Some people have argued that nuclear weapons have brought peace to the world; the threat that they pose, particularly after the arms race and the policy of mutually assured destruction (MAD), being the most powerful deterrent to war available and ensuring that few nations can claim to have 'a reasonable expectation of success' in war, given its likely consequences for the world as a whole. Others label nuclear weapons evil, saying that their very existence is

9 Anthony Kenny, in Nigel Blake and Kay Pole (eds), *Objections to Nuclear Defence: Philosophers on Deterrence*, London: Routledge, 1984, p. 15.

10 http://www.atomicarchive.com/Docs/MED/med_chp10.shtml, accessed 20 April 2012.

unjust and their use could never be part of Just War or justified by the Principles of Proportionality, Discrimination or Double Effect.

Weapons of mass destruction add another level to the discussion. These chemical, biological or 'dirty' weapons are non-discriminatory but capable of being targeted more precisely. For example, current research will probably yield 'ethnic bio-weapons' – biological weapons capable of targeting people of a particular race.[11] If (and only if) one holds that all members of an enemy state are 'guilty', then using such a weapon may be preferable to using nuclear weapons; it would leave infrastructure intact and would not pollute the earth – although it would fail to discriminate and, therefore, could be ethically unacceptable on this ground alone. Another example, highlighted by the Red Cross in 2011, is 'cyber-warfare', which has the potential to bring down networks, destroying civilian air-traffic control capacities along with military communication.[12] Just War theory must stay abreast of such developments and consider whether the use of such powerful and indiscriminate weapons could ever be justified within war.

Situation Ethics

Joseph Fletcher encouraged people to reflect on such questions in order to clarify their moral thinking. In *Situation Ethics: The New Morality*, he describes the following dilemma:

When the atomic bomb was dropped on Hiroshima, the plane crew were silent. Captain Lewis uttered six words, 'My God, what have we done?' Three days later another one fell on Nagasaki. About 152,000 were killed, many times more were

11 http://www.icrc.org/eng/resources/documents/misc/gas-protocol-100605.htm, accessed 20 April 2012.

12 http://www.icrc.org/eng/resources/documents/statement/united-nations-weapons-statement-2011-10-11.htm, accessed 20 April 2012.

wounded and burned, to die later. The next day Japan sued for peace. When deciding whether to use 'the most terrible weapon ever known' the US President appointed an Interim Committee made up of distinguished and responsible people in the government. Most but not all of its military advisors favoured using it. Top-level scientists said they could find no acceptable alternative to using it, but they were opposed by equally able scientists. After lengthy discussions, the committee decided that the lives saved by ending the war swiftly by using this weapon outweighed the lives destroyed by using it and thought that it was the best course of action.[13]

Fletcher also addressed the particular question of espionage in war:

I was reading *Biblical Faith and Social Ethics* (Clinton Gardner's book) on a shuttle plane to New York. Next to me sat a young woman of about twenty-eight or so, attractive and well turned out in expensive clothes of good taste. She showed some interest in my book, and I asked if she'd like to look at it. 'No', she said, 'I'd rather talk.' What about? 'Me.' I knew this meant good-bye to the reading. 'I have a problem I'm confused about. You might help me to decide,' she explained … There was a war going on that her government believed could be stopped by some clever use of espionage and blackmail. However, this meant she had to seduce and sleep with an enemy spy in order to lure him into blackmail. Now this went against her morals, but if it brought the war to an end, saving thousands of lives, would it be worth breaking those standards?[14]

It is worth considering these scenarios and asking whether there are any rules or principles which stand up to such tests, or whether, given the real people in the situation, as Fletcher puts it

13 Joseph F. Fletcher, *Situation Ethics: The New Morality*, London: SCM Press, 1966, p. 167.

14 Fletcher, *Situation Ethics*, p. 163.

'sometimes you have to put your principles on one side and do the right thing'. Natural Law would reject the woman's suggested course of action whereas Proportionalism might well sanction it and Utilitarianism almost certainly would do so.

Kant and War

Thomas Orend (b. 1970) in *War and International Justice: A Kantian Perspective*[15] explores what Kant added to the debate over justice in war. He notes that there is little agreement on this issue; opinions range from seeing Kant as 'a harbinger of world government' to seeing him as a hypocrite, naïvely optimistic but willing to sacrifice his principles at the same time.[16]

It is important to realize that Kant saw his political philosophy (which included consideration of justice, punishment and war) as building on his moral philosophy, but as designed to operate in the real world. In his essay 'On the Common Saying: That May be Correct in Theory, but It Is of No Use in Practice', he explained that pragmatism in government is not enough; states must pursue what is right so far as is possible, though they cannot act as individuals seek to act.[17]

Kant's moral philosophy suggests that coercing another person would always be wrong, that people should 'act externally in such a way that the free use of your will is compatible with the freedom of everyone according to a universal law',[18] thus respecting liberty, which is the cornerstone of Kantian Ethics. Never-

---

15 Thomas Orend, *War and International Justice: A Kantian* Perspective, Toronto: Wilfrid Laurier University Press, 2000.

16 Orend, *War and International Justice*, p. 16.

17 Most of Kant's political philosophy may be found in the first part of *The Metaphysics of Morals*, once published separately as 'The Doctrine of Right' (1797), though Kant added to this in the famous essays *Towards Perpetual Peace* and 'An Answer to the Question: What is Enlightenment?'

18 Immanuel Kant, *The Metaphysics of Morals*, in *The Cambridge Edition of the Works of Immanuel Kant*, trans. and ed. Paul Guyer and Allen W. Wood, Cambridge: Cambridge University Press, 1999, 6:231

theless the Universal Principle of Justice (*Recht*) acknowledges that there is a difference between what an individual may do and what a state may do to protect individual members. He sees the need for the state to have positive laws, restricting some freedoms in order to protect individual liberty[19] and even to coerce people who break them.[20] For example, he is in favour of capital punishment for murderers.

Kant's theory begins by trying to limit the conditions under which nations may ever justly declare war on other nations.

1 Rulers should not have the power to declare war without authorization from the people; if they do so, they would use the people as a means to their own end.[21]
2 War should aim to 'establish a condition more closely approaching a rightful condition',[22] in which states could move beyond their instinctive state of conflict towards a federation or 'league of nations', which recognizes their fundamental value and equality and would seek to make universal decisions.[23] The ideal arrangement would be a 'world republic',[24] though this is a far-off goal or idea.

In *Towards Perpetual Peace*, Kant listed 'six preliminary articles' to reduce the likelihood of war,[25] its duration and recurrence:

1 no temporary peace treaties to mask planning for future wars;
2 no annexation of one state by another;
3 no professional armies;
4 no authorization of national debt to pay for wars;

---

19 Kant, *Works*, 6:231.
20 Kant, *Works*, 6:256, 27:1390–1.
21 Kant, *Works*, 6:345–6.
22 Kant, *Works*, 6:344.
23 Kant, *Works*, 6:351ff.
24 Kant, *Works*, 8:357.
25 Kant, *Works*, 8:343–7.

5 no interference in the internal affairs of another state;
6 no acts in war which breed mistrust and make peace impossible.

The preliminary articles are all negative, so Kant also offers 'three definitive articles':

1 Every state shall have a republican civil constitution,[26] so that the people who decide whether there will be a war are the same people who would pay the price for the war and their self-interest will provide a constraint on war-mongering.
2 Each state shall participate in a union, league or federation of states,[27] giving them a forum to arbitrate disputes peacefully and rationally.
3 There should be a cosmopolitan right of universal hospitality.[28] No state should be allowed to deny foreign citizens a right to travel in its land or to prevent its citizens from entering into links with other peoples or establishing trade with them.

Within the new *league of nations* people should be able to regard themselves as 'citizens of the world',[29] welcome and at home wherever they are, and their rights should be respected.

Kant and Human Rights

Kant believed that each human being has an inalienable right to freedom, from which flows rights to equality before the law, equality of opportunity and the ownership of property. Like Mill, Kant argued that it would be wrong for the state to become

---

26 Kant, *Works*, 8:348.
27 Kant, *Works*, 8:354.
28 Kant, *Works*, 8:357.
29 Kant, *Works*, 8:349.

too unwieldy and prescribe the means by which people exercise their liberty, such as by providing schools and detailing the curricula. Rather, the state must recognize human rights and develop a framework in which people are free to develop autonomously.[30] Kant was the father of what Isaiah Berlin called 'negative' approaches to human rights, and would have supported international intervention to secure the rights of oppressed peoples – though he was reluctant to approve of interference in the internal affairs of one state by another. Kant was hopeful that the French Revolution would result in a patriotic state of free, equal individuals.

Kant's ideas on war, a 'league of nations' and human rights are idealistic and he was obviously ahead of his time in proposing them. Nevertheless, they have been influential and certainly shaped thinking in international politics during the twentieth century.

Kant in and after War

Kant has little to say about *jus in bello*, the means by which a just war may be fought. Although his approach to war was born out of realism, in practice it is difficult to reconcile his theory with his broader ethic. How could he argue that Sergeant A killing Privates B, C and D in order to secure a military target would be 'just' or that Gunner E shelling a village to flush out insurgents would be 'unjust' when the Practical Imperative strictly forbids anyone to use another person as a means to another end? It is perhaps strange that Kant did not give more weighty consideration to pacifism.

Kant does introduce a new principle of '*jus post bellum*' which encourages people to consider how peace must be restored after conflict, and this Orend regards as one of the most distinctive contributions he made to the modern discussion of justice in

---

30 This argument is in *Towards Perpetual Peace*.

THE ETHICS OF WARFARE

war.[31] Kant's ideas on this point are not developed in detail, but have provided a starting point for Orend and others to develop a new branch of Just War theory in recent years.

Jus Post Bellum

Orend suggests that part of Just War thinking must be considering how to end conflicts so that the seeds of future conflict are not sown. In the light of Iraq, Afghanistan or Libya it is clear why such consideration might be thought necessary in the planning stages of conflicts! Orend suggests the following five points:

1 **Just cause for termination**: Has the objective been achieved *or* is the objective now too costly or impossible to achieve? Is the aggressor willing to negotiate, apologize, submit to judgement by the ICC or similar?
2 **Right intention**: The victor state must also submit to judgement if necessary; truth is necessary to make reconciliation after a conflict possible. Sometimes punishment of war-crimes may not be appropriate, but acknowledging that they occurred is vital.
3 **Authoritative declaration**: The terms of peace must be brokered, accepted and announced publicly by a legitimate authority.
4 **Discrimination**: Punishment must be limited to those directly responsible for the conflict; revenge on civilians etc. is not allowed.
5 **Proportionality**: Peace-terms must be proportional to the original offence and the aim must always be to rehabilitate the defeated country.[32]

---

31 http://www.carnegiecouncil.org/media/277_orend.pdf, accessed 28 April 2012.
32 See note 31.

Conclusion

Having its roots in Natural Law, Just War thinking is acceptable to many people, from Catholics to Confucians, as a framework for decision-making and has certain rational appeal. Unlike other applications of Natural Law it is willing to be proportionate and weigh principles in the light of the situation and outcomes. In this way Just War thinking is more acceptable to utilitarians and situationists than other applications of Natural Law. Obviously the application to real situations is a matter of interpretation and debate, yet Just War theory offers useful criteria to shape discussions about highly complex and controversial situations.

CONCLUSION

Ethics Matters

17

Freedom and Conscience

After considering practical questions arising from issues as diverse as contraception and conservation in Part 3, it is clear that none of the normative systems discussed in Part 2 offers clear guidance on how to respond to complex situations. How we make decisions may be informed by insights generated by moral philosophers but, at the end of the day, most people feel that it is their conscience which is most significant in directing their actions.

Nevertheless, what 'conscience' really means and what it may or may not justify is yet another matter for controversy.

Conscience

As Fisher observes:

> the Old Testament has no word for 'conscience', but it does speak of the true heart (lêb) that interiorizes the divine law ... Some Old Testament figures experience God calling them to live his will or Law; at other times they experience him probing or judging their hearts. The shame of sinful Adam and Eve and the repeated remorse of Israel are amongst many Biblical examples of what was later called a retrospective judgment of conscience ... Jesus built on the idea of the right or pure or single heart that allows a man to judge justly and act authentically.[1]

---

1 Anthony Fisher OP, 'Conscience in Ethics and the Contemporary Crisis of Authority', in Elio Sgreccia and Jean Laffitte (eds), *Christian Conscience in*

The first translators of the **Hebrew Bible** introduced the Greek idea of conscience, συνείδησις or *synderesis* into Jewish thought in the third century BC. At that time the word suggested the human faculty of right decision-making; the ability to recognize natural laws and choose to follow them appropriately, possessed by those with *phronesis* (practical wisdom). The translators used the word *synderesis* in both the following passages.

- Job 27.5–6: 'Until I die I will not put away my integrity from me. I hold fast my righteousness, and will not let it go; my heart does not reproach me for any of my days.' (ESV)
- Wisdom 17.11–14: 'For wickedness is a cowardly thing, condemned by its own testimony, distressed by conscience, it has always exaggerated the difficulties. For fear is nothing but a giving up of the help that comes from reason, and hope, defeated by this inward weakness, prefers ignorance of what causes the torment.' (RSV)

Fisher notes, 'For Paul conscience is not some special faculty different from the rest of human thinking and choosing, nor is it some secret wisdom given only to a few.' For Paul conscience is the rational ability to understand what the law, truth, demands of us – which means that we do not need revelation to live a basically good life. Paul used the word *synderesis* some thirty times in his letters, and the word *kardia* (heart) even more often, which seems to have meant much the same thing. In no sense does Paul see conscience as a strange voice in the head or something which would justify individual acts which go against generally accepted moral laws.

Augustine of Hippo wrote that 'human beings see the moral rules written in the book of light which is called Truth from which all laws are copied'.[2] Conscience is our ability to put on 'the mind of Christ', an ability fostered and refined by the Church

---

Support of the Right to Life, Vatican City: Libreria Editrice Vaticana, 2008, pp. 37–70.

2 Augustine, *De Trinitate*, 14, 15, 21.

which counteracts the tendency for human beings to be weak-minded and in error since the Fall. The Catholic Church understood conscience in this sense in documents such as *Gaudium et spes*, which taught that following conscience must be primary, that following orders is no excuse for suppressing it and that coercion in religion or society is wrong.

It was this sort of conscience that **Joseph Ratzinger** (b. 1927), now **Pope Benedict XVI**, referred to in *On Conscience*,[3] two essays in which he argued that it must be our primary guide. **Cardinal John Henry Newman** (1801–90) famously wrote that he would drink to 'conscience first, and to the Pope afterwards', but, according to Ratzinger, he did not mean that the two were or are ever in opposition. Rather, for Newman the papacy (and the Catholic Church) is based on and guarantees conscience, the rational exercise of freedom. For Newman conscience represented the sense of personal responsibility human beings have to God. Human beings feel ashamed when they do some things and, by extension, this means that there must be some being or person before whom human beings are ashamed and the faculty of conscience points to the existence of God.

Ratzinger agrees, writing that conscience should appear 'as a window that makes it possible for man to see the Truth that is common to us all',[4] whether that is moral law or God's basic existence. He sees conscience as obedience to the truth, 'which must stand higher than any human tribunal or type of personal taste'.[5] For Ratzinger (and the mainstream Catholic Church) the perception that living by conscience and living according to rational Natural Law (which they see as identical with the authority of the Church) are opposing choices is false. Ratzinger argues that if conscience is simply subjective and demands contradictory things of different people, then following its demands would negate the existence of truth, make choice meaningless and re-

---

3 Joseph Ratzinger, *On* Conscience, San Francisco: Ignatius Press, 2007.

4 Joseph Ratzinger, *Conscience and Truth: Values in a Time of Upheaval*, New York: Crossroad, 2006, p. 79.

5 Ratzinger, *On Conscience*, p. 26.

move real freedom. The Church and true conscience both testify to the truth and so underpin all rationality and moral autonomy. Conscience, Aquinas said, is 'reason making right decisions' and there is a need to inform conscience by clear, dispassionate enquiry. Conscience in the Catholic tradition is not an inner voice (like Jiminy Cricket in *Pinocchio*) but acting according to reason which arrives at what is morally good and avoids what is morally wrong.

A similar view was put forward by the Anglican scholar **Joseph Butler** (1692–1752) who saw conscience as 'the voice of God speaking in us'. However, he did not mean by this that there was an inner voice from God (a position taken by some Protestant theologians), but rather that all human beings have a moral nature which approves or disapproves of actions dependent on whether they conform to natural laws which are apprehended through reason, independently of revelation.[6] For Butler, conscience, Natural Law and revealed Christianity all point in the same direction: conscience is the voice of reason in moral considerations. The great Islamic philosopher **Avicenna**[7] (Ibn Sina, *c*. 980–1037) also identified conscience with human reason or intelligence, through which God communicates truth to human beings. In the Christian tradition Aquinas developed the distinctive concept of *conscientia*, which he identified as a virtue and *the faculty of moral judgement* by which people choose to follow moral laws.

---

6 *The Analogy of Religion: Natural and Revealed* (1736), Dissertation 1, 'Of the Nature of Virtue'. Discussed in John Creed and John Smith, *Religious Thought in the Eighteenth Century*, Cambridge: Cambridge University Press, 1934, p. 104.

7 Nader El-Bizri, 'Avicenna's De Anima between Aristotle and Husserl', in Anna-Teresa Tymienieka (ed.), *The Passions of the Soul in the Metamorphosis of Becoming*, Dordrecht: Kluwer Academic Publishers, 2003, pp. 67–89. The Islamic philosopher Al Ghazali (1058–1111) similarly identified conscience with that element in the self which enables moral choice and is capable of standing outside ourselves and making judgements, *Nafs Lawammah* as in Qur'an, Surah 75, verses 2–14. See Sami M. Najm, 'The Place and Function of Doubt in the Philosophies of Descartes and Al-Ghazali', *Philosophy East and West* 16:3–4 (1966), pp. 133–41.

This is very similar to Kant's concept of the 'will' (*Willkür*), the free ability of human beings to understand the law and choose to adopt it as the basis of moral decisions. This was also the understanding of the term which was influenced by Spinoza and influenced Hegel. In the *Metaphysics of Morals*, Kant wrote: 'Conscience is practical reason holding the human being's duty before him for his acquittal or condemnation in every case that comes under the law ... an unavoidable fact.'[8] Graphically, he goes on to say that 'incorporated into [a human person's] being ... it follows him like a shadow when he plans to escape'.[9] For Kant everybody has a conscience; they may choose to ignore it, however.[10]

An obvious problem with conscience is what to do when it seems to demand that we do something which is not according to moral norms.

In 1963, **Karl Rahner SJ** (1904–84) argued that people have a duty to follow their conscience, even when it is wrong, although they also have a duty to do everything possible to ensure that it is not.[11] This reflects an ancient tradition which suggests that it is possible for a true calling of conscience to go against the norms of the time, even what seems rational. For **Bonaventure** (1221–74), 'conscience does not command things on its own authority, but commands them as coming from God's authority, like a herald when he proclaims the edict of the king. This is why conscience has binding force ...'.[12]

The idea that a 'knight of faith' may be justified by God in suspending normal ethics was discussed by Søren Kierkegaard in *Fear and Trembling* and by Dietrich Bonhoeffer in *Ethics*, but,

---

8 Immanuel Kant, *The Cambridge Edition of the Works of Immanuel Kant*, trans. and ed. Paul Guyer and Allen W. Wood, Cambridge: Cambridge University Press, 1999, 6:529.

9 Kant, *Works*, 6:560.

10 Kant, *Works*, 6:530.

11 Robert Hodge, 'An Appeal to Conscience', in Karl Rahner (ed.), *Nature and Grace: Dilemmas in the Modern Church*, London: Sheed & Ward, 1963, pp. 49–56.

12 Bonaventure, II Librum Sentent. 39, a 1, q 3.

importantly, neither suggested that conscience is infallible, that we can be certain about what it demands, that it really justifies an action, or even that it is genuine. For Kierkegaard, human beings are called to act *coram Deo* (before God) and in the knowledge that they may be wrong. Hodge records that for Kierkegaard and Newman 'conscience directs a man's gaze towards an authority of law outside of and higher than himself to which he owes obedience. Thus for neither is it a matter of "go as you please".'[13] For a believer, the stakes are so high that adopting personal moral responsibility can never be a matter of convenience, easier than the alternative of following rules.

For Dietrich Bonhoeffer, believing that one is acting in 'good conscience' and that this automatically justifies an action is but a step away from being evil. Hannah Arendt (1906–75) noted that at the Nuremberg Trials the ex-SS commanders seemed without any guilt; they felt they had been doing the right thing, had easy consciences and never allowed the possibility of error to enter their minds. It is reason that should guide conscience – not an inner feeling of certainty.

People who act on conscience often speak of being easy in their mind, not being tormented by the possibility of error. It was perhaps this point which Cardinal Ratzinger (subsequently Pope Benedict) had in mind when he warned that the papal encyclical *Gaudium et spes* would be misinterpreted and used to justify individuals challenging both the authority of the Church and general moral norms, often acting irrationally, out of selfish desires or from some other external motive. Ratzinger was right about the effect of *Gaudium et spes*; liberal Catholics have seen conscience as grounds to reject church teaching on issues ranging from contraception through to adopting Proportionalism (or Situation Ethics) wholesale, much to the chagrin of conservatives such as Grisez. Ratzinger has subsequently made it clear that faithful Catholics need to inform their conscience through the teaching of the Church: the basis for this is that the Church

13 Robert Hodge, *What's Conscience for?: Personal Responsibility in Relation to Conscience and Authority*, Slough: St Paul's, 1995, p. 201.

is more likely to arrive at an accurate and rational evaluation of moral dilemmas than individuals who may be motivated by self-interest and may not have a full understanding of the issues.

However, what opponents of Ratzinger's position might question is whether mainstream Catholic teaching actually does reflect Natural Law. If the Catholic tradition is dominated by authority, culture and custom and does not actually represent the pure, rational position, then it may follow that reason and conscience should stand against it.

Scientific Insights

The psychologist **Sigmund Freud** (1856–1939) famously argued that the conscience is part of the **superego**, along with the 'ego ideal' or projection of what we would like to become and character traits we deem desirable. He wrote:

> The long period of childhood during which the growing human being lives in dependence on his parents leaves behind it a precipitate, which forms within his ego a special agency in which this parental influence is prolonged. It has received the name of 'super-ego'. The parents' influence naturally includes not only the personalities of the parents themselves but also the racial, national and family traditions handed on through them, as well as the demands of the immediate social milieu which they represent.[14]

For Freud, the conscience is formed when we are punished for certain behaviours, giving us negative associations with them, and it creates a sense of guilt which pulls against our instinctive desires (the **id**). In healthy people, people with good ego-strength, the **ego** arbitrates effectively between the superego and the id, ensuring that neither dominates our behaviour. In unbalanced

---

14 Sigmund Freud, *An Outline of Psychoanalysis*, London: Hogarth Press, 1949, pp. 3–4.

people, however, one or the other gains control, leading to dys-functional behaviour. If the superego is in control then people become judgemental and inflexible, guilt-ridden control-freaks.

Freud's ideas influenced the psychologists **Jean Piaget** (1896–1980) and **Lawrence Kohlberg** (1927–87). Piaget saw conscience as something that develops gradually as children move from judg-ing actions always in relation to external authority-figures, rules and consequences (the heteronomous stage) to judging actions in relation to motivation and appreciating the value of and need for rules in managing groups of people (the autonomous stage).

Kohlberg refined these ideas further by arguing that children progress through six stages in their journey to acquire a mature conscience:

1 fear of punishment;
2 desire for reward;
3 desire to be liked or admired;
4 respect for law and order – seeing the need for and value in rules and order;
5 the social contract – seeing the value of rules as dependent on their usefulness to people; that is, having more respect for systems which may be emended or which allow reasonable exceptions;
6 universal principles – which may even challenge the prevailing wisdom.

Sociologists have argued that these stages reflect the develop-ment of religions or societies, with primitive religions being dom-inated by talk of hell and heaven, more developed communities playing on people's desire to set an example and support order and mature societies being willing to discuss shades of grey in morality and take the role of the individual and freedom seri-ously.

Evolutionary theory has always suggested that conscience is developed in order to provide a survival-advantage. Human beings will reason that they have more of a chance of surviving in a group, on the 'you scratch my back and I will scratch yours' principle, described by **Robert Trivers** (b. 1943) as 'reciprocal altruism'.[15] Society will only survive if human beings evolve behaviour which leads them to help and trust others. Conscience, therefore, is the feeling that our actions go against our own genetic interests in the long term in the sense that they may undermine others' trust and willingness to do their bit.

Scientific explanations such as these suggest that traditional philosophical and religious theories of conscience are mistaken, that conscience is subjective and fallible and that it limits human freedom rather than increasing it.

Freedom

The whole discussion of ethics in this book depends of human freedom. All moral philosophies are predicated on the belief that human beings are free and can thus be held responsible for their actions. There seems little point in discussing how people should or should not behave if they are truly determined, whether by God, biology, psychology or social factors. It is, perhaps, interesting that in the Bible Jesus was constantly speaking of bringing people to freedom – thus implying that they are not free in the first place.

The theories of Freud, Piaget, Kohlberg and Trivers may contribute to a **hard determinism** such as that of **Ernst Haeckel** (1834–1919). Hard determinists argue that human freedom is illusory and that philosophers can describe moral norms, but cannot really prescribe them or argue that people can reasonably be judged by norms into which they have not been trained. Rose West, the British serial killer, might be seen to be responding to her abusive upbringing and lack of emotional maturity and intelligence. Any punishment inflicted on Rose for killing one girl and collaborating in the rape and murder of many more would be

---

15 R. L. Trivers, 'The Evolution of Reciprocal Altruism', *Quarterly Review of Biology* 46 (1971), pp. 35–57.

for the purposes of vindicating the law or deterring others rather than because she was really responsible.

Hard determinism is a persuasive position but, if it is true, human freedom is an illusion and discussing ethics is a waste of time since all human actions are determined.

Thomas Hobbes (1588–1679) argued that 'the liberty of the man ... consisteth in this, that he finds no stop in doing what he has the will, desire, or inclination to do';[16] he therefore concluded that although what we have the desire or inclination to do is determined by such factors as our background this was not incompatible with freedom. **Daniel Dennett** (b. 1942) takes a similar **soft determinist** position, arguing that human beings are free to do what they want to do but what they want to do is determined by their background, genetics and education. He argues that freedom is compatible with determinism.

Incompatibilists argue that in order to be free a person must be an 'originating cause' of an action and have entered into it voluntarily. They must originate actions free of external or internal constraint. **Incompatibilism** is directly linked to the more traditional position of **libertarianism**, which argues (whether on the basis of God, transcendent rationality, or dualism) that human beings are more than just material and are capable of overcoming influence and acting in a genuinely free manner. Most normative theories assume freedom because without it they are redundant. Kant's ethic hinges on the issue of freedom, though he acknowledged the difficulty of maintaining this postulate in the face of experience, which suggests that freedom may be radically constrained by past actions and the confusion caused by living in an unjust society. Utilitarianism presumes that people are free to pursue pleasure and avoid pain and that they are capable of making universal rational decisions concerning the greater good, often suppressing immediate desires. John Stuart Mill's famous *On Liberty* shows freedom to be an integral part of any fulfilled human life, a basic idea he shared with Bentham who saw depriving somebody of liberty as a punishment much worse than death.

16 Thomas Hobbes, *Leviathan*, Chapter 21.

Nevertheless, just because people want to believe they are free does not mean that they are. Even if they think and feel that they are free, it is possible that they are mistaken. As Spinoza observed:

[T]he infant believes it is by free-will that it seeks the breast; the angry boy believes that by free-will he wishes vengeance; the timid man thinks that it is with free will that he seeks flight ... All believe that they speak of a free command of the mind, whilst, in truth, they have no power to restrain the impulse.[17]

Peter Vardy has argued[18] that most people are, indeed, determined – they are like the prisoners in Plato's cave (see page 3) but, through philosophy and coming to self-understanding, they may be able to come to freedom. Freedom, therefore, is an achievement which few human beings manage to realize.

Moral Luck

A major problem for all systems of normative ethics is the part that luck plays in ethics. **Thomas Nagel** (b. 1937) argued that most actions are affected by four different kinds of luck:

1 resultant luck – the way things turn out;
2 circumstantial luck – the peculiarities of the general situation, for example, whether one happens to be born in twentieth-century Germany or nineteenth-century New Zealand;
3 constitutive luck – one's existing character traits and dispositions;
4 causal luck – the specific chain of events.[19]

---

17 Baruch Spinoza, *Ethic: Demonstrated in Geometrical Order and Divided Into Five Parts*, Oxford: Oxford University Press, 1930, p. 111.

18 Peter Vardy, *What is Truth?*, O-Books, 2005.

19 Thomas Nagel, *Mortal Questions*, Cambridge: Cambridge University Press, 1979, p. 37.

In spite of these factors, actions continue to be judged on a similar basis, without reference to this complex web of factors. Nagel argued that this was not reasonable and concluded:

> I believe that in a sense the problem has no solution ... as the external determinants of what someone has done are gradually exposed, in their effect on consequences, character, and choice itself, it becomes gradually clear ... that nothing remains which can be ascribed to the responsible self, and we are left with nothing but a portion of the larger sequence of events, which can be deplored or celebrated, but not blamed or praised.[20]

The 2006 film *Babel*[21] explores this idea, showing how small things can have unimagined and life-changing consequences and how unjust it seems when people are held to account for crimes and consequences which seem at odds with their intentions.

- A Japanese hunter rewards his guide by giving him his rifle, not realizing that the rifle will be sold on and end up in the hands of a child.
- A young Moroccan boy takes his father's new rifle and stupidly shoots at a distant coach, not realizing that it is within range. He wounds an American tourist and starts a chain of events which leads to the deaths of both his father and his brother.
- The Japanese hunter leaves his deaf teenage daughter alone in Tokyo for long periods, not realizing that she is descending into an unstable mess and endangering herself.
- American parents leave their children at home in the care of a Mexican nanny in order to go on a trip to heal their relationship after a miscarriage. Their return is delayed by injury caused by the young boy's shot and the nanny chooses to take the children with her to her son's wedding in Mexico as she cannot find anyone else to look after them. The result is that the nanny gets deported and loses everything.

---

20 Nagel, *Mortal Questions*, p. 68.
21 Directed by Alejandro González Iñárritu.

Moral philosophy has difficulty in responding to scenarios such as this. Judging others is easy, but, if placed in the same circumstances, most people might well have acted in the same way or been forced into situations over which they had no control.

Conclusion

Conscience, in the view of most major philosophers, is directly linked to rationality and what it means to be human – it is not to be thought of as a private source of moral inspiration.

Libertarian freedom is essential for any theory of ethics even though, as Kant recognized, it cannot be proved. If determinists are right and human beings are determined then the most that can be done is to understand the evolutionary forces operating on us but, since human beings are powerless to change, talk of ethics and morality is no longer valid.

18

Ethics Matters

It is clear that neither the foundations for ethical decision-making, nor the process by which decisions should be made, are simple. The issues which face human beings are complex and demand mature attention. There are no easy answers, but that does not mean it is not worth asking the questions.

After Certainty ...

In 1994, the great Polish sociologist Zygmunt Bauman, in his book *Ethics after Certainty*,[1] set out the situation people find themselves in today and the challenge they face in trying to live well. He concluded:

We have come a long way in our search for the sources of moral hope, but remain, so far, empty-handed. Our only gain is that we have learnt where such sources are unlikely to be found ... More than two centuries after the Enlightenment promise to legislate for an ethical and humane society, we are left, each of us, with our own individual conscience and sentiment of responsibility as the only resource with which to struggle to make life more moral than it is. And yet we find this resource depleted and squeezed.[2]

1 Zygmunt Bauman, *Ethics after Certainty*, London: Demos, 1994. Available online at http://www.demos.co.uk/files/aloneagain.pdf?1240939425, accessed 19 April 2012.
2 Bauman, *Ethics after Certainty*, p. 28.

Later on in the same book he writes:

> Indeed, the stakes are enormous ... We do not so much move 'forward', as clear the mess and seek exit from the havoc perpetrated by the things we did yesterday ... What makes this already depressing plight near catastrophic, though, is that the scale of the changes we inadvertently provoke is so massive, that the line beyond which the risks become totally unmanageable and damages irreparable may be crossed at any moment.[3]

Bauman sums up the terrifying complexity of ethics and moral philosophy and the problems have become more acute since he wrote the above:

- Medical advances present us with ever more options. The fact that science can do certain things does not imply that it ought to do so. The speed of change is such that taking time to reflect and respond in a measured way is all but impossible. Medical ethics, like King Canute, can sometimes appear to be holding back the tide of progress by shushing back waves at the shore.
- An environmental catastrophe seems to be unfolding yet both political and individual will to act seems to be diminishing. People protect their children, keeping them inside swaddled in sunscreen, organic food and progressive parenting, while being certain that the world they will inherit will degenerate into a chaos in which such lifestyle choices will only be memories.
- Business has come to dominate the world and globalization ensures homogeneity of experience from Bangkok to Belfast. Most people accept the consumer-myth, confusing happiness with material wealth and fulfilment with status. Ethics in business is often seen as a marketing ploy and is seldom taken seriously when it conflicts with the bottom line.

---

3 Bauman, *Ethics after Certainty*, p. 29.

- While war has changed, becoming less a sporadic but all-consuming slaughter and more a persistent threat, it is an ever more important and more difficult issue to discuss. The consequences of modern weaponry and stratagems are huge, long-lasting and difficult to describe or contain. Neither deontology nor consequentialism provides clear direction and Virtue Ethics even less.

What Is the Point of Ethics?

So where can we go from here? Is the whole enterprise of ethics and moral philosophy pointless in the face of overwhelming complexity, a lack of definitive understanding and clear ability to change things? Hopefully this book has shown that there is immense value in reflecting on the meaning of 'right' and 'wrong', the nature of 'a good life' and what characteristics or actions might feature therein, in taking time to reflect on the most difficult of questions even if the answers are not clear.

Sadly, philosophy has become fragmented as a discipline and many people have lost a sense of what it aims to achieve. Some people study history or texts, others delve into the minutiae of linguistic analysis and logic, still others focus on particular issues. What was largely neglected in the twentieth century is the idea that philosophy is more than a professional or academic exercise; it is a way of living. As Kierkegaard observed:

In Greece, philosophizing was a mode of action and the philosopher was therefore an existing individual. He may not have had a great deal of knowledge, but what he did know he knew to some profit because he busied himself early and late with the same thing.[4]

---

4 Søren Kierkegaard, *Concluding Unscientific Postscript*, Princeton: Princeton University Press, 1968, p. 295.

Kierkegaard was inspired by the example of Socrates. In Plato's *Apology*,[5] Socrates remarks that 'I am that gadfly [an insect which bites and bothers horses], which God has given the state and all day long and in all places am always fastening upon you, arousing and persuading and reproaching you.' More than two millennia later, Thoreau wrote: 'I do not propose to write an ode to dejection, but to brag as lustily as chanticleer in the morning, standing on his roost, if only to wake my neighbours up.'[6] This should be the point of moral philosophy, and of philosophy as a whole, to ask difficult questions, provoke discussion and reflection through actions and the example of life well lived as well as through the written word, even if there are no clear answers. As Bauman rightly observes, 'ability to reflect does not translate easily into the ability to act. Even if the mind is perceptive and judicious enough, the will may prove to be wanting; and even if the will is there, hands may be too short'[7] – but that does not negate the value of reflecting, or of moral philosophy.

The Problems of Prediction and Paralysis

Hans Jonas (1903–93) grappled with how to relate moral philosophy to the challenges of the modern world, including bioethics and environmental issues. He argued that the primary role of ethics is 'visualizing the long-range effects of technological enterprise' so that meaningful discussions can be undertaken before events overtake us. For Jonas, the 'categorical imperative' should be 'always act so that the effects of your actions do not destroy the future potential of life on earth'. The difficulty, of course, is to know how things will turn out and not to be para-

---

5 Available online at http://classics.mit.edu/Plato/apology.html, accessed 23 April 2012.

6 Henry Thoreau, *Walden*, Chapter 2, 'Where I lived and what I lived for', available online at http://thoreau.eserver.org/walden02.html, accessed 23 April 2012.

7 Thoreau *Walden*, p. 30.

lysed by the potential that most actions have for causing chaos. Arne Naess recommended that when people cannot be sure of the outcomes they should refrain from acting – but to what extent would that leave all thinking people, certainly all moral philosophers, sitting up Norwegian mountains wringing their hands?

A major shortcoming of traditional normative systems is that they are limited by our understanding of the consequences of actions. Consequentialists struggle to predict the range of results that an action produces, deontologists struggle to classify actions without a clear sense of what will result from them, and even virtue ethicists struggle to relate actions to character via intentions and effects without a full picture of their consequences. As Bauman explained, 'moral life is a life of continuous uncertainty' and 'it takes a lot of strength and resilience and an ability to withstand pressures to be a moral person'.[8]

Brave New World?

The Catholic Encyclical *Gaudium et spes* opens:

> [W]hile man extends his power in every direction, he does not always succeed in subjecting it to his own welfare. Striving to probe more profoundly into the deeper recesses of his own mind, he frequently appears more unsure of himself. Gradually and more precisely he lays bare the laws of society, only to be paralyzed by uncertainty about the direction to give it ... Never before has man had so keen an understanding of freedom, yet at the same time new forms of social and psychological slavery make their appearance. Although the world of today has a very vivid awareness of its unity and of how one man depends on another in needful solidarity, it is most grievously torn into opposing camps by conflicting forces. For political, social, economic, racial and ideological disputes still continue bitterly, and with them the peril of a war which would reduce

8 Bauman, *Ethics after Certainty*, p. 36.

everything to ashes ... man painstakingly searches for a better world, without a corresponding spiritual advancement.[9]

The institutional Church agrees with Bauman, a secular Jewish, ex-communist sociologist, that the loss of certainty should not be the end of ethics or moral philosophy. Doing nothing is not an option in a world where temperatures and sea levels are rising, terrorists are multiplying and scientists are breaking through new frontiers in every field. The need for ethical decision-making has never been greater.

Perhaps what is needed is to accept freedom and moral responsibility positively, either as postulates or articles of faith, to commit to trying to live well even in the knowledge that there may be no recognition or reward, and to believe that this makes a difference. Most major moral philosophers, from Aquinas to Kant, Aristotle to Mill would see in this the basis of a good life. Moral philosophy is not a puzzle like a sudoku, a fleeting pastime to exercise the brain: it should be an eternal struggle, a process which affects all aspects of life.

Bauman concludes that 'one can recognize a moral person by their never quenched dissatisfaction with their moral performance; the gnawing suspicion that they were not moral enough'.[10] Most lives are not made up of textbook dilemmas. They mostly consist in less dramatic choices, about honesty, integrity, prudence or courage. Being good is never about conforming, acting out of habit or fear, following rules or doing what is easy; it is about recognizing complexity, guilt, shades of grey but not being paralysed. Good living is living consciously and conscientiously – the hard way. As Thoreau put it:

I went to the woods because I wished to live deliberately, to front only the essential facts of life, and see if I could not learn

---

9 *Gaudium et Spes* (1965), Introductory Statement. Available online at http://www.vatican.va/archive/hist_councils/ii_vatican_council/documents/vat-ii_cons_19651207_gaudium-et-spes_en.html, accessed 23 April 2012.

10 *Gaudium et Spes*, Introductory Statement.

what it had to teach, and not, when I came to die, discover that I had not lived. I did not wish to live what was not life, living is so dear; nor did I wish to practise resignation, unless it was quite necessary. I wanted to live deep and suck out all the marrow of life.[11]

---

11 Thoreau, *Walden*, Chapter 2, paragraph 16.

Index

CPSIA information can be obtained
at www.ICGtesting.com
Printed in the USA
BVHW040333230721
612375BV00024B/391